Medieval Literature 1300–1500

Edinburgh Critical Guides to Literature
Series Editors: Martin Halliwell, University of Leicester and Andy Mousley, De Montfort University

Published Titles:
Gothic Literature, Andrew Smith
Canadian Literature, Faye Hammill
Women's Poetry, Jo Gill
Contemporary American Drama, Annette J. Saddik
Shakespeare, Gabriel Egan
Asian American Literature, Bella Adams
Children's Literature, M. O. Grenby
Contemporary British Fiction, Nick Bentley
Renaissance Literature, Siobhan Keenan
Scottish Literature, Gerard Carruthers
Contemporary American Fiction, David Brauner
Contemporary British Drama, David Lane
Medieval Literature 1300–1500, Pamela King
Victorian Literature, David Amigoni
Contemporary Poetry, Nerys Williams

Forthcoming Titles in the Series:
Restoration and Eighteenth-Century Literature, Hamish Mathison
Crime Fiction, Stacy Gillis
Modern American Literature, Catherine Morley
Modernist Literature, Rachel Potter
African American Literature, Jennifer Terry
Postcolonial Literature, Dave Gunning

Medieval Literature 1300–1500

Pamela M. King

Edinburgh University Press

For my parents, Eileen and Donald King, with love

Edinburgh University Press Ltd
22 George Square, Edinburgh

www.euppublishing.com

Typeset in 11.5/13 Monotype Ehrhardt
by Servis Filmsetting Ltd, Stockport, Cheshire and
printed and bound in Great Britain by
CPI Antony Rowe, Chippenham and Eastbourne

A CIP record for this book is available from the British Library

ISBN 978 0 7486 3459 0 (hardback)
ISBN 978 0 7486 3460 6 (paperback)

Contents

Series Preface

The study of English literature in the early twenty-first century is host to an exhilarating range of critical approaches, theories and historical perspectives. 'English' ranges from traditional modes of study such as Shakespeare and Romanticism to popular interest in national and area literatures such as the United States, Ireland and the Caribbean. The subject also spans a diverse array of genres from tragedy to cyberpunk, incorporates such hybrid fields of study as Asian American literature, Black British literature, creative writing and literary adaptations, and remains eclectic in its methodology.

Such diversity is cause for both celebration and consternation. English is varied enough to promise enrichment and enjoyment for all kinds of readers and to challenge preconceptions about what the study of literature might involve. But how are readers to navigate their way through such literary and cultural diversity? And how are students to make sense of the various literary categories and periodisations, such as modernism and the Renaissance, or the proliferating theories of literature, from feminism and marxism to queer theory and eco-criticism? The Edinburgh Critical Guides to Literature series reflects the challenges and pluralities of English today, but at the same time it offers readers clear and accessible routes through the texts, contexts, genres, historical periods and debates within the subject.

Martin Halliwell and Andy Mousley

Acknowledgements

Particular thanks are due to the University of Bristol Faculty of Arts for the period of study leave which made the writing of this book possible, to Robert Yeager for pre-publication access to his essay on John Gower, to my colleagues Elizabeth Archibald and Ad Putter who read early drafts of the first chapter, and to Jane Griffiths who read the whole book in draft. Lancaster University English Department kindly arranged the hospitality of their Library where much of the book was researched. I am also grateful to my editors, Andy Mousley and Martin Halliwell, for their support, and to those at Edinburgh University Press who helped to take the volume forward. For everything in this book, I must thank all the teachers, students, and colleagues with whom I have worked over the years: theirs has been the inspiration; the faults are all mine.

Chronology

Precise dating of written works from the period before printing is, in the majority of cases, impossible. Manuscripts can be dated on palaeographical evidence, but the date of the manuscript of a work is not the same as its date of composition. What follows, therefore, dates Middle English works on a 'best guess' principle and sets them alongside a selection of historical milestones.

Historical and Cultural Events		**Middle English and Related Continental Texts**
c.1300	Hereford *Mappa Mundi* constructed	*Cursor Mundi* (c.1300)
1305	Execution of William Wallace	Robert Mannyng of Brunne, *Handlyng Synne* (1303–17)
1306	Coronation of Robert the Bruce	
1307	Edward I dies; Edward II crowned	Dante, *Divine Comedy* (1307–21)
1314	Scots win independence from England at the battle of Bannockburn	
1300– 20s	First War of Scottish Independence	*Prick of Conscience* (early fourteenth century)

Historical and Cultural Events		Middle English and Related Continental Texts
1320	Declaration of Arbroath (Scottish independence)	
1327	Edward II murdered	
1329	Robert the Bruce dies	
1330	Edward III begins his personal rule and has his regent, Mortimer, executed	*Guy of Warwick* (c.1330)
1332	William Langland born	
1332–7	Second War of Scottish Independence	Boccaccio, *Il Filostrato* (1335)
1337–40	Beginning of Hundred Years' War as Edward III declares himself King of France	John Bromyard, *Summa Praedicantium* (1330–52) Stanzaic *Morte Arthur* (mid fourteenth century)
1342	Julian of Norwich born	
c.1343	Geoffrey Chaucer born	
1343	Tournament at Windsor; Order of the Garter established	
1346	Battle of Crecy – England defeats French, and Edward the Black Prince is war hero; England defeats the Scots at Neville's Cross and captures David II	
1348	The Black Death reaches England	
1349	Richard Rolle dies	
1351	Statute of Labourers	
1356	English victory at battle of Poitiers	*The Lay Folks' Catechism* (1357)

Historical and Cultural Events		Middle English and Related Continental Texts
1357	David II of Scotland freed	
1360	Treaty of Calais – Chaucer and Froissart both present	Geoffrey Chaucer trans. *Romaunt of the Rose* (1360s) William Langland, *Piers Plowman* A text (late 1360s)
1361	'The Plague of Children'	
1362	English language required in legal pleading	
1368	Blanche of Lancaster, wife of John of Gaunt, dies of plague	Geoffrey Chaucer, *Book of the Duchess* (1368/9)
1371	Treaty of Vincennes establishes Franco-Scottish alliance	John Gower, *Mirour de l'Omme* (1370s) John Barbour, *The Brus* (mid-1370s)
1373	Margery Kempe born	
1376	The 'Good Parliament'; death of Edward the Black Prince; John Wyclif active at Oxford	
1377	Edward III dies; Richard II is crowned (aged 11) under John of Gaunt's control; the 'Bad Parliament'	William Langland, *Piers Plowman* B text (1377–9) *Livre pour l'enseignement de ses filles du Chevalier de La Tour Landry* [*The Book of the Knight of the Tower*] (1370s)
1378	Great Schism of the Church begins, with rival popes in Rome and Avignon	
1381	'Peasants' Revolt'	*Sir Gawain and the Green Knight*, *Pearl*, *Patience*, *Cleanness* (late fourteenth century)
1384	Death of John Wyclif	
1385	Richard II invades Scotland	
1386	William Langland dies	*The Stanzaic Life of Christ* (late fourteenth century)

Historical and Cultural Events		Middle English and Related Continental Texts
1387	Lords Appellant rebel against the king	Wycliffite English Bibles (1380s)
1388	'Merciless Parliament' condemns advisors of Richard II	Walter Hilton, *The Scale of Perfection* (1380s) *Cloud of Unknowing* (1380s)
1389	Richard II (aged 22) assumes autonomous power	*Wynnere and Wastoure* (reign of Richard II) Geoffrey Chaucer, *House of Fame*, *Parliament of Fowls* (1382), *Troilus and Criseyde*, *Boece*, *Legend of Good Women*, *Canterbury Tales* begun (1380s) John Gower, *Vox Clamantis*, *Confessio Amantis* (1380s) Julian of Norwich, *Showings* (1380s) William Langland, *Piers Plowman* C text (mid-1380s) Gaston 'Phebus', *Livre du Chasse* (1387) Completion of the Wyclif Bible (1388)
1390	Tournaments at Paris in which Richard II took part, and at Smithfield at which Chaucer was Clerk of Works	Julian of Norwich, *Revelation* (1393) *Le Menagier de Paris* [Goodman of Paris] (1390s) *St Erkenwald* (1390s)
1394	James I of Scotland born	*Pierce the Ploughman's Crede* (1390s)
1395	Philippe de Mezieres writes to Richard II urging cessation of Anglo-French hostilities and a joint Crusade	Geoffrey Chaucer, *Canterbury Tales*, *Treatise of the Astrolabe* (1390s) *Alliterative Morte Arthur* (end of fourteenth century)

Historical and Cultural Events		Middle English and Related Continental Texts
1397	Richard II has the Lords Appellant impeached	*Twelve Conclusions of the Lollards* (1395)
1399	Death of John of Gaunt; Richard II abdicates; Henry Bolingbroke (Gaunt's son) crowned Henry IV	Christine de Pisan, *L'épistre au Dieu D'Amours* [Letter to the God of Love] (1399)
1400	Chaucer dies; Richard II murdered	*Mum and the Soothsegger* (1400s)
1401	*De Heretico Comburendi* (Act enabling the burning of heretics)	
1406	James I of Scotland captured and imprisoned	Hoccleve, *La Male Regle* (c.1406)
1407	Archbishop Arundel issues his Constitutions controlling heresies	Nicholas Love, *The Mirror of the Blessed Life of Jesus Christ* (1409)
1410	Owen Glendower of Wales rebels against England	Hoccleve, *Regiment of Princes* (c.1412)
1413	Henry IV dies; Henry V crowned	
1414	Sir John Oldcastle's failed Lollard rebellion; St Andrews University founded	
1415	England defeats France at the battle of Agincourt; Richard Beauchamp jousts at Guines	John Mirk, *Festial* (before 1415) Lydgate, *The Troy Book* (1412)
1414–18	The Council of Constance ends the Papal Schism	The *Ordo Paginarum*, first record of content of the York Plays (1415)

Historical and Cultural Events		Middle English and Related Continental Texts
1420	The treaty of Troyes makes Henry V heir to the French throne	Lydgate, *The Siege of Thebes* (c.1422)
1422	Henry V and Charles VI of France both die; Henry VI crowned at 9 months old with Humphrey, Duke of Gloucester as Regent	*The Book of Margery Kempe* (1420s)
1424	James I of Scotland released	James I of Scotland, *The Kingis Quair* (1424)
1426	Thomas Hoccleve dies	
1429	Philip the Good, Duke of Burgundy, inaugurates the Order of the Golden Fleece; Joan of Arc rescues Orleans from the English	
1431	Joan of Arc burned as a witch; Henry VI of England crowned King of France	*Dance of Death* (1430s)
1436	Henry VI assumes autonomous power	
1437	James I of Scotland murdered; James II succeeds	Lydgate, *The Fall of Princes* (c.1438); Earliest Paston letters and papers
1440	Siege of Harfleur	
1453	Hundred Years' War ends in truce with France	*The Castle of Perseverance* (c.1440)
1454	Richard, Duke of York, appointed regent during Henry VI's insanity;	Gutenberg prints the Bible (1450) Sir Thomas Malory, *Morte D'Arthur* (1451)

	Historical and Cultural Events	**Middle English and Related Continental Texts**
1455	Henry VI (Lancaster) deposes Richard (York) and civil war, the 'Wars of the Roses', ensues	
1461	The battle of Towton fought, with the highest mortality ever on English soil; Edward IV accedes to the English throne	Croxton *Play of the Sacrament* (1460s?) *Wisdom* (c.1460–5) The Register of the York Play (c.1467)
1468	Margaret of York marries Charles the Bold of Burgundy	The N. Town Plays (1468) *Mankind* (c.1465–70)
1471	Henry VI executed; Thomas Malory dies After 1472, Chester Play moves from Corpus Christi to Whitsun	Caxton translates and prints Raoul Lefevre's *Receuils des Histoires de Troyes* (1475)
1476	Caxton sets up the first English printing press	*The Canterbury Tales* printed by Caxton (1478)
1483	Edward V, then Richard III, accede to the throne of England	*The Beauchamp Pageants* (1480s)
1485	Henry Tudor (Henry VII) defeats Richard III at the battle of Bosworth Field	Robert Henryson, *Morall Fabillis* and *Testament of Cresseid* (1480s) Caxton prints *Le Morte Darthur by Syr Thomas Malory* (1485)
1488	James III of Scotland dies, succeeded by James IV	
1492	Columbus 'discovers' America	John Skelton, *The Bowge of Court* (c.1488)
[1501	Prince Arthur marries Catherine of Aragon; 1502 James IV of Scotland marries Margaret Tudor]	William Dunbar, *The Goldyn Targe* (c.1500)

Introduction

MIDDLE ENGLISH LITERATURE

> Many men there ben that, with eeres openly sprad, so moche swalowen the delyciousnesse of jestes and of ryme, by queynt knyttyng coloures, that of the goodnesse or of the badnesse of the sentence [meaning] they take lytel hede, or els non.[1]

So complains Thomas Usk, a less gifted contemporary of Geoffrey Chaucer. It was ever thus. In this volume we will consider some of the concerns that medieval English writers show for 'goodnesse', that is for imparting something improving or enlightening to their readership, whether their subject matter is sacred or secular. We will also spend time exploring how Middle English as a literary language was shaped into different stylistic registers, subtly knitting the colours of rhetoric inherited from Latin. And we will look at Middle English literature as cultural performance, at the overlapping social, political, and spiritual circumstances in which texts were generated and received, and at whose ears (and eyes) were openly spread to receive the vernacular literary culture of the British Isles between 1300 and 1500.

Medieval English literature arguably begins with the earliest surviving texts, around the year 800, but it is conventional to divide it into Old English and Middle English. Old English literature is the body of texts which survive from the period between the time when

England became a politically stable entity under the rule of the heirs of various Germanic and Norse invaders, lately converted to Roman Christianity. The great epic *Beowulf* is probably the best known work of literature in Anglo-Saxon. The conquest of England by William of Normandy in 1066 then caused a huge cultural shift, as the class equipped with the leisure and wealth to commission works of art now spoke a dialect of French. In the ensuing century and a half, literary texts are still written in 'English', but that language shows marked modifications from Anglo-Saxon to accommodate the penetration of the language spoken and written in the British Isles by the languages of its invaders. The English of this period is often referred to as 'Early Middle English', and Layamon's *Brut* stands out amongst the surviving texts. The thirteenth century saw a flourishing literary culture in England amongst the leisured classes, but with a few notable exceptions the medium for imaginative literature was the distinctive insular dialect of French which had developed since the Conquest, known as Anglo-Norman. It is not until the fourteenth century, where our study begins, that English begins to gain a hold as a vernacular considered just mature enough by its users to be a suitable medium for written record and imaginative literature.

Our period pivots tidily on 1400, a year when there was a change of dynasty from Plantagenet to Lancastrian with the deposition of Richard II, and the year in which Geoffrey Chaucer died. We will see how, try as we might to avoid an unreflecting focus on canonical texts, Chaucer's position as the greatest English writer before Shakespeare remains largely unassailable, not only because of the quantity and quality of his surviving output, but because of the unrivalled influence he had on those who came after him. Changes of dynasty do not necessarily have the same, or any, impact on written culture, but the new men brought in in the wake of the early Lancastrian monarchs demonstrably favoured English over Latin and French as the language of written record. The choice of 1300 as a start point is dictated by some of the contextualising material that we need to look at in order to understand where certain written traditions derive from, but is otherwise largely arbitrary. If we were really to seek, or believe in, precisely locatable watersheds, we would have to begin in June 1348, the month in which the Black

Death arrived in Weymouth, leading to a demographic catastrophe that completely changed the social and cultural balance of the nation. Our end point is easier: by 1500 Humanist philosophy was established in northern Europe, news of Spanish and Portuguese discoveries that would change the world map was filtering through, and the new Tudor monarchy had its feet firmly under the table. Periodisation is slippery, however, and it is also worth bearing in mind that 'medieval' Chaucer travelled to Italy, and met with and translated the works of 'Renaissance' Italian authors Francesco Petrarch and Giovanni Boccaccio. We will also consider the works of two poets, one English the other Scots, John Skelton and William Dunbar, whose writing careers span the 'medieval' to 'Renaissance' divide as surely as Rudyard Kipling and Thomas Hardy are both Victorians and modernists. But towards the end of our period we have another precise date that justifies a halt: in 1475, an English merchant, William Caxton, working with Collard Mansion in Bruges, produced the first printed book in English, the *Recuyell of the Historyes of Troye*, and, in the following year, set up his own printing press in Westminster and printed his own edition of Chaucer's *Canterbury Tales*.

Modern editions of medieval texts efface the differentness of pre-print culture. Literary Middle English was a self-consciously fusion language, like modern Yiddish,[2] whose authors knowingly manipulated the etymological sources of their lexical choices to create rich and socially nuanced signs. Modern, largely monoglot, English users, with their comparatively dulled sense of etymology, have to work hard to notice, let alone to decode, these signs. Literary Middle English drew freely on Latin and French, and not only because they were the other languages in which the English had fluency – in the late fourteenth and early fifteenth centuries, large numbers of the population were fluent through trade contacts in Dutch, Flemish and German dialects, which had more linguistic affinity with Anglo Saxon – but because French and Latin were the longer established languages of high culture. The London poet John Gower wrote whole texts in both languages as well as in English.[3]

In manuscript culture every individual book was a unique luxury material object. It was written on vellum – calf or lamb skin – with a quill pen which the writer had to be adept at cutting, with ink made from special recipes. Each page was planned carefully in advance, a frame for the text drawn, and the margins pricked and ruled with a stylus to ensure that the finished text looked tidy. Erasures were unsightly, and had to be laboriously scratched out. Completed folios were gathered, stitched, and bound between boards, which were then covered in leather, often with decorative metal clasps. There is a general presumption that most people in the Middle Ages were illiterate, but illiteracy may have been over-estimated because of the technical skill involved in writing. It is safer to say that, in the Middle English period, more people could read than could write, and writing of anything lengthy was best left to the professionals. The professional scribe wrote a 'book' hand, made up of 'black' letter forms on which moveable type would later be based. As urban culture and trade increased, there was also a growth of more informal 'secretary' hands, the precursors of modern hand-writing, in which private letters, bills of lading, accounts, and other documents were written.[4]

If one were fortunate enough to be able to afford to commission a book in English, one expected it to be written in the English one spoke, and not in the dialect of another part of the country. There was no copyright on written material, and scribes thought nothing of adapting, editing, and 'improving' the material they were working on, introducing their own favourite spellings, to match their market of one, and to bring up to date the material they had to hand. Authors wrote directly for known coterie audiences amongst whom their work would circulate for reading, or be read aloud. Some books wore out physically, for example playbooks used for whole casts to rehearse from, and were replaced by modernised versions. The rise in literacy occasioned by the demographic changes of the fourteenth century led to the increasing professionalisation of the book trade, particularly in London, as the demand for texts broadened, so that the printing press, like many inventions, was impelled by need. Immediately Caxton began to publish multiple identical copies of texts, however, he had to confront the problem of which of the numerous varieties of English he should print in, a problem that he wrote about:

> Certaynly our langage now vsed varyeth ferre from that whiche was vsed and spoken whan I was borne / For we englysshe men / ben borne vnder the domynacyoun of the mone,

> whiche is neuer stedfaste / but euer wauerynge / wexynge one season / and waneth and dyscreaseth another season / And that comyn englysshe that is spoken in one shyre varyeth from another. In so moche that in my dauyes happened that certayn marchauntes were in a shippe in tamyse [Thames], for to haue sayled ouer the see into zelande / and for lacke of wynde, they taryed atte forlond [coast], and wente to lande for to refreshe them; And one of theym named Sheffelde, a mercer, cam in-to an hows and axed for mete [food]; and specyally he axed after eggys; And the goode wyf answerde, that she coude speke no frenshe. And the marchaunt was angry, for he also coude speke no frenshe, but wolde haue hadde egges / and she vnderstode hym not / And thenne at laste a nother sayd that he wolde haue eyren / then the good wyf sayd that she vnderstod hym wel / Loo, what sholde a man in thyse dayes now wryte, egges or eyren / certaynly it is harde to playse euery man / by cause of dyuersite & chaunge of langage.[5]

Here we see Caxton recognising the way in which any language varies by region, and changes through time. What printing did was to impose a 'standard' on written English for the first time. Caxton's anecdote about the eggs suggests that there was already an implied hierarchy of dialects, anticipating his choice to print in the English of his native London, home of the royal court which was the most significant patron of literature, and of Chaucer. Chaucer's status also caused Caxton to choose a variety of London English that was already slightly archaic by the time he was working. The resulting standard decoupled English spelling from current pronunciation for ever.

In this book, quotations from Middle English texts use original spelling, with some assistance in the form of translations of unfamiliar words, rather than attempting modernisation. It helps to read them aloud. They also preserve the handful of obsolete letters which occur in Middle English texts, for the sake of authenticity, and because they are not difficult to assimilate. Hence the reader will encounter thorn in upper case, Þ, and lower case, þ, and learn to pronounce it like the modern digraph <th>; eth in lower case only, ð, also pronounced <th>, and yogh, in upper case, Ȝ, and lower case, ȝ. Yogh, which passed out of use with the coming of the long form of <z> is sometimes confused with it, but generally fulfils the function of modern <y> or the <gh> digraph, or indeed <z>, and can be pronounced like any of these or something like the <ch> at the end of Scottish 'loch'. Thorn's disappearance probably arose because of its confusion with new forms of written <y>, giving rise to the commonly mispronounced 'ye olde tea shoppe', which is of course simply 'the old tea-shop'.

The final <e> on 'shoppe' does not suggest either that the word should be pronounced 'shoppy', as if medieval English people shared the perennial Scots enthusiasm for the diminutive; it is another spelling convention. The evidence that the final <e> was sometimes pronounced is, however, one of the shards of evidence about medieval pronunciation that we can retrieve from the evidence of poetic metre. The metres of Middle English poetry can, and do, form the subject of entire studies in their own right; the reader here needs to know some basic facts. Firstly, the huge majority of texts that survive are written in verse, something that may have arisen originally because of the rareness of books and the concomitant need to commit texts to memory. It is easier to memorise verse than prose. But by the Middle English period it is safer to accept that the predominance of poetry is conventional. Syllable-counted, rhymed verse, written in lines organised into feet, is not a native English way of organising poetry but was inherited from the French. By the Middle English period, however, it had come to dominate almost all London and court-produced poetry, including Chaucer's. The reader should be aware of three forms: the simple rhymed couplet, familiar from The General Prologue to *The Canterbury Tales*; 'Rhyme Royal', a seven-line stanza form associated with elevated subject matter, and in which Chaucer wrote *Troilus and Criseyde*; and the 'tail rhyme'. In 'tail rhyme', long rhymed lines are followed by a short line, the 'tail'. This one is important to recognise as it is associated with romances and, in particular, saints' lives in the 'popular' tradition and is a marker of parody in works of more 'literary' authors, as in Chaucer's Tale of Sir Thopas.

The native English verse form was quite different. Anglo Saxon poetry was written in alliterative metre – that is in a form where the aural patterning depended on the repetition of consonants. The standard line contains four stressed syllables, the first three of which alliterate, while the final one does not. There may be any number of unstressed syllables. Writing in this metre is more difficult when English ceases to be an inflected language, economical with words because variable word-endings carry the codes of grammatical relationship. However in Middle English, particularly from the Midlands and the North, poetry continued to be written in alliterative metre. Again it is important to develop an ear for the alliterative line, so that the reader can recognise, as in the climactic moment in *Piers Plowman* quoted in Chapter 4 below, the poetic effect of an added 'hypermetrical' alliterating syllable. Some poems were, impressively, written in verse that was both alliterative and syllable-counted and rhymed, something worth admiring in the work of the anonymous poet of *Sir Gawain and the Green Knight* and its companion pieces, as well as in some of the pageants in the York Cycle of mystery plays. The stanza form in which *Sir Gawain* is written is often referred to as 'bob and wheel' because of the distinctive way in which the long lines of the stanza are followed by a short 'bob' of typically two words, then a rhymed 'wheel' of short lines that summarise the foregoing stanza. With this bare summary we must leave the metres of Middle English verse to the experts; the variations are myriad, as a quick glance through any anthology of Middle English lyrics will demonstrate.[6]

The same anthology will doubtless throw up examples of macaronic verse, verse in which languages, usually English and Latin, are mixed for effect.[7] The Middle English period is one in which the relationship between Latin and the vernacular was changing and became increasingly politicised, particularly in religious literature, as we shall see in Chapters 3 and 4. The Latin of the liturgy of the Church continued to carry particular resonances, where its authoritative yet familiar sounds probably offered comfort and validation even to audiences who did not understand it, because of its spiritual context. But Latin, which still dominated secular legislation and was the language of education, was equally recognised as an exclusive code used by the corrupt and cynical in positions of power to blind and intimidate their victims. It was, consequently, held in deep suspicion in certain contexts. The amputation of literature in English from its Latin and French counterparts that modern disciplinary boundaries and linguistic skills dictate, remains, for the Middle Ages, a relatively artificial exercise which might have surprised the authors discussed in the following pages.

THE ORGANISATION OF THIS BOOK

A guide to the literature of any modern culture may be organised relatively easily according to genre and/or author; Middle English literature demands to be addressed according to a different organisational principle. To begin with, the names of many of the authors have been lost; then, almost everything is 'poetry', that is written in verse, including narrative material that according to modern conventions would generally be the matter of prose. Nor is the present study a 'history', so it is not organised chronologically, either overall or within individual chapters, although dates are made clear and can be matched against the accompanying timeline to avoid the sense that everyone in the Middle Ages lived at the same time, or thought with one 'medieval mind'.

This book has been designed around chapters which are loosely organised on thematic principles. It aims to provide contexts for the best known works and authors of the period, but also to lead the reader beyond them to consider the increasingly wide range of texts available in accessible editions as a part of a distinct material culture. There are some close readings of the customary canonical texts, some *Canterbury Tales*, *Troilus and Criseyde*, *Piers Plowman*, *Sir Gawain and the Green Knight*, and Malory's *Morte D'Arthur*, and there is also close study, sometimes in as much detail, of other less frequently read texts, such as the short but perfectly formed *St Erkenwald*, and a number of works, long poems, lyric verses, and plays, from the post-Chaucerian period. The project is always to reach beyond a sense of 'set texts' to provide readers with a cumulative and accessible introduction to the intellectual, devotional, and political fabric of the society in which the texts were produced, as well as something about that production and the climate in which they were received. Consequently not everything discussed is narrowly 'literary', although there is a continuous focus, brought together in the last chapter, on what it meant to be a writer of imaginative literature in the period immediately before the invention of the printing press, on developments in literary form, and on the changing status of the book as precious object and cultural artefact. The aim is, in short, to offer both ways into the detail of individual texts, and ways out to broader theoretical and critical issues. Readings of texts are thus clustered in each chapter to suggest they can be related in a variety of ways; categories, as well as chapter divisions, should be regarded as provisional and permeable.

Chapter 1, 'The Ideal World', considers how elite medieval society fashioned its image through the literature of the leisured classes. It is, therefore, largely concerned with romance and pageantry. It contextualises fourteenth and fifteenth-century aspirations for a revival of chivalry and a new Crusade, against the background of perpetual war in Europe. It treats romance as a genre, providing a guide to the French books which influenced the English tradition, particularly the *Roman de la Rose*, and looks at the great 'matters' of romance.[8] Texts chosen for particular focus include the Tale of Gareth from Malory's *Morte D'Arthur*, the anonymous romance of *Guy of Warwick*, The Knight's Tale from *The Canterbury Tales*, and, also by Chaucer, *Troilus and Criseyde*, the anonymous *Sir Gawain and the Green Knight*, and Chaucer's Tale of Sir Thopas.

Chapter 2, 'Social Change', explores the impact of the demographic changes brought about by the Black Death, the breakdown of the manorial system, and the growth of a society based around moveable wealth in England's growing cities. It also glances at how official society's inflexibilities at a time of sudden social change led eventually to the events of 1381 conventionally known as 'The Peasants' Revolt'. The chapter begins with a close reading of the topical debate poem, *Wynnere and Wastoure.* It is in this chapter also that the idea of *The Canterbury Tales* will be discussed, with a particular focus on The General Prologue. *Fabliau* is discussed as a genre, and the uses to which Chaucer puts it in exposing and lampooning the upwardly mobile for the entertainment of his audience of courtiers in The Miller's Tale. The role of lay women in late medieval society is considered through the (fictional) Wife of Bath, and the real Margery Kempe. The chapter will end with an examination of the York Cycle, in which the city and its citizens are site and subject of literary production.

Chapter 3, 'Religion and Morality', opens with a discussion of the dominance of the Church in late medieval society, its structure, from papacy to parish, and the profession of religion. We consider a variety of types of religious writing: literature of catechesis, sermons, saints' lives, visionary and contemplative texts. The large number of focus texts covered here includes *Patience, Cleanness*, and *Pearl*; a section of John Gower's *Confessio Amantis*; one of Robert Henryson's *Moral Fables*; Chaucer's Prioress's Tale; *St Erkenwald*; *The Mary Play* from the East Anglian N. Town compilation; Julian of Norwich's *Vision* and *Revelation of Love*; *Mankind*, *The Castle of Perseverance*, and *Wisdom*, morality plays also from East Anglia, and a selection of religious lyric verse.

Chapter 4, 'Complaint and Dissent', is devoted to texts, and authors, which criticise and satirise authority, particularly the Church and the Court. It opens with an account of the radical religious movement known to its detractors as 'Lollardy', the most identifiable node of dissenting opinion in the period. Singled out for special attention is William Langland's long and challenging *Vision of William concerning Piers the Plowman* as a non-aligned and comprehensive imaginative reflection of a climate of anxiety which generated the range of texts in the chapter. Like Langland, through texts which are very different in tone and style, Chaucer also expressed his dissatisfaction with spiritual authority, attacking the shortcomings of the Church in The Friar's Tale, The Summoner's Tale, and The Pardoner's Tale, all of which are also discussed. Some of the more radical literary responses to the call for change in Church and State, *Pierce the Plowman's Creed,* and *Mum and the Soothsegger*, are also considered, but the chapter ends by returning to the question of whether there can be truly dissenting literature in a literary culture dependent on patronage and in which punishments for speaking out of turn were draconian.

The book's final chapter, 'The Literary World', returns to issues of production and reception, and develops the discussion of literary patronage. Chaucer once more provides the focus through examination of his occasional poems *The Book of the Duchess* and *The Parliament of Fowls*, and his excursions into literary theory in *The House of Fame* and The Nun's Priest's Tale. There is a consideration of who constituted the Chaucer circle at court, the writers he followed and who followed him, leading up to a study of two works by his immediate successor, Thomas Hoccleve: *Regement of Princes* and *La Male Regle.* Later developments of the self-consciously Chaucerian tradition will be explored through one of John Lydgate's Mummings, and through the works of writers who come at the end of our period: William Dunbar, particularly his poem *The Golden Targe*, and John Skelton's early poem, *The Bowge of Court.* The book ends with a return to the middle of the period under consideration, and an analysis of one of its most extraordinary and self-reflexive pieces of writing, one which happens to have been written not for but by a monarch: James I of Scotland's *The Kingis Quair.*

NOTES

1. Thomas Usk, *The Testament of Love*, extracted in Jocelyn Wogan-Browne et al., *The Idea of the Vernacular* (University Park, PA: Pennsylvania State University Press, 1999), p. 29.
2. Benjamin Harshav, *The Meaning of Yiddish* (Stanford, CA: Stanford University Press, 1990).
3. Robert Yeager, 'The Poetry of John Gower', in Corinne Saunders (ed.), *The Blackwell Companion to Medieval Poetry* (Oxford: Blackwell, 2010), pp. 463–82 (p. 464).
4. For an account of the growth of literacy in the Middle Ages, see M. T. Clanchy, *From Memory to Written Record: England 1066–1307* (Oxford: Blackwell, 1993); for a succinct account of the medieval book, see Julia Boffey, 'From Manuscript to Modern Text', in Peter Brown (ed.), *A Companion to Medieval English Literature and Culture, c.1350–c.1500* (Oxford: Blackwell, 2007), pp. 107–42, or, more comprehensively, Jeremy Griffiths and Derek A. Pearsall (eds), *Book Production and Publishing in Britain, 1375–1475* (Cambridge: Cambridge University Press, 1989).
5. William Caxton, *The Prologues and Epilogues*, ed. W. J. B. Crotch, Early English Text Society OS 176 (Cambridge: Boydell and Brewer, 1999 [1928]).
6. See Donke Minkova, 'The Forms of Verse', in Peter Brown (ed.), *A Companion to Literature and Culture* (Oxford: Blackwell,

2007), pp. 176–98; Thorlac Turville-Petre, *The Alliterative Revival* (Cambridge: D. S. Brewer, 1977).

7. See further Elizabeth Archibald, 'Macaronic Poetry' in Corinne Saunders (ed.), *The Blackwell Companion to Medieval Poetry* (Oxford: Blackwell, 2010) pp. 277–88.
8. The 'matters' are listed in Richard Morris (ed.), *Cursor Mundi*, Part I, Early English Text Society, OS 57 (Oxford: Oxford University Press, 1961 [1874]), pp. 9–11.

CHAPTER I

The Ideal World

PAGEANTRY

> Now gracious God he save oure kinge,
> His peple, and alle his well-willinge,
> Yef him gode life and gode ending;
> That we with mirth mowe safely singe,
> *Deo gratias Anglia,*
> *Redde pro victoria.*[1]

So ends the 'Agincourt Carol', celebrating Henry V's victory over the French in 1415. When Henry returned to London he was welcomed with pageantry imitating the soul's entry into paradise. Pageants representing heaven were set up in the streets he passed through, and at each he was welcomed as God's faithful servant.[2] The splendour of the occasion, burnished in the telling by the author of the *Gesta Henrici Quinti,* recollects the modesty with which the triumphant monarch presented himself to a grateful nation, 'with an impassive countenance and at a dignified pace, and with only a few and trusted members of his household in attendance . . . silently pondering the matter in his heart'.[3] The account thereby encodes precise messages about Henry's comportment as the Christian king, responsible leader, and merciful conqueror.

Henry's reception was devised for an audience of one, the monarch, as he moved from installation to installation, addressed by the performers on each. But he was also a critical part of that performance, the royal protagonist without whose presence and credentials the city of London's efforts had no purpose. Royal pageantry was the late medieval equivalent of what we have learned to call 'spin'. 'Impression management', as a mechanism for asserting and maintaining the power and exclusivity of an elite group, is fundamental to human behaviour, and to the performativity of public life in particular.[4] In his classic work on the self and social performance, *The Presentation of Self in Everyday Life*, Erving Goffman observed: 'it is always possible to manipulate the impression the observer uses as a substitute for reality because a sign for the presences of a thing, not being that thing, can be employed in the absence of it.' Furthermore, '[in these circumstances] the observed become a performing team and the observers become the audience. Actions which appear to be done on objects become gestures addressed to the audience'.[5] The power groups of the English Middle Ages had their own media for impression management. They consisted of triumphal entries and other performances in which notable events, such as royal weddings, or monarchs' visits to provincial cities, were celebrated by displays in the streets. These displays took the form of symbolic constructions, peopled by fabulous beings who spoke lines directed at underscoring the splendour of the occasion. The monarch or returning hero moved processionally through a temporary landscape as both protagonist and particular audience, turning civic space into a particularised and meaning-laden place.

Performances such as Henry's triumph were ephemeral; we inherit the written record of the event in the *Gesta*, laced with markers of approval which signal in turn its intended audience of knowing connoisseurs. There are other reports of such events that adopt so many of the tropes of contemporary poetry that they have passed into the literary canon. For example, the Scots court poet William Dunbar's dream-vision poem *The Thrissel and the Rose* offers a highly stylised allegorical reflection on the marriage between James IV of Scotland and Margaret Tudor in 1503, inspired by the poet's participation in the pageantry surrounding the real nuptial event.[6] In this chapter we look at the literary resources that secular elites in late medieval English society drew on to reflect, affirm, critique, refine, and fashion their worldly image of the secular ideal, both in their own aspirations and for their public. It will be largely concerned with 'courtly' literature, with texts loosely categorised as romances, particularly those allied to contemporary understandings of 'history'. It will, thus, focus on the twin ideals of chivalry in its martial aspect, and related ideals of refined erotic love, looking at how these ideals are encoded and then by turns celebrated, promoted, and finally problematised in the literary output of the English in the real fourteenth- and fifteenth-century world of perpetual strife for sovereignty in Europe.

The primary medium of historical record for the late Middle Ages is the chronicle. Chronicles, though frankly partisan in point of view, generally adopt a plain middle style in describing triumphs, disasters, storms, plagues, portents, and the passing of princes. They are an invaluable resource for modern historians, but, for the period itself, 'histories' were texts of a different order, and a close cousin of the wholly fictional 'romances' enjoyed by an elite readership who made no clear distinction between the two. At the beginning of the long early fourteenth-century poem *Cursor Mundi*, which aims to tell the whole history of the world, the author lists the 'iestes' men yearn to hear, the stories of historical 'matter' told as 'romance'. Here we can observe how the past is selectively idealised as an aspirational reference point for the present, as the author itemises Alexander, Julius Caesar, the war between the Greeks and Trojans, Brutus the Trojan who conquered England, King Arthur and his knights, Tristram and Isolde, and other related 'storyes of dyuerse þinges / of princes prelates & of kynges'. He goes on to observe that everyone seeks personal affirmation in these texts, but his own book will be different, as all of good and evil will be inescapable, because it contains everything.[7]

Socially affirmative and self-congratulatory, the discourse of the kind of 'history' or romance that the *Cursor Mundi* author references, is aimed at the coteries from which it is generated so that they are flattered into believing their own mythologies. Some of the 'best' texts, however, and many of the most read in our own time, also stretch this mould, critiquing the values they represent. Courtiers living in Chaucer's lifetime preferred to read 'histories' and romances in French, and Chaucer's own romance writings were read by the intellectual elite only amongst his contemporaries, having to wait until after his death to join the mainstream. Romance is a conservative mode, so innovative interventions, the rich texts which stand up to the passage of time, had in their turn to acquire the patina of age before they found a wide audience.

THOMAS MALORY, *THE MORTE D'ARTHUR*

The most durable stories which lie at the centre of medieval English romance literature are those concerning King Arthur and the Knights of the Round Table.[8] What the 'matter' of Arthur offered was a set of stylised ideals for aristocratic conduct, wrapped up in an array of gripping narratives, and catering to a wide range of preferences from the most brutal details of warfare to some of the most sentimentally affecting love stories ever told. Chaucer and Gower largely ignored the matter, but Sir Thomas Malory, passing the time while he was in prison, took on the feat of synthesising the whole Arthurian story. The resulting work became one of the earliest printed for mass consumption by Caxton in 1485.[9]

Malory's sources, as he acknowledges, were problematic, for he was dealing with more than one discrete tradition. The 'English' Arthur, enshrined in the fourteenth-century poem known as the *Alliterative Morte Arthure*, had remained true to the 'history' written by Geoffrey of Monmouth, and focused on Arthur as superlative martial leader. This poem provides the framing narrative of the rise of Arthur as the great king to unite Britain, of epic military victories, and the king's heroic death and transportation to the Isle of Avalon. The other Arthur which Malory inherited comes from a very different fourteenth-century English poem, the stanzaic *Morte Arthur*, itself drawing on the French *La Mort Artu*, to which Malory also had direct access (the 'French boke'). The stanzaic *Morte* is a condensed version of the French original, and in its plangent evocation of individual distress provides Malory with the tragic adulterous love affair of Lancelot and Guinevere.[10] Malory's work, particularly if judged by the anachronistic standards of literary 'unity', is a glorious failure:

> Knights seem to be almost involuntary agents in the stories in which they act; stories split and fragment so that the whole

> landscape through which knights-errant move seems to be littered with the residues of narrative. This, along with an overwhelming sense of unhistoricalness and unrealness and the almost narcotic or balletic repetition of the rituals of jousting and fighting, is part of the dominant experience of reading Malory.[11]

Yet the work has its own coherence. The inevitable tragedy of the end of the Round Table and the deaths of Arthur and Lancelot acquire dimensions of psychological drama that override the individual adventures of which it is comprised. It is a story of human strengths and weaknesses, of greater goods and lesser evils. And Malory returns repeatedly to his preoccupation with chivalry as a moral code for guiding action, which is for Malory applicable to real-life situations. His central characters speak like ordinary political beings, capable not only of emotive oratory, but also of laconic or evasive dialogue. For him, the Arthurian world is at once nostalgic and a blueprint for a realisable ideal.

The word 'chivalry' derives from *cheval*, so applies to the elite military class who were able to turn up to fight for their overlord with horse, armour, and full accoutrements. Because of the cost involved for the individual in contributing thus to national overseas military ventures, participation was restricted to aristocrats, and thus chivalry as a code of conduct became synonymous with gentle behaviour across the spectrum of aristocratic life. It adapted the awkwardly ascetic morality of medieval Christianity to provide a virtuous ideal that was compatible with the ownership of vast wealth, and, like all mores associated with the 'best sort of people' its finer details were closely scrutinised by those who aspired to join their ranks.[12] The fourth part of Malory's *Morte D'Arthur* is the 'Tale of Sir Gareth of Orkney That Was Called Bewmaynes'. Because it is relatively free-standing, and because its hero accumulates his chivalric reputation as the Tale progresses, it is a good starting-point from which to observe how a system of social and political ideals is conveyed through romance narrative.

The Tale begins with Arthur and his knights celebrating Pentecost, a feast-day of significance to the company, as it celebrates the commencement of the apostolic mission to spread the gospel of Christ around the world. The analogy between Christ and his disciples and Arthur and his knights is constantly suggested if never explicitly stated. The feast is interrupted, as is often the case, by an incursion from the world outside, the fairest man anyone present had ever seen, 'large and longe and brode in the shuldyrs, well-vysaged, and the largyste and the fayreste handis that ever may sye' (177: 25–7). Thus enters Sir Gareth, who in direct opposition to Sir Lancelot in the immediately preceding Tale, arrives with no credentials. Susan Crane's observation that 'status can be bequeathed, but virtuous conduct must complement it before true gentility can be claimed' will perfectly gloss Gareth's story.[13] The intruder decorously asks Arthur for three gifts. The first is food and drink for a year. Arthur is discomfited by the menial request, but Sir Kay is convinced that the visitor is a peasant, names him 'Bewmaynes, that is to say Fayre Handys', and gives him a job in the kitchen. Kay will of course be proved wrong and Arthur right about the anonymous visitor's lineage; Kay has judged him superficially, whereas Arthur recognises innate nobility, conveyed to the reader by 'Bewmaynes' physique and refined conduct. Both Gawain and Lancelot offer to supplement the visitor's uncouth diet, a marker of Gawain's subconscious recognition of his as yet unidentified brother, and of Lancelot's innate 'jantylnesse and curtesy' (179: 5–6). Thus, as Bewmaynes joins the kitchen servants, a number of nuanced assessments of what it is to be one of a knightly fellowship are opened up.

A year later, a maiden asks Arthur to help her sister who is being oppressed by the Red Knight. The maiden is refused a knight, but given the exemplary Bewmaynes who requests this as an adventure by which to prove himself. His third request is to be knighted by Lancelot. To general astonishment, Bewmaynes is miraculously supplied with horse and full armour by a dwarf, and embarks with the lady. As soon as he adds knightly apparel to his noble speech and behaviour, all but Kay and the maiden recognise him as a 'goodly' man. Bewmaynes is courageous in the face of dangerous tests on the journey, but the true challenge to his knightly comportment is the maiden. She takes over from Kay as the figure of discourtesy against which Gareth's speech and actions are thrown into relief. Her repeated sneering, goading insults directed at the stinking, sluggardly, spit-turning ladle-washer, are communicated in direct speech (182: 6–12) to the reader to promote direct appreciation of Gareth's forbearance. Moreover, the maiden not only demonstrates discourtesy in her own speech and action, but her distorted accounts of Gareth's exploits provide hypothetical instances of bad knightly conduct in action to compare with the actual exemplary conduct of her significantly unsung champion. Throughout the ensuing action, cognates built around 'hap', fortune, are particularly loaded, as it is clear that Gareth's success is providential. And so he fights and kills the Black Knight, and subjugates his brothers, the Green and Red knights, sparing them only when the maiden pleads for their lives. Finally, the maiden relents, admitting that he must come from gentle blood because of his forbearance towards her, which Gareth brushes off nonchalantly, remarking that 'a knight may lytyll do that may nat suffir a jantyllwoman' (191: 9–10); she gave him motive to prove 'what I was'.

Gareth then meets a new challenge: he wakes after he has defeated his fourth adversary to find his host's eighteen-year-old virgin daughter naked in his bed. Gareth sends her off with a chaste and courteous kiss, thus passing the harder knightly test of sexual continence, before setting out with his maiden, Lyonet, to meet the Knight of the Red Lands who has imprisoned her sister, Lyones. The Knight hoped to encounter Lancelot, Tristram, Lamerok de Galys, or Gawain, but is faced instead by the still-to-be-proved Gareth. The latter is promised that if he prevails he will be renowned as the fourth best knight in the world, which prompts Gareth to reveal to his host and to Lyonet that he is Sir Gareth of Orkney, son of King Lott and of Arthur's sister Morgawse, and youngest brother of Gawain, Aggrevayne, and Gaherys. At this juncture his dwarf goes off to tell Lyones of Gareth's approach and who he is, reprising all his feats, and supplying all his adversaries with names and identities, drawing to a conclusion the movement in the Tale in which all the agents are identifiable only through appearance and action and all other identifiers are withheld.

The Knight of the Red Lands provides another foil for Gareth's perfect chivalry. Lyones describes her jailor as a 'full nobel knight', but one who 'is nother of curtesy, bounté, nother jantylnesse; for he attendyth unto nothing but to murther' (195: 15–17). This is illustrated by the grisly sight of the forty knights he has hanged from trees. Gareth condemns the knights' deaths as disgrace to the knightly profession, vowing to die in 'playne batayle' rather than meet such a fate. He also falls in love at first sight with Lyones. It is his hardest battle so far, as the extended technical details of its description make clear, and he would have been overcome but for a well timed taunt from Lyonet. Gareth then gains access to Lyones's tower, only to be sent off by her for a year to prove himself. The potential continuing adventures are cut short, however, when Gareth's kidnapped dwarf tells Lyones's brother the true lineage of her would-be lover which makes him immediately acceptable. The united lovers are, however, thwarted in the desire to make love precipitately – a further temptation prompted this time by Lyones – by a magic knight sent by Lyonet. Gareth defeats him, but the household is awoken by the disruption, and the opportunity for furtive love-making is averted. This is the first battle that Gareth has had to fight from a position of shame, and the beheading of the knight stands as a figure of the sexual incontinence which Gareth must learn to tame. The events are repeated in ten days' time, and Gareth's 'old wound' reopens. His attempt to obliterate his conscience by cutting his adversary's head into 100 pieces and throwing them out of the window fails, as Lyonet reassembles the knight for a second time. It is in keeping with Malory's wider preoccupations that Gareth should find sexual temptation hardest to resist, as everything that goes irreparably wrong in the *Morte D'Arthur* as a whole arises as a result of ill-judged erotic love.

Next Pentecost Gareth's defeated adversaries are all admitted into the Fellowship. His mother, the Queen of Orkney, then arrives, and complains about her youngest son's treatment and is upbraided by the king for not warning them he was coming. She responds that he left her well-armed and horsed, but he was always 'mervaylously wytted', and so, it becomes clear, Gareth's trials have all been of his own contriving as a means to prove his worth. The Queen's words also draw out the whole theme of 'what's in a name?' which has threaded its way through the Tale all along. The reader may be forgiven for being puzzled that those who are told who Gareth really is seem to suffer bouts of amnesia in the Tale, but the repetition of the motif of identity-revelation serves to make a wider point. The knight's 'name' is as important to him as the

Victorian maidservant's 'character', something that has to be lived up to and which can be taken away for bad behaviour. Finally, the reader is given to understand explicitly that 'hands' have particular connotations here. One of the interlocking five fives in the pentangle on Gawain's shield in *Sir Gawain and the Green Knight* stands for the fact that he never fails in his five fingers (641), which amounts to the same thing. The moral conduct of Gawain in that poem and of Malory's Gareth 'Beaumains' is signalled by their use of their hands only for the good; they use force, take up arms in just causes only, and perform with skill, elegance, and success. Thus Gareth performs under two names: like many people in the Middle Ages, notably successive dukes of Burgundy, he has a patronymic which proves his noble lineage, but also another name which signifies his innate quality.

As the lovers are married before an emotional Arthur, Malory, as is customary, withdraws to a distance from the narrative, addressing his audience in the second person, reminding them that these events took place long ago, and that he is working from a French source (225: 25–31). The Tale is wrapped up with a plea to God for the good deliverance of the author, a reminder that Malory is writing from prison in circumstances that, despite an abundance of theories, remain obscure. His Tale has, however, characteristically imbued the remote world of Arthurian romance with many sharp realistic details, particularly as the characters interact with, and speak to, one another. He has not only shared his nostalgia for a time long ago and his admiration for the values of that world, but has presented them as a model for the kind of ideal world that he believes remains, with a little effort from those in power, truly attainable.

GUY OF WARWICK

Malory, and Arthur, supply us with our starting point, but the *Morte D'Arthur* and its printing by Caxton, come right at the end of our period, and Malory writes, uniquely amongst English medieval romancers, in prose. Most romances were written in verse, as is the case with one of the book-owning elite's instant runaway favourite thrillers, *Guy of Warwick*, which directly influenced the personal 'style' of at least one real fifteenth-century English magnate. *Guy of Warwick* and the other long English action-packed romance, *Bevis of Hamptoun*, survive, along with a number of other romance narratives, in the Auchinleck Manuscript.[14] *Guy* is, therefore, an early fourteenth-century Middle English text, written partly in couplets and partly in tail-rhyme stanzas. It is also one of a number of romance narratives in Middle English that can be traced back directly to a twelfth-century Anglo-Norman source. *Gui de Warewic* is one of the 'foundational texts' of insular romance, as well as the originator of one of the most enduring and popular romance tales to survive right through the Early Modern period, to be printed in chapbooks until the eighteenth century, and abridged for children.[15]

Despite its patriotic reputation there is little in the story that is either set in England or about England, and the association depends rather on Guy being assimilated later into the culture-myth of the English. The real focus is the hero, as he roves Europe experiencing a range of adventures and winning hearts. The Middle English poet inherits from the Anglo-Norman original a story which is a true *aventure* concerned with 'the unplanned setting out with no goal other than proving oneself against all comers and taking what fortune offers'.[16] Embedded within the construction of the hero, however, are a number of latent readings; Guy is no simple adventurer, but occupies a series of overlapping and recognisable exemplary identities which could be appropriated and celebrated by various aspirant groups within the culture in which the story circulated. These include Englishness, chivalric excellence, saintliness, and a particular identification with Warwick. Thus Guy became a 'culture-hero', emerging from a narrative whose progress may be defined as a series of transformational actions as he accretes his various exemplary identities.[17] Three complete manuscripts and two sets of fragments of the romance survive in Middle English representing five quite separate translations from one or other of the Anglo-Norman originals, suggesting that the survivors represent a sorry fragment of an originally extensive body of manuscripts.[18]

The Auchinleck Manuscript belongs to the immediately pre-Chaucerian world of London during the reign of Edward III in which civic and royal court culture overlapped. In this context, *Guy of Warwick* plays perfectly to a mixture of legal and historical interests, combined with models of nationalistic heroism, and is aimed at an audience who are practised readers of romance, understanding its procedures as a literary tradition.[19] *Guy of Warwick* has everything. Its eponymous low-born hero eventually makes good, fighting knights, traitors, Saracens, giants, and dragons. He is selfless, loyal, popular, patriotic, and pious, and even has a pet lion. Both his prowess and his penance are extreme: he spends the first half of the story fighting in order to gain the approval and hand in marriage of Felice la Belle, then sets out again to fight for God, contriving to die in the end both as a holy hermit and in the arms of his wife.[20] The Middle English poem inherited from its Anglo-Norman source a story which already offered insular nationalistic appeal and included all the elements of *aventure* which found a ready audience. It is a long and complicated story, so it took a long time to write in the first place, and the author may well have introduced some of its ingredients in response to audience demand and reaction as he went along.[21] Moreover, the romance generated subsidiary offshoots which testify to the complexity of its reception and to the variety of different interest-groups it accreted, in particular inspiring the devotional texts *Speculum Guy de Warwick* and John Lydgate's *Guy of Warwick*.[22]

Recent scholarship recognises the function of romance as exemplary narrative in the later Middle Ages, just as the tournament had become increasingly theatrical, as combatants dressed themselves up in symbolic guises and adopted fanciful names, revealing a complex two-way traffic between real life and fiction. Central to the project of impression management was the assertion through a range of cultural signifiers, of association and identification with the heroes and actions of romance narratives which encoded all that was admirable and worthy to the milieux in which they circulated. Romance, and particularly the large 'matters' set out by the author of *Cursor Mundi*, took on the status of secular scripture with models for imitation which supply its accompanying hagiography. In this climate, *Guy of Warwick* was a powerful image-building asset for the real earls of Warwick, despite offering little to convince the reader that the author knew anything about Warwick. The first Beauchamp earl of Warwick, William (1268–98), clearly familiar with the Anglo-Norman romance, named his son Guy.[23] The

Beauchamp earls accumulated various material goods associating themselves with their legendary, if specious, ancestor, and these became useful tools in their continuing assertion of status during vicissitudes in their fortunes. The family project reached its apogee with Richard Beauchamp, Earl of Warwick (1389–1439), soldier, statesman, diplomat, and tutor to the young king Henry VI. He inherited family artefacts celebrating Guy and refounded the chapel dedicated to St Mary Magdalene at Guy's Cliffe outside Warwick, for which he commissioned a huge sculpture of the hero, dressed as a knight. Richard, the last Beauchamp to hold the title, used literature as a tool with which to construct and shape his reputation, by association and by emulation. This feat of self-fashioning was taken up by his daughter, Anne, with whose marriage the Warwick title passed to Richard Neville (the 'Kingmaker'). When the family lost the title after Neville died fighting for Henry VI, his widow called upon the distinguished history of her father in petitions to Richard III and Henry VII during the 1480s, commissioning the manuscript known as *The Beauchamp Pageant.* It depicts Beauchamp as the model of chivalry, giving particular prominence to his role in the tournament held on Twelfth Night 1415 at Guînes near Calais at which he appears, 'in Gy ys armes and Beauchamps quarterly'.[24]

It is a matter of perspective whether one remarks on the high degree of historical accuracy in the sequence of events set out in the *Beauchamp Pageant*, or on the manner in which they set out to fashion and present the life of their protagonist as if it were a romance narrative. The book is both historically accurate and highly stylised. Like all life-writing it selects particular events from the life according to its underlying agenda, in this instance the desire to present Richard Beauchamp as a peerless example of English chivalry. That in his lifetime he had taken pains to present himself as the descendant of the legendary Guy, whose only real existence was always as a literary construct, means simply that the *Pageant* brings the story full circle. Small wonder then, that it has been proposed, albeit contentiously, that Richard Beauchamp provided Malory with his model for Sir Gareth, and that more plausibly the author of the *Pageant* drew on Chaucer's Knight in *The Canterbury Tales.*[25] The Tale that knight tells again treats the ideal chivalric world in complex relationship to real people and events from the generation before Richard Beauchamp adopted the legendary Guy as his model ancestor.

THE KNIGHT'S TALE

The Knight's Tale from *The Canterbury Tales* predates the *Tales* as a whole, as Chaucer mentions it as a separate entity in *The Legend of Good Women*. It has been suggested, however, that Chaucer revised the Tale, and in particular the description of the great tournament at its centre, as a direct result of his own experiences of a real tournament.[26] In the Tale, Duke Theseus devises elaborate lists, modelled on the zodiac, at which the rival brothers Palamon and Arcite, accompanied by their attendant lords, fight for the hand of Emily. Unchivalrous scrapping has already broken out between the rival lovers, so Theseus appoints a day for them to meet in a full-scale and civilised tournament. In the meantime, each has prayed to his chosen deity: Arcite to Mars for victory, Palamon to Venus for the winning of his love, Emily. The commendably chaste Emily has also prayed to Diana to be permitted to remain a maid, but has discovered her goddess's complex identity, embracing Luna and Proserpina, goddesses of childbirth, and has received the gentle divine rebuke that indicates that the time has come to marry. The gods will choose whom.[27] Both contestants achieve their desires, as Arcite wins the day but falls off his horse and dies, so Palamon gets the girl.

Synopses of The Knight's Tale can thus suggest that the plot is less than compelling: the resolution of a dispute between two virtually identical lovers, between whom Emily refuses to distinguish, is needlessly deferred, then resolved on a technicality generated by powers higher than the great Duke who aims to control all, and finds he is merely an agent of some larger providential plan. This is not a story with the narrative drive of *Guy of Warwick*, but all its interest, and Chaucer's literary reputation, rests on the manner of the telling. In The Knight's Tale Chaucer constructs an ideal pageant of refined behaviour in literary form. The characters are drawn from the great classical 'matter' of Thebes and their behaviour is carefully choreographed. The unfolding of the Tale is equally stylised, as Chaucer matches the mode of delivery to the elevated nature of the matter. Emotions are exquisitely refined, and characters matched to appropriate landscapes, times of day, and planetary deities. There are no conversations, just speeches, and, in the case of Theseus and his father Egeus, they reflect on the human condition in philosophical terms transparently Boethian, although they live before his time.[28] Moreover, the reader is made aware of the control that the narrative voice self-consciously exercises over his subject matter, and that this is always done out of solicitousness for the reader. Transitions in the text are drawn attention to and embroidered with appropriate topoi, such that, as here, when it is judged time to return to look at what is happening to Arcite, he is presented rising in the morning with the lark and the sun, and without the shared superior knowledge of narrator and reader that a certain fate awaits him:

> Now wol I turne to Arcite ageyn,
> That litel wiste how ny that was his care,
> Til that Fortune had brought him in the snare.
> The bisy larke, messager of day,
> Salueth in hir song the morwe gray,
> And firy Phebus riseth up so bright
> That al the orient laugheth of the light,
> And with his stremes dryeth in the greves
> The silver dropes hangynge on the leves.
> And Arcita, that in the court roial
> With Theseus is squire principal,
> Is risen and looketh on the myrie day . . . (1488–99)

Not only is The Knight's Tale modelling the perfect match of style to subject matter, but a narrator is constructed by the text whose solemnity is perfectly in keeping with the portentous actions of his characters. The climax of this highly designed construct is the description of another construction, the lists for the tournament (1881–5). The conceit is that the matter of the Tale is recollective rather than inventive, lying outside the narrator's imagination but being shaped into a coherent selective telling for his reader. The lists mirror cosmic order, and represent the supremely admirable, but ultimately fallible, attempt of Theseus to impose a model of the stable providential ideal universe on the real, haphazard sublunary sphere.

The real tournament Chaucer experienced took place in summer 1390, when he was Clerk of the King's Works for Richard II. The major job of the season was the erection and dismantling of scaffolds for jousts in Smithfield. It seems likely that as a result of his experiences he expanded the architectural description of the ideal jousting arena, walled around with stone rather than the rickety second-hand construction he was involved in overseeing in reality.[29] Richard II's reign was a troubled one, and he made particular efforts to court popularity with the city of London, on whose financial support in time of war he depended.[30] The form that the jousts at Smithfield took was derived, according to the chronicler Jean Froissart, from the pageants and jousts organised for the entry of Queen Isabella into Paris in June 1390 in which Richard had participated.[31]

Richard's attempts to secure peace with France, and to substitute shows of chivalry for pitched battles in which Christian knight killed Christian knight, were well supported by the advice literature of his day. War veteran Philippe de Mezieres, Counsellor to French kings and prolific writer on chivalric topics, wrote his *Letter to Richard II* in 1395 urging both Richard and Charles VI to end hostilities and to join together in battle against the infidel.[32] Chaucer's portrait of the Knight in The General Prologue presents a picture of a military career that has more in common with what De Mezieres urges than with the real experiences of English fighting men in the late Middle Ages. Terry Jones confronted the apparent problem that the Knight's battles are those in which soldiers fought as hired adventurers, rather than as defenders of national interests, by suggesting that the portrait is satirical.[33] Scholars have subsequently made sense of the same list in ways more consonant with the Knight's positioning as the representative of the chivalric ideal amongst the Canterbury pilgrims, and Maurice Keen has pointed out that the Knight's battles were campaigns against the heathen. Drawing on evidence from the Courts of Chivalry, he shows that a number of English knights participated in crusades in Spain, the Eastern Mediterranean, and Prussia, and that Geoffrey Chaucer appeared in a case before the Courts bearing witness 'as one who had seen honourable war service and could recall what old knights and esquires worthy of credence in points of chivalry had retailed in his hearing'. Neither Edward III nor any of his sons ever went on crusade, but Henry of Grosmont, father-in-law to John of Gaunt, went twice, and John of Gaunt's sons, Henry Bolingbroke, later Henry IV, and John Beaufort, both took part in major campaigns.[34] Territorial disputes in Europe meant that, for real English knights, crusading was not the dominating military experience, but the ideal of the crusade remained live in the aristocratic culture of Chaucer's age. Crusading involved setting off on campaign at one's own risk and cost without prospect of the financial spoils that fighting in France might generate from the lucrative trade in ransomed prisoners; the rules of engagement advised that infidels should be massacred in the field. Crusading was the noblest kind of military life, risk taken for the advancement of the faith alone. The chivalric ideal was Christian, martial, and aristocratic, and Chaucer's Knight, who went on more crusades than any real Englishman, therefore stands alongside Gareth and Guy as a model of chivalry.

FIN AMOR

The ideal chevalier earns social and moral capital by putting himself in perpetual physical jeopardy, and is judged according to a finely nuanced range of criteria surrounding whom one fights for, whom one fights against, and in what arena. Fighting in service of one's liege-lord, or of God, is relatively straightforward, but when knightly service is impelled by service of a woman, the protagonist is subject to a whole different order of jeopardy. In a secular literature that is largely driven by the action of *aventure*, the chief focus of introspection, and the main source of moral hazard, is the problem of erotic love. In romance literature, erotic love is as superlative, as refined, and threatens to be as mortally wounding, as military endeavour. 'Courtly love' has been conventionally read in contradistinction to gender relationships in 'real' aristocratic society,[35] but that reading suggests that romance reading is merely escapist. If, as is proposed here, romance production and reception are part of a seamless world of aristocratic impression-management, the fiction of *fin amor* will also have its counterpart in the conduct of real people.

The medieval landed elite was concerned with preserving the status quo, which meant breeding the next generation, preferably of sons. Naturally aristocratic marriages were arranged, but as with arranged – as opposed to forced – marriages in all cultures, this does not mean that they were contracted without genuine affection. Both parties after all had much in common. Richard Beauchamp, earl of Warwick married twice, first to Elizabeth, one of the Gloucestershire Berkeleys, then to Isabel Despencer, heiress to the Despencer and Abergavenny fortunes. Elizabeth Berkeley's Household Book provides an illuminating account of the life of an aristocratic wife.[36] She ran the earl's household while he was abroad, travelling with large retinues between their extensive estates, while at home she received tradesmen, clergy, strolling players, and estate officials, and also entertained female friends of noble blood, deans and bishops, a Master of Theology, a prioress, and several friars, as well as the goldsmiths and embroiderers who travelled from London to fulfil her commissions. She dispensed lavish hospitality and was a node of conspicuous consumption. Elizabeth Berkeley's life not only typifies that of the elite laywoman in England, but supplies an imaginary back-narrative to the life of Felice la Belle, engaged in charitable works while Guy of Warwick roams the known world on *aventures*. The earl's second wife, Isabel, married him when he was the foremost lay magnate in England. How much she was swept up in her second husband's cosmopolitan life is unclear, but she did travel abroad, spending Christmas with him in Paris in 1431. In the posthumous *Pageant* of his life, she features only once, bound to the mast in a shipwreck which the family survived on their return from France.[37] Her husband also wrote, and his 'Balade to the Lady Isabel' is a proficient and conventional poem of idealised love, addressed to a real woman.[38] Theirs is one example of a real aristocratic marriage in which genuine affection was expressed in the stylised terms of the literature of love. Equally, romance literature offers a range of cautionary models for relationships between the sexes. What is consistently idealised is not the relationship, but the condition of being in love, the extreme emotional response of the (male) lover, whose refinement displays itself here as much in his debility as it does in his invincibility in war. The poem of idealised love from which later texts drew their inspiration is the French *Roman de la Rose*, begun by Guillaume de Lorris around 1230, continued by Jean de Meun around 1275, and translated in part by Chaucer as *The Romaunt of the Rose*.

Over 200 manuscripts of the *Roman* survive, including many with lavish illustrations. The 'story' is relatively simple: a young man falls asleep and dreams that he enters the garden of Pleasure, where, shot by Cupid's arrows, he falls in love with the reflection of a perfect rosebud. Fair Welcome, son of Courtesy, allows him to pick a leaf, but he is shortly seen off by Rebuff. Reason advises him to abandon his goal, but he refuses to listen, turning instead to Friend. Fair Welcome secures him a kiss, but is then imprisoned by Jealousy. As Jean's text takes over from Guillaume's, Reason reappears and is again turned off, while Friend advises the lover on tactics to win the rose and warns him to avoid marriage. The Rose has come to stand not simply for the unattainable woman but also for her virginity. Wealth refuses to allow the lover to employ Lavish Giving, but Cupid organises an assault on the castle of Jealousy, supported by False Seeming and Constrained Abstinence who disable Evil Tongue. Then, just as the lover is about to win over Fair Welcome, he is assaulted and beaten back by Rebuff, Fear, and Shame, and Fair Welcome is again imprisoned. Venus arrives to help her son, and they all swear to defeat Chastity. Nature then confesses to Genius that she has failed to persuade man to make proper use of his equipment to perpetuate the species. Genius, dressed as a bishop, joins forces with those opposing the union of the lover and the Rose. Rebuff, Shame, and Fear are put to flight by Venus's fiery arrow which passes between two pillars, and sets fire to the castle of Jealousy. The lover introduces his pilgrim's staff through the same opening, plucks the rose, and wakes up.[39]

The poem has been read as an allegory of the perfect love affair, a satirical and misogynistic attack on the moral dangers of sensuality, and a philosophical work on the perils of trusting in fortune and the consolations that may be found in looking beyond ephemeral gratification. The dual authorship further complicates interpretation, calling into question any consistent unity of purpose. Many recurrent themes and motifs in the literature of romantic love from the later Middle Ages can, however, be found here. The refining effect of the state of being hopelessly in love, as well as the procreative need for the sexual act, are set in tension with the danger sensuality poses to reason, and the biblically-sanctioned virtue of chastity. Setting the narrative as an allegory within a dream framework draws on earlier philosophical models (see Chapter 5) to support the idea that dreams can be revelatory but require correct interpretation. And the May-time garden topos comes to be universally adopted as a signifier of auspicious erotic fantasy. In English literature, Genius reappears in John Gower's *Confessio Amantis* as confessor to Gower's lover-protagonist Amor. There confession becomes a framework for eight books directed at the seven deadly sins, each exemplified by stories of human love adapted from Ovid and other classical sources (see Chapter 3). Chaucer's great work of romantic love, reworking many of these themes, is *Troilus and Criseyde.*

TROY

The sack of Troy was one of the great 'matters' of medieval romance, partly because of the myth that Ascanius's son, Brutus, founded Britain. Troy stood for the epitome of an ideal society, tragically destroyed by the unchivalric ruse of the wooden horse. As with the matter of Arthur, stories of Troy first appear in 'histories'. Geoffrey of Monmouth derived the version in his twelfth-century *Historia Regum Britannicum* from the ninth-century *Historia Britonum*, by the Welsh chronicler Nennius. Three anonymous histories of Troy survive in English from the late medieval period: *The Seege or Batayle of Troye*; the alliterative *Gest Historiale of the Destruction of Troy*; and the *Laud Troy Book*, a long English metrical romance.[40] All seek to make history accessible in its contemporary detail. They suggest wealthy audiences who like stories to which they can relate, enjoy accounts of action, do not require moralising digressions, and have the money to purchase books on a subject which has a status born of antiquity. These three poems throw into sharp relief the project that Chaucer took on in *Troilus and Criseyde,* where he dispatches the events of the Trojan war with an efficient bibliography:

> But how this town come to destruccion
> Ne fallen naught to purpos me to telle

> For it were a here a long digression
> Fro my matere, and yow to long to dwelle.
> But the Troian gestes, as they felle,
> In Omer, or in Dares, or in Dite,
> Whoso that kan may rede hem as they write. (I, 141–7)

Homer was available only in Latin abridgement and inconveniently favoured the Greeks, but sixth-century Dares and fourth-century Dictys provided more usable 'eye-witness' accounts, available in Latin. Both omit the supernatural elements in the *Iliad*, and stress the love story of Paris and Helen. The sources that Chaucer does not mention are Benoit de Saint-More's *Roman de Troie* (1160), an inspirational text for crusaders in the twelfth-century West, and its popular Latin prose abridgement by Guido de Colonna. But it is Giovanni Boccaccio's Italian vernacular romance, *Il Filostrato*, that is the major narrative source for *Troilus and Criseyde*. The oft-told story of Troy was for Chaucer chiefly an authenticating context which he used in two love stories: *Troilus and Criseyde* and the story of Dido in the *Legend of Good Women*.[41]

Chaucer's innovation is not simply to turn a story of heroic warfare into a love story, but to set that account within a Boethian philosophical framework that measures human endeavours, erotic love, and the vicissitudes of fortune against the eternal. *The Consolation of Philosophy*, by the fifth-century Latin Christian philosopher Boethius, is a source of a different order, permitting the extension of a single historical instance to something of universal application. Chaucer translated the *Consolation*, with Nicholas Trevet's commentary of 1307, into his *Boece*, and drew on it not only in The Knight's Tale and *Troilus*, but in his short lyrics 'Fortune' and 'Truth'. The *Consolation*, written while Boethius was in prison awaiting execution, considers the triviality of earthly success. He is visited by Lady Philosophy who points out that it is in the nature of fortune to change, and that only fools rely on consistent good luck. Fortune, apparently random, is part of the eternal plan of a benign God, so, while apparent disasters are all part of God's providential plan, it is best to rely only on those things which are beyond change. The work is part monologue, part Platonic dialogue, a mixture of prose and verse in which the verse complements the argument by appealing to the senses. There are also interesting debates on cause and effect which Chaucer experiments with in *Troilus and Criseyde* through his hero who, because he is pagan, is unaware of the answers because he is ignorant of the existence of God.[42]

Troilus and Criseyde takes romance into new and challenging territory.[43] Yet Chaucer innovates without sacrificing the style and topoi which characterise the literary construction of an ideal aristocratic world, for the poem's use of philosophy is fundamentally aesthetic, and integral to the construction of affecting narrative. *Troilus and Criseyde* debates the view that true love does not change just because the circumstances of the lovers change. Troilus as the hero grows into his role as vehicle for Boethian musings, facing the problem of maintaining moral firmness in a changing world, remaining faithful to Criseyde once she has gone to the Greek camp and transferred her affections on to Diomede. Through maintaining truth in earthly love, he moves towards the God he cannot know, but before he can learn that God is the only fitting and reliable object for his love, Troilus has to be constructed as the ideal lover. Thus, in Book I, he is presented as the supreme warrior who, like Guy before him, succumbs to love in a manner that is life-threatening and annihilating. To learn that 'sexti tyme a day he loste his hewe [fainted]' (I: 441) may seem exaggerated to modern sensibilities, but the earlier address to the audience as 'ye loveres that bathen in gladnesse' (I: 22) is surely an injunction to read with a connoisseurship for the kind of refined sentiment embodied in the hero. The 'Canticus Troili' (I: 400–20), Troilus's lyric expression of the effect of falling hopelessly in love, borrowed directly from Petrarch, has all the qualities in its placing, its stylistic virtuosity, and its detachability, of an operatic aria. Troilus is also, in the manner of all ideal lovers, ennobled by the effects of love (I: 1079–82). Later, when Criseyde has received his suit, but the love is yet to be consummated, Troilus's joy is compared to the springtime landscape (III: 351–7).

Chaucer assumes knowledge of the Troy story, but draws on a mixed tradition of epic, romance, and moralised stories of pagan archetypes that resists drawing monolithic conclusions about anything. Narratorial evasion is presented as a scrupulous attention to sources, and leads to creative openness in the matter of apportioning blame for the collapse of the love affair. Troy's world of superlative warriors and refined love is placed within a philosophical perspective that forces the audience to see the story from a critical distance; its central action also introduces its own kind of realism, where war and violence produce painful consequences, and where erotic love makes demands that those caught up in it find themselves unable to meet. Both of these dimensions of the narrative turn it from romance to 'tragedie', and tragedy which, unlike those in The Monk's Tale, cannot be dismissed as exemplifying the wounds of fortune in the sublunary world to which Boethian philosophy may be applied as a plaster. The experience of reading *Troilus and Criseyde* is less tractable than that because of the creation – and the problem – of Criseyde.

Viewed from a distance, Criseyde is the archetypal betrayer, the shallow fickle woman who bows out of the poem with the wholly inadequate message of her last letter, promising Troilus enduring friendship (V: 1623–4). Criseyde has sometimes sounded shy, refined, and retiring (III: 159ff), at other times garrulous and demanding (II: 456; III: 169ff). With Guy's imperious Felice, or with Gareth's unrelentingly bitchy Lionet, the reader knows what the hero is up against, but Criseyde's voice is inconsistent, seducing the modern reader into believing in her as an individuated character, demanding sympathy and judgement. The narrator withholds judgement, which has led many critics to transfer the impulse to find characters on to a naïve narrator, in love with his own creation. The stanza on which these arguments focus is V: 1093–9:

> Ne me ne list this sely woman chide
> Forther than the storye wol devyse.
> Hire name, allas! is punysshed so wide,
> That for hire gilt it oughte ynough suffise.
> And if I myghte excuse hire any wise,
> For she so sory was for hire untrouthe,
> Iwis, I wolde excuse hire yet for routhe. (V: 1093–9)

The larger problem here, and the poem's continuing power to generate critical interest, is that individual stanzas can be invoked to support any number of incompatible readings. Other readings recuperate Criseyde by reading her against 'real' history, the position of women in medieval society at war.[44] The relationship between romance and 'history' was, after all, a close one throughout the period. As Corinne Saunders aptly puts it:

> Romance is a genre of extraordinary fluidity: it spans mimetic and non-mimetic, actuality and fantasy, history and legend, past and present, and is striking in its open-endedness, if frustrating in its capacity to defy classification and resolution. It is about wish-fulfilment, nostalgia, and social ideals, but it is also 'socially pertinent'.[45]

Of course, there are enchanting stories that inhabit an ethereal world in which supernatural intervention drives the turn of events, exemplified particularly in the short romances known collectively as Breton *Lais*, but the literature that presents a secular ideal world to late medieval English society runs closer to 'history', with a concomitant playing-down of the para-normal.

Malory's Lancelot and Chaucer's Troilus inhabit privileged positions in a public world which is fundamentally aggressive and where initiative for action is exclusively masculine. Both heroes stoically absorb setbacks in their private lives for the public good. In the case of Lancelot's adulterous love for Guinevere, the collateral damage remains considerable, for not only does the Round Table fall, but Elayne of Astolat finds her place in Arthurian legend as the archetypal naïve who dies of love, having refused the consolation of 1000 pounds a year when Lancelot evasively tells her, 'I caste me never to be a wedded man' (638: 20). Yet it is the damage to Lancelot's own career that is weighed in the end. When he visits Guinevere in her nunnery for their final meeting, he reminds her that 'in the queste of the Sankgreall I had that tyme forsakyn the vanytees of the worlde, had nat youre love bene'. Sir Ector's obituary sums him up as

> the curtest man that ever bare shelde! And thou were the truest frende to thy lovar that ever bestrad hors, and thou were the trewest lover, of [for] a sinful man, that ever strake with swerde, and thou were the kindest man that ever strake with swerde. (725: 18–22)

Perhaps by the time he has almost completed his flawed synthesis of the whole Arthurian story, the ambivalences here that strike the modern reader had also begun to trouble Malory himself.

Chaucer's Troilus, on the other hand, acts, or rather does not act, before his inappropriate love affair can damage the state: he abstains from moving to prevent Criseyde's exchange with Antenor, 'Syn she is changed for the townes goode' (IV, 553). He consoles himself with philosophical generalisations, and gets on with being a fighting man. Unlike Guinevere, who enjoys the inviolability of being Arthur's consort whatever her capriciousness, Criseyde is a widow, daughter of a traitor, and, although she is assured within the private world of the household, in the public world is understandably diffident and fearful, wholly subject to the self-regarding actions of men. Her father Calchas betrays and deserts her, leaving her in the care of uncle Pandarus, master of emotional blackmail and the audacious lie. By the time she reaches the Greek camp and meets Diomede, her transfer of affection may disappoint, but can hardly have surprised. Criseyde belongs to the world of superhuman heroism that is projected on to ancient Troy, but also to the world of political expediency in which England was chronically at war with France. Chaucer's granddaughter, Alice, duchess of Suffolk, lost three husbands directly and indirectly, to that war, but survived to cut a formidable political figure in her own right. Some of her associates were less fortunate. For example, Eleanor Moleyns, who grew up with Alice, married Sir Robert Hungerford, lost her fortune ransoming him, saw him and their son executed, and went on to marry one Oliver Manningham, considerably her social inferior, but providing a safe alliance in which she lived into her fifties in respectable obscurity.[46]

'Quha wait gif all that Chauceir wrait was trew?' (61) wrote the fifteenth-century Scots poet Robert Henryson in his *Testament of Cresseid*. 'Truth' can be read in a number of ways. Chaucer, tongue in cheek, authenticated his story of Troilus by selective reference to some, but by no means all, of his mixed heritage of sources, but he also fashioned – 'fenyeit of the new' (*Testament*, 64) – his Criseyde and his Pandarus from other imaginative material, doubtless coloured by the truths of contemporary court politics with which he lived. Henryson projects the story of Cresseid forward into a life of prostitution, for which a parliament of planetary deities punishes her with leprosy.

The disease, reflecting her moral condition, disfigures her physically, reduces her socially to the status of a beggar, and thus prompts a process of contrition and self-knowledge. Henryson does not even attempt to confer the status of authorised truth on the matter of his poem, writing openly about the inspiration of fiction, of one fellow innovator's effect on another. If one were to read simply this trajectory of the history of Troy in Middle English, from Boccaccio, to Chaucer, to Henryson, one would see it as a progressive freeing of the matter of romance from the stranglehold of authority and convention. Chaucer's Troilus is an ideal hero, exemplifying the medieval ideal of a differently nuanced kind of *trouthe*, in love, in war, and in devotion to the Christian God. Criseyde pulls the poem in another direction: in her, Chaucer created a social, private individual whose notorious act of bad faith was impelled by the society of which she was victim.

Retelling the story of the siege of Troy to exemplify ideal values did not, however, vanish in the wake of Chaucer's story of lost love. John Lydgate was commissioned in 1412 to write his *Troy Book* for Henry, Prince of Wales, later Henry V. Henry could have read the story in Benoit or Guido, but his desire to revive the values of chivalry possibly prompted his desire for a new version in the vernacular. With Lydgate the Troy story became once more England's national story, and an exemplum of truth.[47] For Chaucer, the 'matere' of poetry is the search for ethical truth in human complexity, his 'digressioun' (*Troilus*, I, 140–7) is the large background of the historical narrative. Chaucer's 'digressioun' was revived as Lydgate's 'matere'. The events themselves matter to Lydgate, and the reason is plainly stated at the end of his poem: Christ alone can fortify princes and defeat tyrants. He prays to Christ for Henry:

> So that his name may be magnified
> Here in this lyf up to the steres clere,
> And afterward above the ninth sphere,
> Whan he is ded, for to han a place. (V, 3580–3)

The Troy story is not only a useful encomium of chivalric behaviour, it is genealogical information, its sacred letter is Henry's personal heritage. The *Troy Book* is a status symbol in the narrowest sense, as the past is used to corroborate the present. Narrative digression, the padding Lydgate puts on the bones of Guido's story, further illuminates the special social function of the book. Lydgate is partisanly pro-Trojan, because of the genealogical importance of the story, moralising selectively. In avoiding historical narrative, Chaucer avoided overburdening his audience with facts; not so Lydgate. The *Troy Book* is not written to problematise the aspiration to chivalric perfection, but as an academic showcase of the high style to glorify the subject matter, so that the present can bask in the reflected glory of the past. This is undoubtedly why its numerous luxury manuscript versions enjoyed the status of being the aristocratic commodity of the time, despite its challenging length.

Lydgate's commission ran in parallel with an abiding fascination exhibited in the Burgundian court, renowned for its library and for the employment of historians, from which Benoit's version had first gained popularity. Henry shared with the dukes of Burgundy the desire to revive chivalry on the Trojan model and to embark upon a new and final crusade. The alliance of Burgundy and England was signed in 1420 at the Treaty of Troyes, in Burgundian territory, which was where Henry V and Catherine were married. Moreover, in 1429, on his marriage to Isabella of Portugal, Philip the Good founded the Order of the Golden Fleece in answer to the English Order of the Garter, as the highest Burgundian order. The Troy story remained popular in the related courts of the kings of England and the dukes of Burgundy, whose ostentatious habits of conspicuous consumption and revival of nationalistic chivalric values were unrivalled in the fifteenth century. Those who went on crusades had found their pagan past there as a tangible heritage, against whose exotic splendours they experienced military rigours comparable to those of the old stories. The last duke was Charles the Bold, and his third wife was Margaret of York, Edward IV's sister. She rescued Caxton's attempts to translate Raoul Lefevre's *Receuils des Histoires de Troyes* in 1471, to which we shall return at the end of this chapter.

SIR GAWAIN AND THE GREEN KNIGHT

The mid-twentieth-century literary theorist Northrop Frye commended Chaucer as an author of romances, warning that we must not 'think of him as a modern novelist who got into the Middle Ages by mistake' just because of 'his mastery of low mimetic and ironic techniques'.[48] Frye, unlike his near-contemporary Erich Auerbach, who found romance characters 'limited by their isolation from political reality',[49] suggests that romance is 'more revolutionary' than the novel. The bourgeois novelist may parody romance as something outgrown in favour of dealing with personalities within 'stable society', but the romancer too deals with individuality, 'with characters *in vacuo*, idealised by revery'.[50] The next two texts for consideration here are no more nascent bourgeois novels than is *Troilus and Criseyde*, yet *Sir Gawain and the Green Knight* and Chaucer's Tale of Sir Thopas in *The Canterbury Tales* stand as pointed critiques of the values of romance. Yet although both demonstrate modal counterpoint between the ideal and the real, the second being a sustained parody, their access to this counterpoint is wholly contained within the conventions of romance.

The anonymous late fourteenth-century poem, *Sir Gawain and the Green Knight*, is a remarkable and eccentric contribution to the 'matter' of Arthur. It takes material from Celtic mythology, and from the hunting manuals of the aristocratic playground, to generate a perfectly made tale of suspense. Its reference points involve a playful alternation between the motifs and conventions of Arthurian romance, and the experience of living on the northern Welsh March in the late fourteenth century. It then presents this whole literary game, the poet's 'gomen', as a deeply serious and pertinent moral conundrum. In its sole manuscript witness, British Library MS Cotton Nero A. x, the poem ends with the motto of the Order of the Garter, *hony soit qui mal pence* [shame be to he who thinks evil of this]. The Order was founded in 1343 as part of Edward III's grand tournament at Windsor and his attempt to found his own Round Table there. Edward drew on the legends of Arthur to justify the protracted war with France: 'Arthur's legendary knights had won their fame not by patriotic self-sacrifice but rather in the vendettas of those who had been injured in their rights, and that was how Edward and his captains talked about their war too'.[51] The Garter motto's inclusion at the end of this poem is extra-textual, so could be scribal, but also seems to sit in ironic relationship to the poem's denouement in ways that suggest that it is part of the original plan.

At the centre of the poem, the hero is tested by his host, Bertilak de Hautdesert, whose wife comes to Gawain's bedchamber on three consecutive days and attempts to seduce him. Gawain is sworn to exchange what he 'wins' each day for whatever Bertilak has killed while out hunting. In the hunting scenes the poet presents his audience with vivid blow-by-blow accounts taken straight from the idealised world of chivalry and recounted with the knowing authority of an insider for the vicarious pleasure of a connoisseur audience. Hunting was the leisure pursuit of the arms-bearing class designed to hone skills of stealth and weaponry, and Bertilak's three hunts, of deer, boar and fox, are tightly tied into the poem's central motif-system of entrapment and testing. They are also full of technical detail drawn from manuals in circulation amongst the social elite of the day such as the *Livre du Chasse* (1387), associated with Gaston III of Foix (Gaston 'Phébus') and dedicated to Philip the Bold, duke of Burgundy, on which the first comprehensive English hunting manual, the *Master of Game*, drew heavily.[52] The manuals are not purely technical in their focus, but also offer reflection on the social refinements and moral benefits of the hunt.

On the third day when Bertilak hunts and Gawain stays at home in bed, although he resists the lady, he accepts the gift of her girdle, which she claims will save his life in his forthcoming encounter with the Green Knight. He has already been tricked into this encounter, as the Green Knight invited him to an exchange of beheading blows in which Gawain, invited to strike first, found that his headless adversary remained inconveniently alive. Desperate not to die, Gawain fails to relinquish the girdle in exchange for Bertilak's prize, a fox's brush. The Green Knight – Bertilak de Hautdesert's alter ego – regards the girdle's retention as the hero's one minor display of weakness. Gawain considers that he has compromised his entire code of values set out symbolically in a pentangle device painted on his shield and surcoat, and returns to Arthur's court cross, deflated, and ashamed, with the girdle draped across the pentangle in the manner of a 'mark of distinction', which in heraldry indicated, if not actual bastardy, at least questionable claim to heirship.[53] His welcoming comrades, however, with limited comprehension of its implications for Gawain, adopt the girdle, an intimate item of ladies' clothing rather like a garter, as a badge of triumph. The origins of the blue Order of the Garter itself are obscure, as the records were destroyed by fire. According to tradition, Edward III retrieved a garter that a woman dropped at a dance, and wore it himself to spare the woman embarrassment. His courtiers felt that in doing this the king compromised the dignity of his office, so he retaliated with the motto. If the legend is true, there are, as Susan Crane has pointed out, a number of interesting parallels between this event and Gawain's situation, as both involve a crisis in the interpretation of chivalric conduct.[54] Conversely, current historians of the Order treat the legend with scepticism, believing that the 'garter' was a stylised representation of the straps used to connect pieces of plate armour, an obvious symbol for the binding together of an elite brotherhood.[55]

Binding imagery abounds in the poem, both good and bad. The pentangle is described as an 'endeles knot' (630), and turns out to be more of a liability, a trap, than a protection. Its five points, representing the five sets of five values that Gawain follows, are formed by a single continuous line, so that one breach compromises the whole. Consequently when Gawain is ensnared by the lady of Hautdesert in his bed – and she too uses the language of binding and trapping (1211–40) – and when he has to exchange his winnings with Bertilak, he finds himself in a dilemma which is at least social, but which is also morally serious. For example, behaving with courtesy to the lady who offers sexual favours is hard to balance against his fellowship with his host, not to say the implicit demands of sexual continence that his devotion to the five wounds of Christ and the five joys of the Virgin make of him. From the moment he is strapped into his armour – useless on a mission to bare his neck – Gawain is all tied up. So too, however, is the reader, as a story unfolds into which we are more than half way before we are afforded superior knowledge over the hero. One of the traps set by the poet, in his poem 'loken' together by its alliterative verse-form (35), is that the long-awaited climax of this knight's quest to exchange beheading blows with the Green Knight, turns out to refer back to the exchange of winnings game at Hautdesert, which was presented as a narrative digression along the way.[56] 'Shame be to he who evil thinks of this' is, then, a reasonable gloss on a poem which exposes the hubris of an ideal knight's aspiration to the perfection implied by the pentangle, while simultaneously teasing the readers of his *aventure* into admitting that they have fared no better in untangling its knots.

The rapprochement the poem contrives between hero and reader is reinforced by its extraordinary treatment of geographical setting, not as a backdrop to action, nor as a list of features, but as a landscape which is moved through and experienced. As Northrop Frye further observed, the binary opposition between realism and romance is a by-product of the nineteenth-century fashion for realism as the favoured order of correspondence;[57] approaching *Sir Gawain and the Green Knight* from the point of view of that opposition is a particularly futile critical exercise. On Gawain's journeys he encounters a number of potentially lethal and/or fabulous adversaries: 'worms', 'wolves', 'wodwos', 'bulls', 'bears', 'boars' and 'etaynes' [giants] are perfunctorily listed (720–3). Yet this is not an author who is ironically presenting a tired convention, as the whole narrative also hangs upon the initial appearance of a knight who is 'ouerall enker grene' (150), who invites a representative of the court to cut off his head, and who then rides off on his green horse with his head under his arm. Gawain's two destinations are distinctly fabulous too, not only in physical detail but in association: the glistening white castle that rises up before him, superlatively fortified yet insubstantial, as if 'pared out of papure' (802), and the Green Chapel of indeterminate location and shape (2171–84) but where the Devil might well recite his matins about midnight (2187–9). In both cases the reader 'reads' the unexpected sight through the eyes of Gawain. The reader is also led to experience the very 'real' desolation and loneliness that Gawain feels on his journey through the winter landscape on Christmas Eve:

> Hiȝe hillez on vche a halue, and holtwodez vnder
> Of hore okez ful hoge a hundreth togeder.
> Þe hasel and þe haȝþorne were harled al samen,
> With roȝe raged mosse rayled aywhere,
> With mony bryddez vnblyþe vpon bare twyges,
> Þat pitosly þer piped for pyne of þe colde.
> Þe gome vpon Gryngolet glydez hem vnder
> Þurȝ mony misy and myre, mon al hym one,
> Carande for his costes, lest he ne keuer schulde

To se þe servyse of that Syre, þat on þat self nyȝt
Of a burde watz borne oure baret to quelle. (742–52)

[[There were] high hills on each side, and woods below of rimy oaks, a hundred together. Hazel and hawthorn were tangled altogether, with rough ragged moss suspended everywhere, and with many unhappy birds on bare twigs, pitifully twittering in misery from the cold. The man on Gringolet glided under them through bog and mud, all on his own, worrying about his religious observances, in case he shouldn't return to see the service of that Lord who on that same night was born of a girl to put an end to our strife.]

The illusion is of uneasily taking in the topography of the comfortless surroundings with the lone horseman as he moves silently through the snow, of being perhaps slightly reassured to have a familiar horse for company, and of feeling simultaneously the self-pity of a young man separated from friends, family, and ritual at Christmas. The winter landscape is much less threatening experienced from within the exciting camaraderie of a hunting party, or casting sharp winter light across the walls of a warm castle bedroom (1126–81). The seamless mixing of modes derives surely from the poet's insistence that the reader experience the quest, the hunts, the temptations, alongside their respective protagonists, imaginatively uncovering through accumulating detail what it is really like to live in a romance world. The discomfiting experience of receiving the attentions of a predatory female, who you think is your host's wife, who might be a fairy mistress, and who certainly seems to be able to offer magic accessories, but who turns out to be the agent of a vindictive aunt, is similarly evoked. Internally and contextually cryptic, *Sir Gawain and the Green Knight* respects the nostalgia of romance while subjecting its conventions to a sophisticated make-over which reeks of fashionability.

Less respectful of the conventions of romance is the open parody that is the Tale of Sir Thopas in *The Canterbury Tales.* Chaucer's crusading Knight is given a Tale to tell possibly inspired by the poet's not altogether ideal experience of real tournament organisation, but also by the great 'matter' of Thebes, and the product is a narrative of a world so refined that the planetary deities and even the weather collaborate in the tide of human affairs. The Knight-pilgrim has a son, the Squire, whose later attempt to tell a refined Tale of the love between Canacee and Cambalus, is so overburdened with romance motifs that it is decorously brought to a premature conclusion just as its sub-plot about a tragic love triangle between three birds of prey is being wound up. In The Squire's Tale, Chaucer is just warming up in his project to expose the excesses of fashionable refined stories.

The Tale of Sir Thopas points up the larger conceit within *The Canterbury Tales* that they are retold from memory by Chaucer, the most inept story teller in the company. Sir Thopas is so bad that Harry Bailey, not a subtle brain, ventures, 'This may wel be rym doggerel' (925), and nobody disagrees. The Tale of Sir Thopas is an explosive parody of knightly *aventure* in which the hero sets out with no motive and no goal. The story is told with such lack of attention to proportionality, that, as Harry Bailey further observes, 'Thou doost noght elles but despendest tyme' (931). To categorise Sir Thopas simply as a parody of romance is, however, to understand romance to be a homogenous genre with a convergent readership, where in fact it is quite an unhelpful literary category. 'Romance' collects together a wide variety of texts whose commonality lies more in the social mores they seek to encode than in any single set of formal structural or thematic characteristics. The narrator of Sir Thopas certainly betrays his lack of social nous, topping his hero's accomplishments at hunting, for example, with the news that he is also an unbeatable wrestler. Thopas's appearance is ridiculous, not to say unmasculine, and the landscape through which he pointlessly 'pricketh' is full of referants from the kitchen garden. Even the traditional arming scene is accompanied by a snack of gingerbread.

The Tale of Sir Thopas's plot is profoundly pointless. When Thopas is exhausted and his horse lathered in sweat, he falls asleep on the grass and falls in love with an elf-queen, a clear but ludicrously unprepared-for reference to the more mechanical plot devices of numerous 'fairy mistress' tales. On waking, Thopas is confronted by a giant, Olifaunt, who claims to have the Queen of Fairies, and requires to be fought. Thopas promises to fight him the next day, once he has been home to put his armour on, and retreats under a shower of stones from the giant's sling-shot in a ludicrous reversal of the story of David and Goliath. The first fitt ends abruptly, but is immediately followed by the second, which repeats all the injunctions to listen that have already been liberally scattered through the rather short first fitt. Thopas, with a lily stuck in his helm 'glood' upon his way, mysteriously managing to strike sparks from the ground as he goes. Like other heroes on quests, he sleeps out of doors, not because he can find no harbourage but because it is the done thing, with his horse browsing the good grass beside him.

At the beginning of the truncated second fitt, the narrator digresses to compare Thopas to others – Horn, Ypotys, Beves, Guy, Lybeux, and the untraceable 'Pleyndamour' – running through a stock list of romance heroes. It was long thought that Chaucer's poem was, therefore, written as a simple burlesque of the diet of tail-rhyme romances this represents. John Burrow has suggested, however, that the influences Chaucer drew on were more complex, and that the Tale may have sources which are themselves burlesque, proposing the French text, *La Prise de Nuevile*, a parody of the French *chansons de geste*, as a likely candidate. The targets of the two poems are too disparate to argue for a direct relationship, but the point that Chaucer was familiar with a polyglot literary world in which he might readily find models of parody and burlesque is worth remembering.[58]

ROMANCE READERS

Like the durable representatives of any literary genre, all the texts discussed in this chapter demonstrate that the 'typical' romance is a literary mirage, although from its mutant variants it is clear that there was, and indeed is, a common understanding of what constitutes the mores, structural properties, topoi, motifs, themes, and characterisations belonging to these literary reflections of a secular ideal. Furthermore, the hallmarks of that ideal involve a refinement of manners associated with elite social groups and are nostalgically presented as having been better in the story's 'then' than they are in the reader's 'now'.[59] In the space available here, the desire to treat well-made texts has crowded out many which might be regarded as more commonplace, and some small gems like *Sir Orfeo*.[60] In pre-print culture there was no 'popular' demotic literary culture, as most people could not afford books. There was nonetheless a kind of 'popular', easy-to-read and not particularly intellectually challenging entertainment material which found favour with much of the wealthy reading public. What constitutes this body of material is supported by the rather unreliable census of surviving manuscripts, including texts chosen for inclusion or excerpting in compilations, as well as the few surviving booklists of private libraries. The 'reading public' is generally defined as the immediate court circle, the circles surrounding the provincial courts of great magnates, and the top ranks of mercantile wealth concentrated principally in London. There is a growing literature on the make-up of these groups, and on what can be learned about manuscript ownership and literary tastes from them. It must suffice here to consider briefly who was and was not reading what, for, if we are considering literary portrayals of ideal worlds, it helps to know whose ideals.

It is often assumed that Gower and Chaucer wrote in response to court tastes, but, as John Scattergood has cautioned, 'the poetry of Gower and Chaucer . . . appears to have been written, on occasions with an aristocratic courtly audience in mind; but its more significant readers appear to have been career diplomats, civil servants, officials and administrators who were attached to the court and government'.[61] This was the intellectual elite who read and wrote for each other, and who were interested in poetry which pushed the boundaries of conventional genres into the philosophical territory typified by Chaucer's *Troilus*. It was not until after their deaths and well into the fifteenth century that manuscripts of Chaucer and Gower's works were commissioned by the book-owning 'mainstream', that is the aristocracy at large.[62] Richard II, in whose reign Chaucer wrote his major works, inherited a number of romances from his Arthurophile grandfather, Edward III, but there is no evidence that he read them. He may not have read the love poems presented to him by Froissart. Books were precious objects, significant gifts and bequests, but this does not mean that their recipients wanted them, let alone read them. Richard II's tastes may have lain elsewhere, in, for instance, the *Forme of Cury*, a recipe book which he is known to have owned.[63] Then as now, the social and the intellectual elites were not the same, and the ideals espoused by each, although they overlapped, were not identical either.

The clear test of 'popularity' is marketability, and we find that in what Caxton printed; the advantage of printing over manuscript production was the production of multiple identical copies. Caxton chose first the history of Troy, not Chaucer's love story, nor Lydgate's *Troy Book*, but a translation of Raoul Levefre's *Receuils des Histoires de Troyes*. Caxton was Governor of the English Nation in Bruges and had sound commercial knowledge of the prestige of art works associated with the Burgundian court. In his Prologue to the work, he alleged that he secured the help and patronage of Margaret of York, duchess of Burgundy and Edward IV's sister. Given the timescale he outlines and the length of the work, it seems more likely that he prepared it earlier, but waited for the right commercial circumstances. The Prologue, Norman Blake has pointed out, is better read not as a true history of the enterprise, but as the first 'publisher's blurb'. Margaret did not personally need the book in English, preferring to commission books in French. Whatever the precise sequence of cause and effect, when Caxton had finished the book with these credentials in place, he took it to Cologne and learned to print.[64] He went on to look for other books in an elegant style written for influential European aristocrats, which included two other Trojan books, *Jason* and the *Eneydos*. The double bond of trade and fashion between England and Burgundy secured his initial market. Inevitably Caxton also recognised the commercial appeal of Arthuriana, so adapted and printed Malory's *Morte D'Arthur* in the only version known until the discovery of the Winchester manuscript of the original in 1931.

If Chaucer used his romance narratives to expose the difference between the then and the now, his fifteenth-century successors used a nostalgic return to the same stories to goad their elite readership into recognising how far short their own chivalric class fell of the ideal models to which they aspired. In his Epilogue to the *Book of the Ordre of Chyvalry*, Caxton's famous address to the 'knights of England' reads as a memorable challenge to his contemporaries:

> O, ye knyghtes of Englond, where is the custom and vsage of noble chyualry that was vsed in tho dayes? What do ye now but

> go to the baynes [baths] & playe att dyse? And some, not wel advised, vse not honest and good rule ageyn alle ordre of knyghthode. Leue this, leue it and rede the noble volumes of the saynt grail [holy grail], of Lancelot, of Galahad, of Trystram, of Perse Forest, of Percyual, of Gawayn & many mo. Ther shalle ye see manhode, curtosye & gentylnesse. And loke, in latter dayes, of the noble actes syth the conquest, as in kyng Rychard dayes cuer du lyon; Edward the fyrste and the third, and his noble sones; Syre Robert Knolles; Sir Iohan Hawkwode; Syr Iohan Chaundos; & Syre Gaultier Manny, rede Froissart. And also behold that vyctoryous and noble kynge, Harry the fyfthe, and the captayns vnder hym; his noble bretheren, therle of Salysbury Montagu, and many other whoos names shyne gloryously by their virtuous noblesse & actes that they did in thonour of thordre of chivalry. Allas, what doo ye, but slepe & take ease, and ar al disordred fro chyualry . . . [65]

The address has great emotive power, but it also drops a prodigious list of names: caution must be exercised in attributing any personal sincerity to it; more probably it signals Caxton's shrewd instinct for what would appeal to his target market. The address is surely a calculated part of the merchant-printer's own project in product placement.

Let's give the last word on the subject instead to Malory, with whom we started. Quirky, racy, and in prose, the *Morte D'Arthur* is not typical in style of the English romance tradition, as we have already seen, despite the conservatism of its aims. Malory's reward for his labours was that his name became synonymous with Arthurian legend as it passed to future generations. It is also the matter of Arthur that has proved the most tenacious of the English romance matters, evoking the ideal world of chivalry and refined love for future generations through the mediation of others from Spenser to Tennyson and on into that democratiser of idealised fantasies, the Hollywood film industry. The larger-than-life world of Malory, like that of all the best romances, offers up a model that is as much cautionary as it is exemplary, a demonstration of the conservative values which the elite can use as a touchstone for their own fashioning and presentation, but also a wistful meditation upon a fickle human nature which so easily lets all that is splendid in its achievements trickle away, insufficiently regarded until it is too late. As Northrop Frye put it, romance is about the wish-fulfilment dream, but it is also 'curiously paradoxical' as it is a projection of the ideals of the ruling social or intellectual class and yet it is 'never satisfied with its various incarnations', and it turns up again and again 'hungry as ever, looking for new hopes and desires to feed on'.[66] Caxton may exhort his contemporaries to be more like knights of old; for Malory, despite the pageantry, there never was a time when chivalry was free of realpolitik:

> Lo ye all Englysshemen, se ye nat what a myschyff here was? for he that was the moste kynge and nobelyst knight of the worlde, and moste loved the felyshyp of noble knyghtes, and by hym they all were upholdyn, and yet might nat thes Englyshemen holde them contente with hym. Lo thus was the olde custom and usayges of thys londe, and men say that we of thys londe have nat yet loste that custom. Alas! thys ys a great defaughte of us Englysshemen, for there may no thynge us please no terme. (708: 34–41)

NOTES

1. R. T. Davies (ed.), *Medieval English Lyrics* (London: Faber and Faber, 1973), pp. 168–9.
2. Gordon Kipling, *Enter the King: Theatre, Liturgy, and Ritual in the Medieval Civic Triumph* (Oxford: Clarendon Press, 1998), pp. 205–9.
3. *Gesta Henrici Quinti*, ed. and trans. Frank Taylor and John S. Roskell (Oxford: Oxford University Press, 1975), pp. 112–13.
4. See Michel de Certeau, *The Practice of Everyday Life*, trans. Steven Rendall (Berkeley: University of California Press, 1984); Pierre Bourdieu, *Outline of a Theory of Practice*, trans. Richard Nice (Cambridge: Cambridge University Press, 1977), both cited in Susan Crane, *The Performance of Self: Ritual, Clothing, and Identity during the Hundred Years War* (Philadelphia, PA: University of Pennsylvania Press, 2002), p. 5.

5. Erving Goffman, *The Presentation of Self in Everyday Life* (Harmondsworth: Penguin, 1971), p. 229; p. 243.
6. William Dunbar, *Selected Poems*, ed. Harriet Harvey Wood (London and New York: Routledge, 2003), pp. 3–8.
7. Richard Morris (ed.), *Cursor Mundi*, Part I, Early English Text Society, OS 57 (Oxford: Oxford University Press, 1961 [1874], pp. 9–11.
8. For accessible introductions, see Elizabeth Archibald and Ad Putter (eds), *The Cambridge Companion to Arthurian Legend* (Cambridge: Cambridge University Press, 2009); and Derek A. Pearsall, *Arthurian Romance: A Short Introduction* (Oxford: Blackwell, 2003).
9. See Thomas Malory, *The Works of Sir Thomas Malory*, ed. Eugene Vinaver (Oxford: Oxford University Press, 1966), for the original spelling text from which all references here are taken, by page and line number, or Thomas Malory, *Le Morte Darthur: The Winchester Manuscript*, ed. Helen Cooper (Oxford: Oxford University Press, 1998) for a modern spelling text.
10. For both poems, see Larry D. Benson, (ed.), *King Arthur's Death: The Middle English Stanzaic Morte Arthur and the Alliterative Morte Arthure* (Kalamazoo, MI: Medieval Institute Publications, 1994).
11. Derek A. Pearsall, *Arthurian Romance* (Oxford: Blackwell, 2003), pp. 83–4, following Jill Mann, *The Narrative of Distance, The Distance of Narrative in Malory's 'Morte Darthur'*, the William Matthews lectures (London: University of London, Birkbeck College, 1991).
12. See Maurice Keen, *Chivalry* (London and New York: Yale University Press, 2005).
13. Susan Crane, *The Performance of Self* (Philadelphia, PA: University of Pennsylvania Press, 2002), p. 107. See further James Simpson, 'Violence, Narrative and Proper Name: *Sir Degaré*, 'The Tale of Sir Gareth of Orkney' and the *Folie Tristan d'Oxford*', in Ad Putter and Jane Gilbert (eds), *The Spirit of Medieval English Popular Romance: A Historical Introduction* (London, New York: Longman, 2000), pp. 122–41.
14. Edinburgh, National Library of Scotland Advocates MS 19.2.1,

produced in London c.1330, contains a number of romances alongside devotional and moralising texts and hagiographical material.

15. Rosalind Field, 'From *Gui* to *Guy*: The Fashioning of a Popular Romance', in Rosalind Field and Alison Wiggins (eds), *Guy of Warwick: Icon and Ancestor* (Cambridge: D. S. Brewer, 2007), pp. 44–60 (pp. 44–5).
16. Ibid. pp. 54, 47.
17. See Susan Dannenbaum, 'Guy of Warwick and the Question of Exemplary Romance', *Genre*, 17 (1984), 351–74, and R. A. Rouse, 'Guy of Warwick as Medieval Culture-Hero', in Field and Wiggins (eds), *Guy of Warwick*, pp. 94–109.
18. For the manuscript tradition, see Alison Wiggins, 'The Manuscripts and Texts of the Middle English *Guy of Warwick*', in Field and Wiggins (eds), *Guy of Warwick*, pp. 61–80.
19. Julius Zupitza (ed.), *The Romance of Guy of Warwick*, Early English Text Society ES 42, 49 and 59 (Oxford: Oxford University Press, 1883, 1887, 1891), an edition of the text on facing pages as it appears in the Auchinleck MS from ff. 108r–175v, and Cambridge, Gonville and Caius College, MS 107/176. For a recent assessment of the Auchinleck Manuscript, see Ralph Hanna, *London Literature 1300–1380* (Cambridge: Cambridge University Press, 2005), pp. 104–47.
20. For critical readings of the romance's internal structures and themes, see Velma Bourgeois Richmond, 'Guy of Warwick: a Medieval Thriller', *South Atlantic Quarterly*, 73 (1974), 554–63; David N. Klausner, 'Didacticism and Drama in *Guy of Warwick*', *Medievalia et Humanistica,* 6 (1975), 103–19; and Susan Wittig, *Stylistic and Narrative Structure in Medieval Romance* (Austin: University of Texas Press, 1978).
21. Field, 'From *Gui* to *Guy*', p. 54.
22. For further details of these texts, see A. S. G. Edwards, 'The *Speculum Guy de Warwick* and Lydgate's *Guy of Warwick*: The Non-Romance Middle English Tradition', in Field and Wiggins (eds), *Guy of Warwick*, pp. 81–93.
23. See Yin Liu, 'Richard Beauchamp and the Uses of Romance', *Medium Aevum*, 74 (2005), 271–87; and David Griffith, 'The

Visual History of Guy of Warwick', in Field and Wiggins, *Guy of Warwick*, pp. 110–32.

24. London, British Library, MS Cotton Julius E.IV, art. 6; published as Alexandra Sinclair (ed.), *The Beauchamp Pageant* (Donington: Paul Watkins, 2003), pp. 112–13.
25. Respectively Lynn S. Martin, 'Was Richard Beauchamp, Earl of Warwick, the model for Sir Gareth?' *Studies in Medieval Culture*, 4 (1974), 517–23; and G. A. Lester, 'Chaucer's Knight and the Earl of Warwick', *Notes and Queries*, 226 (1981), 200–2.
26. Derek A. Pearsall, *The Life of Geoffrey Chaucer* (Oxford: Blackwell, 1992), p. 212.
27. For a close analysis of the astrological meaning of The Knight's Tale, see Douglas Brooks and Alastair Fowler, 'The Meaning of Chaucer's *Knight's Tale*', *Medium Aevum* 39 (1970), 123–46. See also Alastair J. Minnis, *Chaucer and Pagan Antiquity* (Cambridge: Cambridge University Press, 1982).
28. The philosophical speeches in The Knight's Tale draw on Boethius's *Consolation of Philosophy*. Chaucer's use of this work is discussed at greater length below.
29. See Pearsall, *Life of Chaucer*, p. 212; *The Westminster Chronicle 1381–1394*, ed. and trans. L. C. Hector and B. Harvey (Oxford: Clarendon Press, 1982), pp. 438–9; 470–2; Martin M. Crow and Claire C. Olsen (eds), *Chaucer Life Records* (Oxford: Clarendon Press, 1966), pp. 473–89.
30. See James Gillespie, *The Age of Richard II* (Stroud: Sutton, 1997); and James Gillespie and Anthony Goodman (eds), *Richard II: The Art of Kingship* (Oxford: Oxford University Press, 2003), especially ch. 7, Caroline M. Barron, 'Richard II and London'.
31. Jean Froissart, *Chronicles of England, France, Spain and the adjoining countries from the latter part of the reign of Edward II to the coronation of Henry IV*, trans. Thomas Johnes, 2 vols (London: William Smith, 1848), vol. 2, pp. 449–505.
32. Philippe de Mezieres, *Letter to Richard II: A Plea made in 1395 for Peace between England and France*, trans. G. W. Coopland (Liverpool: Liverpool University Press, 1975), pp. 31–2.

33. Terry Jones, *Chaucer's Knight: The Portrait of a Medieval Mercenary* (London: Eyre Methuen, 1980).
34. Maurice Keen, 'Chaucer's Knight, the English Aristocracy and the Crusade', in V. J. Scattergood and J. W. Sherborne (eds), *English Court Culture in the Later Middle Ages* (London: Duckworth, 1983), pp. 45–61.
35. C. S. Lewis *The Allegory of Love: A Study in Medieval Tradition* (Oxford: Oxford University Press, 1937) has the most influential study on the subject, though now considered misleading.
36. C. D. Ross, 'The Household Accounts of Elizabeth Berkeley, countess of Warwick, 1420–1', *Transactions of the Bristol and Gloucester Archaeological Society*, 70 (1951), 81–105.
37. Sinclair (ed.), *Beauchamp Pageant*, f. 25v.
38. London, British Library, Additional MS 16, 165, ff. 245v–46r.
39. See Guillaume (de Lorris) and Jean (de Meun), *The Romance of the Rose*, ed. and trans. Frances Horgan (Oxford: Oxford University Press, 1999), and Sylvia Huot, Alastair Minnis and Patrick Boyde (eds), *The Romance of the Rose and Its Medieval Readers: Interpretation, Reception, Manuscript Transmission* (Cambridge: Cambridge University Press, 1993). I am indebted to Horgan for this summary.
40. Mary Elizabeth Barnicle (ed.), *The Seege or Batayle of Troye: A Middle English Metrical Romance*, Early English Text Society, OS 172 (Oxford: Oxford University Press, 1926); G. A. Panton and D. Donaldson (eds), *The Gest Hystoriale of the Destruction of Troy*, vols I and II, Early English Text Society, OS 39 (Oxford: Oxford University Press, 1869); J. E. Wulfing (ed.), *The Laud Troy Book*, Early English Text Society, OS 121 (Oxford: Oxford University Press, 1902).
41. See Piero Boitani (ed.), *The European Tragedy of Troilus* (Oxford: Oxford University Press, 1989); Geoffrey Chaucer, *Troilus and Criseyde: A New Edition of 'The Book of Troilus'*, ed. B. A. Windeatt (London and New York: Longman, 1984).
42. Scc further Alastair J. Minnis, *Chaucer's Boece and the Medieval Tradition of Boethius* (Woodbridge, Suffolk: D. S. Brewer, 1993); and Minnis, *Chaucer and Pagan Antiquity*.
43. *Troilus and Criseyde* attracts large amounts of critical activity

which cannot all be referenced here. See C. David Benson (ed.), *Critical Essays on Chaucer's Troilus and Criseyde and his Major Early Poems* (Toronto: University of Toronto Press, 1991); Piero Boitani and Jill Mann (eds), *The Cambridge Companion to Chaucer* (Cambridge: Cambridge University Press, 2003), especially essays by Lambert, pp. 78–92, and Mann, pp. 93–111; Lee Patterson, *Chaucer and the Subject of History* (Madison, WI: University of Wisconsin Press, 1991), pp. 84–164; Richard J. Schoeck and Jerome Taylor (eds), *Chaucer Criticism II: Troilus and Criseyde and the Minor Poems* (Indiana: Notre Dame University Press, 1961); Barry A. Windeatt, *Troilus and Criseyde*, Oxford Guides to Chaucer (Oxford: Clarendon Press, 1992).

44. Stephen Knight, *Geoffrey Chaucer* (Oxford: Blackwell, 1986), pp. 32–65.
45. Corinne Saunders (ed.), *A Companion to Romance: From Classical to Contemporary* (Oxford: Blackwell, 2007), pp. 2–3.
46. See M. B. Rudd, *Thomas Chaucer* (Minneapolis, MN: University of Minnesota, 1926), pp. 12–13; G. E. Cokayne and Vicary Gibbs (ed.), *The Complete Peerage*, 14 vols (London: St Catherine's Press, 1926), vol. IX, pp. 42–3, and vol. VI, pp. 619–21.
47. John Lydgate, *Troy Book – Selections*, ed. Robert R. Edwards (Kalamazoo, MI: TEAMS Middle English Texts, 1998).
48. Northrop Frye, *Anatomy of Criticism* (Princeton, NJ: Princeton University Press, 1957), p. 51. See also *The Secular Scripture: A Study of the Structure of Romance* (Cambridge, MA: Harvard University Press, 1976).
49. Erich Auerbach, *Mimesis: The Representation of Reality in Western Literature*, trans. William R. Trask (Princeton, NJ: Princeton University Press, 1974), p. 133.
50. Frye, *Anatomy of Criticism*, pp. 305–6.
51. Maurice Keen, *English Society in the Later Middle Ages, 1348–1500* (Harmondsworth: Penguin, 1990), p. 141.
52. For detailed analysis of the hunting scenes in the poem, see further Anne Rooney, *Hunting in Middle English Literature* (Cambridge: Boydell Press, 1993), pp. 159–93.
53. The 'bend sinister', which the girdle emulates, was one of

a variety of indicators used to show degrees of 'cadence' which compromised the bearer's right to heirship. See Arthur Charles Fox-Davies, *A Complete Guide to Heraldry* (New York: Skyhorse Publishing, 2007), p. 510.

54. Crane, *The Performance of Self*, p. 136.
55. See Frances Ingledew, *Sir Gawain and the Green Knight and the Order of the Garter* (Notre Dame, IN: University of Notre Dame Press, 2006).
56. For this dimension of the poem's structural trickery, see further Ad Putter, *An Introduction to the* Gawain *Poet* (London and New York: Longman, 1996), pp. 38–102.
57. Frye, *Anatomy of Criticism*, p. 45.
58. John Burrow, '"Sir Thopas" and "La Prise de Nuevile"', *Yearbook of English Studies*, 14 (1984), 44–55.
59. See further Derek Brewer, 'The Popular English Metrical Romances', in Saunders, *A Companion to Romance*, pp. 45–54.
60. *Sir Orfeo*, loosely based on the story of Orpheus and Eurydice, is one of the group of romances with a high incidence of supernatural events known as the 'Breton Lais'. See Thomas C. Rumble (ed.), *The Breton Lais in Middle English* (Detroit, MI: Wayne State University Press, 1965).
61. V. J. Scattergood, 'Literary Culture at the Court of Richard II', in Scattergood and Sherborne (eds), *English Court Culture*, pp. 29–44 (p. 38).
62. Ibid. pp. 40–1.
63. Ibid. pp. 32–5.
64. N. F. Blake, *Caxton: England's First Publisher* (London: Osprey, 1975), pp. 20–4.
65. William Caxton, *The Book of the Ordre of Chyvalry*, ed. A. T. P. Byles, Early English Text Society, OS 168 (Oxford: Oxford University Press, 1926), pp. 122–3.
66. Frye, *Anatomy of Criticism*, p. 186.

CHAPTER 2

Social Change

WYNNERE AND WASTOURE

Lydgate, Malory, and Caxton paint wistful rhetorical pictures of a past and compare it with a comparatively degenerate present, despite Chaucer's earlier warnings of the ultimate unknowability of the inhabitants of remote cultures. The texts in this chapter express little interest in the past, but subject the present day to a long cool stare of appraisal. As the court becomes that of Edward III, Richard II, or the Lancastrian monarchs, rather than that of Arthur, or of Theseus, or of Love, so barter takes over from service as the represented mode of effective social and political interaction.

Wynnere and Wastoure takes the form of a debate in which competing voices are matched to competing estimations of social worth.[1] The comportment of the aristocracy, represented in the person of Wastoure, is subjected to a blistering if unfocused attack by Wynnere, a representative of the newly powerful merchant class whose ethics and social behaviour are in turn attacked by his adversary. Wastoure is a portrayal of the profligacy of the upper classes from Wynnere's point of view; his defence is that the liberality and significant expenditure of his class oil the wheels of production. Wynnere, on the other hand, is portrayed as miserly and avaricious by his opponent, while presenting himself as a prudent and responsible manager of resources. The poem's 500 lines break off before the king can pronounce his verdict on who has won. The derogatory connotations of 'wasting' and favourable connotations of 'winning' might suggest that the poet favours the latter, but all other aspects of the text reveal a partisan and conservative point of view which places him in Wastoure's camp. All the detail of the dispute and its setting are rooted not in an exemplary past, but in a materially detailed political and economic present in which the very form of the poem as a debate reveals that social worth was a subject of contestation. The unique copy of the poem survives in Robert Thornton's mid-fifteenth-century manuscript (British Library Additional MS 31042), but internal evidence places its composition in the late fourteenth century.

The poem opens, like *Sir Gawain and the Green Knight*, with Brutus's flight from Troy, but this poet jumps immediately into an apocalyptic vision of his own times. He draws on contemporary 'signs of Doomsday' to mix eerily superstitious portents with concrete evocations of post-Plague society in which families and social hierarchies are collapsing.[2] Past and future are, here and throughout, reference points for an intense focus on the present moment. The king in this poem is Edward III, whose war with France put under constant stress an economic and political system already in shock following the profound changes impelled by the Black Death. The major outbreak in 1348, and subsequent return epidemics throughout the fourteenth and fifteenth centuries, present a temptingly simple explanation for all the preoccupations, including the aesthetic, of the times; it will provide a persistent context in this chapter.

The causes and origins of the pandemic known as the Black Death are well documented. Its arrival in the south west of England from the Crimean steppes via Gascony, carried by the flea whose favoured host was the sea-going *ratus ratus*, need not be rehearsed.[3] Its psychological impact was intensified by contemporary explanations for its cause, from atmospheric miasma and inauspicious astrological conjunctions, to the wrath of God. It is estimated to have eliminated around a third of the English population in its first visitation, with some regional and class variations. The exceptional losses sustained by communally living religious communities added to general unease and suggested an imminent apocalypse. For those who survived the disease, however, there were new opportunities. Standards of living rose, but so did geographical and social mobility.

In particular there was a mass move from the countryside to the towns as the manorial system disintegrated. Plague had an emancipating effect on the female population, as a shortage of suitable marriage partners drove women into the towns where they found economic independence born of the general labour shortage, and particularly as household servants for the newly emergent middle classes. Increased female economic autonomy appears to have been a contributory factor in the failure of the birth-rate to rise and a continued depression of population numbers. At the same time, civic amenities improved and town life prospered.

The landed classes were being impoverished by the Crown's demand for resources to finance war, while civic prosperity brought with it the growth of new wealth, held not in land, but in moveable goods, a potential resource which Crown systems of taxation proved inadequate to tap. These are the circumstances directly reflected on by the poet of *Wynnere and Wastoure*. The Crown had to curry favour with the new 'winners', while also attempting to control soaring wage levels, through the Statute of Labourers of 1352, and to suppress popular discontent by the Statute of Treasons of 1353. Both pieces of legislation were implemented during the time that William Shareshull was Chief Justice of the King's Bench, whom the poet incidentally attacks as a suppressor of popular feeling (317). There was also an inevitable freeing of the class-based marriage market, as the newly wealthy intermarried with the impoverished arms-bearing classes:

> And eke boyes of no blode, with boste and with pryde,
> Schall wedde ladyes in londe, and lede at hir will. (15–16)

What can only tenuously be attributed to the plague, however, is degeneration in poetry itself, which the poet goes on to deplore as his Prologue progresses:

> Bot now a childe appon chere, with owtten chyn wedys
> Þat neuer wroghte thurgh witt thies wordes to gedire,
> Fro he can jangle als a jaye, and japes telle,
> He schall be leuede and louede and lett of a while
> Wele more þan þe man that made it hym seluen. (24–8)

Good poetry was traditionally associated with truth-telling and wisdom,[4] and the narrator establishes his persona through an association with poetic tradition as a sign of his wider conservatism. He demonstrates his mastery by how he manipulates the conventional dream-vision. He is alone in a landscape, and lies down on a grassy bank to sleep, but significant deviations in the description prepare a knowing audience for the satirical nature of what follows. Instead of being lulled to sleep by babbling water and sweet birdsong, he is prevented from sleeping by the raucous landscape. Among the birds 'singing' to him are woodpeckers and a jay that 'janglede one heghe' and charmed the 'foles'. The jangling jay is a commonplace for empty words, and the pun on fowls/fools a parting shot directed at bad poetry. Contention in nature anticipates the contending armies of Wynnere and Wastoure encountered in the dream itself; strife in nature is treated with humour, whereas political strife will be a serious matter.[5]

The poet moves from courtly dream-vision into debate, drawing on scholastic method as practised in contemporary courts of law.[6] The whole poem is driven by dialectic, framed by the poet's testing and rejecting of idealising poetic forms in favour of a form which analogises actual juridical practice. His own initial unbalanced descriptions of the opposing armies also alert the reader to the tensions inherent in receiving an account of opposed cases from a single and evidently prejudiced voice. The desire to locate a precise context for the poet's prejudice also leads the modern reader into attempting to decode what are evidently precisely encoded details in the opening section of the dream before the debate proper opens. The poem's first editor, Sir Israel Gollancz, dated it to 1352 or shortly thereafter, as the poem includes the Garter motto rendered in English as an integral line of alliterative verse – 'hethyng haue the hathell þat any harme thynkes' (68) – and makes detailed references to the Statute of Treasons. However Elizabeth Salter questioned this dating, convincingly placing the poem much later, in the reign of Richard II. Her argument, which suggests a particular connection with one aristocratic family, the Wingfields of Leatheringham, opened up a speculative case for the poet's patronage relationship with a prominent martial dynasty, which in turn supports the evident authorial bias in favour of Wastoure, and the old aristocratic values he represents.[7] The closest parallel to his line on the degeneracy of poetic composition is the opening to Chandos Herald's *Vie et Gestes du Prince Noir* [Life and Exploits of the Black Prince], written in 1385.[8]

The problems of locating the precise references in the opening section of the dream are, presumably, problems for the modern reader rather than for the original target audience. As a context, however, the underlying aggression of the scene anticipates the poem's end, when the King is asked not to judge which of two debaters is right, but which should live, suggesting that, for the poet and his audience, the class struggle represented in the debate is more gladiatorial than academic. When the two armies themselves are then described, the poet's bias, which is never directly declared, is clear. He devotes fifty lines to Wynnere's forces, in which all participants are inappropriate in a martial context – for example friars and lawyers. Wastoure's forces, on the other hand, are drawn from the martial class and described in only four lines, devoid of satirical implication and vigorous enough to eclipse the account of Wynnere's:

> And sekeere one þat other side are sadde men of armes,
> Bolde sqwyeres of blode, bowmen many,
> Þat if they strike one stroke, stynt þay ne thynken
> Till owthir here appon hethe be hewen to dethe. (193–6)

The debate itself, though presented as direct reportage, also reveals the narrator's prejudices. Wastoure frequently invokes assumptions about the nature of hierarchical society and the desirability of the status quo that Wynnere sneers at, ignores altogether, and fails to counter.[9] Chiefly Wastoure argues that spending his wealth benefits the poor, and is, at any rate, better than keeping it under lock and key (296). Wynnere's 'arguments', by contrast, are a great deal less subtly constructed or backed by authority, relying instead on visceral responses to descriptions of Wastoure's excesses (325–65), and undercut by the narrator's description of him as 'this wrechede wynnere' (324).

Despite the narrator's prejudice, the debate is expediently inconclusive. Late medieval monarchical government was a model of absolute authority, yet in practice, and particularly during the Hundred Years War, the monarch was vitally dependent on his support in the country. From the reign of Edward III onwards, that support consisted of the two groups exemplified in the poem, and in reality in constant tension. The poem grudgingly acknowledges the monarch's increasing dependence upon new non-noble reservoirs of wealth, and the need to effect access to them, the 'wynneres' represented variously by religious communities and particularly by new urban merchant wealth concentrated chiefly in London. *Wynnere and Wastoure* articulates social crisis in post-Black Death England by resisting, through form, metaphor, and subject matter, convergent patterns of orderliness. The inconclusive debate is an example of how an open conclusion is based on Aristotelian models of teleological moderation whereby temporal good is actualised as social practice. Cases have been made for the conclusion being that both winning and wasting have their place in a vibrant economy, and, conversely, that the poem condemns both excessive hoarding and spending.[10] Medieval philosophical ideologies would support a third conclusion favouring moderation, even if the debates between Monetarism and Keynesianism, saving versus spending, that drive modern economic theory had not yet arrived in medieval economic thought.

William Langland's exploration of the related problem of reward and bribery in a contemporary court, through the personification of Lady Mede in *Piers Plowman*, suggests unsurprisingly that common understanding ran in advance of formal theory.[11] *Wynnere and Wastoure* also, however, stands as a warning to the reader not to equate topicality with radical ideology. Signalled by the poet's initial identification of himself with 'old school' standards in poetic composition, the poem unfolds as an example of radically structured satirical writing from a deeply conservative point of view. Debate is simply a discourse through which to propose that social order and individual identity are not givens, but are provisional constructs subject to contestation and defended by repeated affirmation. Debate, therefore, turns the business of impression management into a competitive performance.

THE CANTERBURY TALES

More elaborate than the two- or three-part debate poem is the signature work of the whole period, *The Canterbury Tales*. The voices of the pilgrims on Chaucer's imagined expedition to the shrine of St Thomas Becket are set in competition with one another as story-tellers, but the overarching construct is a test not just of the individual performers, but of the skill of the narrator and the judgement of the reader. We have seen how Chaucer sets up the Knight as premier pilgrim, validated by chivalric history and by romance decorum, and also how skills in romance-telling are honoured in the breach in the failed Tale of Sir Thopas. Unlike the narrator of *Wynnere and Wastoure*, who parades his opinions and credentials, the narrator of *The Canterbury Tales* presents himself as deficient in literary skill and discrimination but prodigious in memory. The search for order in his book falls doubly on the reader, for not only does he withhold judgement, of pilgrim and of story-telling skill, but he left *The Canterbury Tales* unfinished and unsorted. He did, however, write the beginning and the end. In the end, he retracted much of what he had written on grounds that it 'sownen into synne' (X (I), 1085), but in the beginning he laid out a complete catalogue of the performers in the forthcoming competition in order that his readership might study their form for themselves.

The poem claims to be recollective of an event which 'bifel' in real time. The occasion was a perfect spring day when 'smale fowles' sang, although the place, the Tabard Inn in Southwark, is not rural but part of the unregulated urban sprawl that occupied the south bank of the Thames. It is a convenient gathering-point from which to embark on the popular pilgrimage route to the very English shrine of the martyred Archbishop Thomas Becket. The pilgrimage frame displaces the whole ensuing substance of the book into its own margins, as activity undertaken to pass the time before the performers arrive at the real business they were engaged in upon arrival in Canterbury. The readers of *Sir Gawain and the Green Knight* learn only after the event that what they took to be displacement activity at Hautdesert was the hero's real test; in *The Canterbury Tales* the reader's focus on the tale-telling competition is engaged from the outset. There is no suggestion that the visit to the shrine will play any significant part in the narrative, although it provided a fertile opportunity for at least one of the fifteenth-century continuators of the book.[12]

The modern reader of *Wynnere and Wastoure* is forced into a relationship of surrogacy with the reader to whom the work was addressed, as the narrator assumes not only knowledge of contemporary persons and events, but complicity of opinion. By contrast, *The Canterbury Tales* creates its own society, containing its own closed internal systems of telling, receiving, and judging. On the comparatively rare occasions on which any external audience is addressed, such as in the Prologue to The Miller's Tale, it is a non-specific reading audience of whose tastes and opinions the narrator is unsure:

> And therfore every gentil wight I preye,
> For goddes love, demeth nat that I seye
> Of yvel entente, but for I moot reherce
> Hir tales alle, be they bettre or werse,
> Or elles falsen som of my mateere.
> And therfore, whoso list it nat yheere,
> Turne over the leef and chese another tale;
> For he shal fynde ynowe, grete and smale,
> Of storial thyng that toucheth gentillesse,
> And eek moralitee and hoolynesse.
> Blameth nat me if that ye chese amys. (I (A), 3171–81)

Paul Strohm associates the apparent distance between Chaucer and his audience with a period in which he was isolated from his immediate circle of coterie readers, which may explain why *The Canterbury Tales* gives the modern reader the illusion of direct access to the world Chaucer creates.[13]

That life itself is a pilgrimage is a commonplace of medieval devotional writing, whether or not the author endorses the physical journey to a sacred shrine as meaningful.[14] Chaucer's own views on the value of physical pilgrimage are irrecoverable. It has become a commonplace in modern criticism to find implied moral judgements of the fictional pilgrims by noting that the spring pilgrimage to Canterbury was too easy, and then to impute suspect motives to a number of the participants. It may just be possible to read some irony in the audaciously postponed principal clause in the long sentence that opens The General Prologue, but otherwise to invoke the relative challenge of pilgrimages to the Holy Land and Rome, or the radical outpourings of some of Chaucer's contemporaries against all forms of physical pilgrimage, is wilfully to read alongside the text. On the other side is the evidence of genuine belief in the efficacy of venerating shrines of the saints, and the earnest endeavours of those who maintained and beautified them as a devotional act that many in England fought to preserve beyond the Reformation.[15] To read *The Canterbury Tales* against some nebulous medieval moral absolute is comparable with assuming that characters in modern literature are to be judged according to Western totemic beliefs in, for example, their commitment to renewable energy or ethical food production. What is explicitly available within Chaucer's text is a narrative stance that *refuses* totalising judgement of the overarching event and its participants. Its permissiveness of intra-textual response, freed from the particularities of any assumed community of external reception, is what makes *The Canterbury Tales* as a whole, and The General Prologue in particular, rich in available readings of late medieval social fluidity.

Formally The General Prologue is a list. The binary oppositions that used to be the focus of critical studies, between whether the portraits in it are individuals or types, rooted in Chaucer's social world, or in some eternal understanding of the human condition, have now largely been abandoned. Jill Mann's suggestion that Chaucer was working with a ready-made generic model, medieval estates satire, importantly moved the debate along.[16] Estates satire has as its reference-point the three overarching categories which were taken to be divinely ordained, reaching back in English tradition to Alfred the Great,[17] and defined as those who pray, those who fight, and those who work. By 'estate' is further understood an individual's social position, or membership of a class, with particular reference to their dominant occupation. The portraits Chaucer paints of his pilgrims are dominated by a fascination with the quiddity of what they do, and generates more lists. The reader is treated, for example, to a list of different culinary techniques in the portrait of the Cook – 'He koude rooste, and seethe, and broille, and frye,

/ Maken mortreux, and wel bake a pye.' (I (A), 383–4) – and in the portrait of the Physician, to a bibliography of medieval medical education:

> Well knew he the olde Escupalius
> And Deyscorides, and eek Rufus,
> Olde Ypocras, Haly, and Galyen,
> Serapion, Razis, and Avycen,
> Averrois, Damascien, and Constantyn,
> Bernard, and Gatesden, and Gilbertyn. (I (A), 429–36)

Estates satires generally sought neither to be complete nor to achieve absolute hierarchical order, which may explain why, in The General Prologue, Chaucer exercises some freedom with selection and ordering. Yet at the end he apologises to his audience, 'al have I nat set folk in hir degree' (I (A), 744), suggesting that he has pushed the model to some limit of perversity. The pilgrims do not represent a cross-section of late fourteenth-century society, any more than they represent a balanced representation of each of the three overarching estates, but rather appear to problematise the estates model. The second estate, with which Chaucer himself had most dealing in his own working life as a royal servant, is significantly under-represented, perhaps because he devised a model to engage the market for expensive secular manuscripts by concentrating on voyeuristic portraits of the 'other orders'. One of the difficulties made acute by the social changes impelled by the Black Death was, of course, that the third estate became increasingly diverse, with many of its members challenging the other two for power and position. There is a high concentration in The General Prologue of individuals who fail to conform to any tidy model. Representing the first estate there are, for example, the Summoner, who works within the Church but has no clerical vocation, and the Pardoner, who is personally and professionally defined by his outsider status. The Physician and the Sergeant at Law, as medieval university graduates, properly also belong within the clerical estate, but their vocations are wholly secular in focus. The Franklin sits uneasily between the second and third estates, and the prominent women on the pilgrimage, one a very secular nun, the other a barren, much-wedded wife, both expose the gender bias of the estates system and defy other traditional categorisations of women.[18]

The diversity of *The Canterbury Tales* themselves is a diversity of genre. Traditional criticism enjoyed speculating about how far each given tale 'fits' its teller, largely ignoring the fact that the work is unfinished, that no manuscript of it survives from Chaucer's lifetime, and that the earliest manuscript witnesses vary in the ordering and attribution of the Tales.[19] The material circumstances of the manuscript witnesses, smoothed over in modern editions, suggests that a fully dramatic reading of *The Canterbury Tales* is not possible. On the other hand, each Tale has the internal auspices of a performance, an experiment in a particular narrative genre with a more or less constructed narrative voice. Good modern readings are careful to balance the palpable sense of performance conveyed by the book, though concentrated in the transitions between Tales, against the evidently 'bookish' nature of the whole experiment, as signalled by injunctions to, for example, 'Turne over the leef and chese another tale' (I (A), 3177).

THE MILLER'S TALE

Fragment I of *The Canterbury Tales* survives in finished form, which means that the transitions from The General Prologue to Knight, and Knight to Miller, are securely authorial. The Knight's status is affirmed by God, as he draws the first lot and opens the competition. The Miller's following intervention signals a disruption of the implied social order; the host wishes 'som bettre man', namely the Monk, to speak next (I (A), 3130). The Miller's breach of decorum is anticipated within the narrative as a kind of noise: 'That I am dronke, I knowe it by my soun' (I (A), 3138). The cause, Southwark ale, and its effects become a burlesque motif for the social disruption played out in what follows. References to sound are reinforced by the Reeve's intervention: 'Stynte thy clappe!' (I (A), 3144), which also establishes a rivalry within the dramatic fiction which provides a different ordering principle in the tale-telling competition. Balanced against the noise is the narrator's reminder that the Tale is part of a book, its main focus its variety of 'storial thing' (I (A), 3179). Thus the Miller and the Reeve's *ad hominem* rivalry is balanced by the intertextual rivalry between the Tales of the Miller and the Knight.

The source, structure, and imaginative world of The Miller's Tale make it a *fabliau*. *Fabliaux* were fashionable comedic French thirteenth-century narratives, written to amuse the aristocracy by exposing the customs and social climbing habits of the urban classes. The typical *fabliau* is racy in pace, and low on descriptive embellishment. It usually centres on a practical joke, often scatological and/or sexual, as its denouement, exposing the social pretensions of the protagonist. In The Miller's Tale, the story ends as John, the old, ignorant, but well-to-do carpenter, falls from roof to floor, cuckolded by Alisoun, the young sexy wife he was vain enough to believe he could retain. The mechanics of getting to this point have been set up as an elaborate ruse perpetrated by Nicholas the lodger. The plot combines three source story types: the story of the man who was persuaded that he had been selected to be the second Noah; the story of the lover who, expecting to kiss his loved one's mouth, was misdirected into kissing his rival's backside; and the story of the adulterous lover who was branded on his bare backside by his rival. All have French analogues.

In a number of ways, however, The Miller's Tale breaks the formal bounds of the traditional *fabliau*. For example, the narrative halts to itemise the heroine's physical attractions. The imagery in this passage of *effictio* may reflect the farmyard where she was born and the tradesman's counting-house into which she married, but this type of narrative digression is much more typical of romance. There is also a detailed description of Absolon, the unsuccessful suitor, again privileging the reader with a level of background information beyond the usual scope of *fabliaux*. The real difference is, however, that the putative narrator, the Miller, is not a young aristocrat mocking his social inferiors, but a character drawn straight out of the *fabliau* tradition himself, a boorish know-all, put (by his occupation and his accomplishments) irredeemably outside the honour group. So this is at once a *fabliau* told by a *fabliau* character, and a show-piece of narrative erudition enhanced with embellishments more common in romance. The formal rapprochement between romance and *fabliau* as genres, and between literature by and for the aristocracy and a more demotic palimpsest, sets the bar for the other genre experiments that will follow.

Chaucer's presentation of The Miller's Tale is a faux performance, its point-of-view signalling an intellectual snobbery that implies an anticipated audience drawn from Chaucer's immediate circle. Nicholas, the student lodger and seducer of Alisoun, contrives a plot involving the frivolous application of arcane knowledge, which mirrors the construction of the Tale itself. The targets of Nicholas's manipulation – a provincial carpenter, a flighty young gold-digger up from the country, a fastidious parish clerk with small-town aspirations, and the bit-part given to a peculiarly dense monk at Osney Abbey – also coincide with the likely targets of Chaucer's metropolitan coterie of readers, real or projected. The real performances in The Miller's Tale are not the Miller's, but those of the deftly presented actors within the Tale. The burlesque treatments of John, Alisoun, and Absolon are all devised around the performance of lives fashioned to create an impression motivated by social aspiration that seriously misses the mark. John as a successful tradesman has married his trophy wife and set her up in a modern house in the suburbs; Alisoun has used her very uncourtly sexiness to move herself from the countryside to the suburbs and to deck herself out in ostentatiously vulgar fashion, and Absolon has accreted a range of effete accomplishments, and contrived a physical appearance to match, which allows him to enact a personal fantasy of courtly style in the same unpromisingly suburban setting. The only character to escape ridicule is Gervase the Smith, whose laconic detachment from the after-dark shenanigans of the young would-be lovers may, perhaps, reflect the respect with which Chaucer, sometime Clerk of Royal Works, held the professional artisan who knows his place. In all the other cases the Tale encodes the characters' socially aspirant performances by reference to real contemporary theatre.

The Miller's Tale is shot through with references to dramatic performance. There are two direct references to alert the reader to what is going on: the Miller is first heard crying 'in Pilates voys' (I (A), 3124) when he disrupts the transition from Knight to Monk, and then it is improbably claimed that Absolon 'pleyeth Herodes upon a scaffold hye' (I (A), 3384). Modern readings which assume that Chaucer's reference point is guild drama like the York, Chester, and Coventry cycles ignore the fact that these are geographically and chronologically problematic. Yet Chaucer must have anticipated an audience who would find the idea of a New Testament play, performed on a scaffold in the vicinity of Oxford, meaningful and funny. Research into the records of medieval drama in the Thames Valley has found small-scale biblical plays to have been a common provincial entertainment used for bringing in revenue for the parish at Easter.[20] The surviving records are late, but the scale, the parish as the organisational structure, and the mode of performance all suggest a playing tradition that provides a context for Absolon's dramatic activities. Chaucer may have been a detached bystander at just such a parish biblical play on one of his visits to the environs of Oxford to visit friends.[21] On the other hand, he need not have left London to see biblical dramas performed by clerks. In Clerkenwell throughout the late fourteenth century the independent confraternity of parish clerks of London regularly put on plays, performing, for example, 'the Passion of Our Lord and the Creation of the World' before Richard II in 1391.[22] Clerkenwell is close to Smithfield where Chaucer was engaged in superintending the construction of the scaffolds for the lists for Richard II's tournaments in 1390.[23] He could not have avoided knowing about, if not watching, the elaborate amateur theatricals of the parish clerks at Clerkenwell as he moved between Smithfield, Westminster, and the Tower engaged in employment which gave him familiarity with carpenters, their materials, tools, and work. It thus becomes possible to see The Miller's Tale as a companion piece to The Knight's Tale in more ways than one, each employing a different kind of contemporary theatricality as a sign of social distinction, the Knight's aristocratic Tale focusing on the ultimate courtly performance, the idealised tournament, while The Miller's Tale draws on references to parish plays in order to mock the middle orders for their social and aesthetic aspirations.

The two overt allusions to playing in The Miller's Tale and its frame are only signals of a range of more oblique references. Although Absolon is the only character in the Tale labelled as an actor, all are preoccupied with dressing up and role playing.[24] The precise effect Alisoun's costume is designed to achieve is difficult to excavate from the ephemerality of fashion, but the fussy over-dressing which contrivedly reveals and draws attention to body-parts, is all about vulgar display. Absolon's curious hair-style – fanned-out, curly, and golden (I (A), 3314–15) – has been interpreted as either mocking the minor clergy for disobedience in relation to the tonsure, or referring to Absolom in 2 Samuel, to whom Adam of Usk compared the deposed Richard II, a possible, now lost satirical allusion.[25] At any rate, Absolon's appearance is contrived and outlandish, and his varied accomplishments – letting blood, barbering, drawing up legal documents, dancing twenty kinds of dance, singing falsetto, playing the 'rubible' and the 'giterne', and acting (I (A), 3216–36) – are added to the performance of his ecclesiastical duties as part of a larger self-fashioned performance to which he ill-advisedly adds the affectation of playing the courtly lover. Nicholas is a more enigmatic force within the narrative, not being subjected to the same level of belittling descriptive detail, but still presented as a role-player who sets up his own downfall: the student whose business is the assimilation of the authorities of the past pretends to be a foreteller of the future. His activities are directed at persuading John and Alisoun to play at Noah and his wife, and so we are back with biblical drama.

Performing provides a set of metaphorical resonances based on the idea of pretending to be what you are not, which supply the mainspring of The Miller's Tale's attack on those who exploit the social fluidity that flourished in post-Plague England. Moreover, the Tale extends its examination of the fluidity of individual social identity from the social to the sexual. With his splendid hair, his fastidiously customised shoes, his goose-grey eyes, and his falsetto voice, Absolon is persistently interpreted by modern readers as effeminate. This response is triggered by the burlesque *effictio* which Chaucer uses to describe him, as the convention, cataloguing body parts for admiration, is used in romance to describe the object of the gaze, which is almost exclusively female. There is, however, no innuendo about Absolon's sexual orientation comparable with Chaucer's other blond falsetto, the pilgrim Pardoner; Absolon is a show-off who seeks to attract women, and indulges heterosexual fantasies, albeit sanitised. Woefully miscast as Herod, he matches the requirements of the ideal female impersonator, particularly one who played the Virgin Mary and chose to grow his own hair in order to perfect his part. We may assume with some confidence that, in the Clerkenwell plays at any rate, all roles were played by men, which may have supplied Chaucer with some further comedic inspiration.

The climax of the burlesque analogy between inept theatricalities and ineptly fashioned social identities is perfectly synchronised in the proto-play of Noah's Ark. John and Alisoun, like January and May in The Merchant's Tale, belong to the well-worn traditional gag of the old cuckolded husband and the young wife whose reference point is the counter-example of the marriage of Joseph and Mary. Biblical typology associated the counter-example with two Old Testament bad marriages, Adam and Eve, and Noah and his wife. In The Miller's Tale, John and Alisoun perform the parts of Noah and his wife in a 'play' directed by clerkly student Nicholas as surrogate for the author who revels in putting this provincial Noah and Mrs Noah into kneading tubs in a village duck-pond. Just as the scaffolds knocked together for the lists at Smithfield may have been a poor substitute for Theseus's perfect arena, so too Chaucer here suggests that epic biblical events are hard to produce convincingly on a domestic scale.

Noah's wife is one of the pseudo-biblical archetypes of the shrewish wife, a role in which Alisoun is better typecast than Absolon is as Herod. Demure speech, or preferably silence, was an important dimension of idealised contemporary female comportment. Chaucer elsewhere illustrates the shortcomings of complying with the ideal in the fates of Griselda in The Clerk's Tale and Virginia in The Physician's Tale.[26] His counter-examples are his two Alisouns, the Wife of Bath, and the Miller's heroine whose voice is 'as loude and yerne / As any swalwe sittinge on a berne' (I (A), 3257–8). Bold speech is permitted in female virgin martyrs, and Alisoun threatens to cry 'out! harrow!' and 'allas' (I (A), 3286) when Nicholas grabs her by her 'haunchebones', but although she is noisy, she is no virgin. And if she is Noah's wife in this drama, she also needs to be a man. The description of Alisoun's body contains details that cannot be accounted for as part of the satirical description of an upwardly-mobile suburban woman; it is neither that of the ivory-breasted courtly ideal nor yet of its broad-hipped carnivalesque opposite to be encountered by the testosterone-charged students in The Reeve's Tale. Alisoun is 'long as a mast, and upright as a bolt' (I (A), 3265), and thin as a weasel (3234), more like a youth, a 'joly colt', than a voluptuous girl. The loud voice, the elaborate figure-concealing dress, in particular the broad collar and the apron, and the plucked eyebrows all contribute to a picture which, for all it is soft, sweet-smelling, tactile, and sexy, is sexually ambiguous. As a number of recent critical studies have observed, nobody inhabits their gender identity in a simple way in The Miller's Tale. If social roles within the Tale are exposed as being synthetically constructed, it stands to reason that this will also entail various versions of what it is to be male and to be female.[27] Chaucer's interest in the cultural construction, and attendant vulnerability, of the female is apparent elsewhere and is the main driver of The Wife of Bath's Prologue and Tale. Fashions at the court of Richard II also incidentally indicate that heterosexuality may not have been the only acceptable sexual practice. The ambiguous bodies that inhabit The Miller's Tale may derive their humour from topical reference to cross-dressing practices in plays in the city or at court, real performances that Chaucer may himself have witnessed.[28]

THE PEASANTS' REVOLT

As a citizen of London throughout the reign of Richard II, Chaucer must also have observed more earnest social performances, notably the violent eruption of the Kentish rebels in the revolt of 1381.

> So hydous was the noyse, a, *benedicitee!*
> Certes, he Jakke Straw and his menyee
> Ne made nevere shoutes half so shrille
> Whan that they wolden any Flemyng kille,
> As thilke day was maad upon the fox. (VII, 3393–7)

Thus he describes the pursuit of Reynard the fox and attempted rescue of Chanticleer the cock, by the poor widow and her dogs in The Nun's Priest's Tale. We will return to that in Chapter 5, but what of 'Jakke Straw and his menyee'?

The social and economic changes following the Black Death inspired satirical attacks from within the establishment on the opportunists who had gained new financial and social agency thereby. We can presume that they preached to the converted. Many of the features of his contemporary society illustrated by Chaucer in *The Canterbury Tales* were, however, symptomatic of a more serious crisis of authority in late fourteenth-century England. The bad fit between seigneurial obligations and burgeoning commercial activity extended to all levels of society, and the discontents provoked thereby came to a head in the events of 1381. The country had gone through extreme demographic change: there was high social mobility, a change in the balance between town and country, and an increase in trades and services. The Church was also affected by these changes, and, in particular, the lower clergy became increasingly integrated into the urban micro-cultures of the parishes they served.

The three foremost canonical literary authors of the period witnessed the events of 1381 in London at close quarters. Chaucer, lodging in Aldwark throughout the events, is the most reticent. His contemporary John Gower uniquely foresaw trouble, writing in his French work, *Mirour de l'omme*:

> There are three things of such a sort
> That they produce merciless destruction
> When they get the upper hand:
> One is a flood of water,
> Another is a raging fire
> And the third is the lesser people,
> The common multitude;
> For they will not be stopped
> By either reason or by discipline. (26498–506)[29]

Gower was finishing his Latin *Vox Clamantis* when the rebels from Kent passed his house in Southwark on their way to burn John of Gaunt's palace at the Savoy and to storm the Tower, where they seized and executed archbishop and chancellor Simon Sudbury. The book was devised to give a consensual authoritative voice to the people of England, with Gower as their self-appointed representative, complaining of political corruption amongst those close to the king. But the Revolt caused him to append a new dream-vision to the beginning of the poem, aligning the voice crying out with all those under attack. In this nightmarish vision he encounters in the fields crowds of poor people whom God changes into domestic farm animals that then run wild. He imitates the noises the animals make in a passage of contrived poetic ugliness. It has been suggested that The Nun's Priest's Tale parodies the farmyard imagery of Gower's response to events.[30]

William Langland, author of *Piers Plowman*, to which we will give detailed attention in Chapter 4, was resident at Cornhill in London in the 1380s when he wrote the latest of the three surviving versions of his poem. It demonstrates that he was anxious about the misappropriation of his earlier 'B' version by the rebels.[31] Whether Langland knew that the radical preacher of 1381, John Ball, had used the poem in letters to the rebel leaders and in his sermons as part of his provocation to action, we cannot know. Ball's sermons and letters survive only in the 'transcripts' of unsympathetic chroniclers. However, the reported text of Ball's famous sermon on Blackheath does quote the harangue of Wit from *Piers Plowman* 'B' Text, passus 9, a passage later revised by Langland to remove the reference to all three estates having come from one man. It was this passage which Ball adopted as the inspiration for what has become a rallying cry for popular political movements since:

> When Adam delved and Eve span, Who was then the gentleman? From the beginning all men by nature were created alike, and our bondage or servitude came in by the unjust oppression of naughty men. For if God would have had any bondmen from the beginning, he would have appointed who should be bond, and who free. And therefore I exhort you to consider that now the time is come, appointed to us by God, in which ye may (if ye will) cast off the yoke of bondage, and recover liberty.[32]

Langland's attempts to distance himself from rebel ideology whilst striving to understand the rebel cause have been subject to detailed critical study,[33] but he, along with Gower and Chaucer, offers only recollective reflections on the events of 1381. For contemporary accounts of events, and for the reported voices of the rebels themselves, we depend on the chroniclers Froissart, Henry Knighton, and Thomas Walsingham, as well as the anonymous authors of the

Westminster and Anonimalle chronicles.[34] Modern historiography of the revolt problematises these sources because of their evident anti-rebel bias, and has found in local judicial records new and more nuanced sources on which to base an understanding of the rebels and their motivations. Their studies have revealed the dispersed nature of the revolt, and the different patterns of cause and effect that predominated in different regions.[35]

Despite the occluded voices of the rebels themselves, the fundamental textuality of the risings is inescapable. Judicial records reveal that one of the rebels' major goals was to burn records, particularly the green-sealed escheat rolls and documents facilitating the collection of the poll tax. They thereby demonstrated a technical familiarity with forms of written culture out of keeping with their designation as 'peasants' by the hostile chroniclers, with all its associations of non-literate culture. The same records also reveal that those prosecuted as rebels were as diverse a group in terms of social background as the representatives of the third estate in *The Canterbury Tales*, including minor gentry, well-to-do merchants and craftsmen, and members of the lower clergy. The most famous of the latter group is John Ball, again for reasons that relate to textuality, as letters ascribed to his hand were transcribed by Thomas Walsingham who had direct access to them when present in St Albans at Ball's trial and execution.[36] Ball's letters are included with three others, attributed to the presumably pseudonominous Jack Milner, Jack Carter, and Jack Trueman, all quoted by Henry Knighton. Certain patterns occur across this small body of texts written for wide circulation, possibly by copying, possibly in the form of broadsheets displayed in public places to be read silently or aloud by the literate to those unable to read or simply unable to get close enough to see.[37] What the texts afford access to more broadly is the performative dimension of political rebellion: the rebels were as self-conscious in the performance of their public identities as any other social group in late medieval society.[38]

> Man be ware and be no fool:
> Thenke apon the ax, and of the stool.
> The stool was hard, the ax was scharp,
> The iiij yere of kyng Richard.[39]

So writes an anonymous Londoner, laconically reflecting on the events and subsequent executions of 1381, but the populace was not to be silenced, and voices from outside the first two estates who were the traditional custodians of written authority continued to express social discontent. Spreading vernacular literacy was a form of empowerment that came particularly with the practice of trade. Not only was the third estate growing in fiscal power in the period following the Black Death, it was becoming noisier, and its noises were not those of barnyard animals; they have left stylised, enthusiastic, and subversive textual traces. This is an area we will return to in Chapter 4.

THE WIFE OF BATH

The chroniclers were particularly affronted by the refusal of Kentish rebel-leader, Wat Tyler, to show deference to his monarch. One of the side-effects of fourteenth-century demographic change was an evident new sense of self-worth amongst groups that formerly made up the labouring poor. The discourse of market value permeated all human relationships, as service tested its power to name its price and to become both commodity and merchant. This change also, and particularly, affected the position of women. We have seen literary reflections of the elite marriage market already. Felice, Emilye, Criseyde, and other literary reflections of the varied lot of the aristocratic woman, all show in common how woman was subject to the initiative of men, of fathers, uncles, and brothers, in the marriage market. But in The Miller's Tale it is unclear who did the deal that delivered young, pretty Alisoun into the house of elderly, rich John. Similarly, in The Merchant's Tale, January finds his May, as 'in a commune market-place' (IV (E), 1583), and contracts marriage with her without reference to any male intermediary. In the more refined Franklin's Tale, Dorigen condescends to take Arveragus as her husband, 'of swich lordeshipe as men han over hir wyves', without recourse to any higher authority. The absence from their narratives of Alisoun, May, and Dorigen's fathers, is, in its own way, as significant as the absence of the mothers of Prospero's Miranda or the three daughters of King Lear. One does not have to subscribe to the view that Chaucer created a 'marriage debate' within *The Canterbury Tales*[40] to understand that these are portraits of women whose submission to the lordship of their husbands is as conditional as that of the former bondsman to his lord.

The Wife of Bath is the only secular woman on the pilgrimage to Canterbury. Her presence is a marker of female social and material autonomy and geographical mobility. Bath, 100 miles (160 km) from Southwark, was an important centre in the English cloth industry, which along with brewing, was a late medieval industry in which women found work. The Wife's connection with the marketplace is not, however, focused on her trade or craft but on the commodification of her own body. Her Prologue's confessional account of her five barren marriages is shot through with references to trade. She has controlled, manipulated, and offered for sale sexual favour through a subversive rereading of the patriarchal biblical idea of the 'marriage debt': 'wynne whoso may, for al is for to selle' (III (D), 414), she says; 'greet prees at market maketh deere ware [goods]' (522); 'blood bitokeneth gold, as me was taught' (581), and, 'The flour is goon, ther is namoore to telle; / The bren, as I best kan, now moste I selle' (477–8).

Just as the baronage's loss of control over the bondsman is variously signalled in the textual environment of the Revolt, the man's loss of control over the newly empowered woman is signalled through reading the palimpsests of resistant texts. This is what Chaucer pre-prepares for his reader in The Wife of Bath's Prologue, confecting a show performance from a textual melange. An audience of knowing males would recognise the portrait of the Wife as an animated cut-and-paste of contemporary anti-feminist writing, so that the Prologue presents her as *exemplum*. The Latin sources present the classic case for a man to avoid marriage. Chaucer adds in some Ovid, some *Roman de la Rose*, and material from *Le Miroir de Mariage*, a diatribe against marriage by his French contemporary, Eustace Deschamps, as well as a number of biblical texts, especially Proverbs 7: 10–12; 31: 10–31, and St Paul's first letter to the Corinthians 7.[41] The intertextual references do not have to be unearthed as they are directly referenced and enacted in the book within the book, Jankyn's book of wicked wives. The Wife's assertion, that lived experience is preferable to written authority, is performed by the emblematic action of the Wife, who tears a leaf from the book, causing Jankyn to hit her, which in turn causes her to go deaf. The 'deafness' of the voice of female resistance to male written authority, like the leprosy contracted by another transgressive woman in Robert Henryson's *Testament of Cresseid*, enters the narrative at a particular point, but signals a perpetual condition. It is an absence, a defect, a negation, which affirms the established values of the texts in Jankyn's book.

In the advice literature of the period there are a number of texts on proper female conduct addressed to women by men. All preach restraint and deference. The *Livre pour l'enseignement de ses filles du Chevalier de La Tour Landry*, written in the 1370s, proved sufficiently popular to merit translation and printing by Caxton over 100 years later as *The Book of the Knight of the Tower*.[42] Its narrator, a widowed father, instructs his daughters on their deportment at court. It focuses on the wife's absolute duty to support her husband no matter how badly he behaves, adducing biblical examples, such as Abigail, who devoted herself to appeasing people her husband upset. All instances show that the woman has no innate value except insofar as she adds value to her husband. She, unlike Eve, is a true rib of Adam. The *Menagier de Paris*, or Goodman of Paris, similarly wrote an advice-book in the 1390s, this time for the young wife whom he expected would remarry after his death. Amongst the advice he offers her to perfect her wifely skills is that she should observe and emulate the behaviour of domestic animals:

> you shall see how that a greyhound or mastiff or little dog, whether it be on the road, or at table, or in bed, ever keepeth him close to the person from whom he taketh his food and leaveth all the others and is distant and shy with them; and if the dog is afar off, he always has his heart and his eye upon his master; even if his master whip him and throw stones at him, the dog followeth, wagging his tail and lying down before his master to appease him, and through rivers, through woods, through thieves and through battles followeth him.[43]

Of the few female voices to which we have direct access, Christine de Pisan, Chaucer's French contemporary, is the best known. In her

Epistre au Dieu d'Amours [Letter to the God of Love], she complains that women's reputations are tainted because they are written about by men.[44]

The Wife of Bath is, however, not a 'real' woman but a textual construct. What leads to the illusion of a fully individuated dramatic character is not the content of her opinions, nor the credibility of the lived experience described, but the manner of the telling. Like the other Alisoun's, this is a noisy voice: 'Allas! Allas! That evere love was synne!' (III (D), 614). She is rendered garrulous and emphatic by frequent insertions of 'By God!', and 'Fy!', and by the raconteur's validating technique of recreating the exact words spoken in a recounted incident in all its phatic detail. In the Wife, Chaucer again frames social comment within performance, allowing the fictional performer's voice to obliterate the narrator's, so that the reader must negotiate his or her response without overt direction. Moreover, the whole Prologue is presented in the form of an unprompted confession. Confession, the revelation of past thoughts and actions for the scrutiny of an authoritative audience, is a discourse used by the patriarchal authority of the Church to control access to the real and imagined privileges and punishments it administered. Dyan Elliott writes about the exploitative ways (male) ecclesiastical authority used the confessional to assert power, often sexual power, over women. Yet, as she has also shown, women's reputation for zealous confessing paradoxically opened up opportunities of empowerment, as a number of female sham mystics, working with their attendant priests, created a lucrative theatre of spirituality in which the woman was the centre of attention, like the Wife of Bath, controlling the response of a credulous and voyeuristic audience.[45]

The Wife of Bath's Tale itself is another genre-experiment which enacts the Wife's speculation:

> By God! If women had written stories,
> As clerkes han withinne hire oratories,
> They wolde han written of men moore wikkednesse
> Than al the mark of Adam may redresse. (III (D), 693–6)

The Tale is the retelling of a fairy mistress tale in which a knight finds that he can save his life only if he can find the answer to the question of what women want most. He goes on a quest in search of the answer and meets a loathsome old hag who tells him that women most want to have control over men. The knight escapes death at the hands of his enemies, but in return must marry the old hag. In bed on their marriage night, she persuades him to face her, whereupon he finds that she has transformed into a beautiful young girl. She asks him whether he would prefer to have her beautiful by day or by night, but tired by now of trick questions, the knight leaves the decision in her hands. Because he has capitulated to her, she promises to stay young and beautiful always, and they live happily ever after.

What a synopsis effaces is the way in which this story can be adapted to prompt various responses. In the anonymous *Wedding of Sir Gawain and Dame Ragnall*, the narrative framework is deployed to allow Gawain, as hero, to demonstrate extreme chivalric behaviour and win audience approval. A subtler range of responses is prompted by John Gower's adaptation in his Tale of Florent in *Confessio Amantis*, Book I, where the romance becomes an exemplum of obedience, as Florent is eventually rewarded for exercising nobility of mind and moral discernment. Chaucer's adaptation is more radical. The hero is a rapist, forced into the bargain set by the ladies of the court to save his life. In all other versions, the testers are malign; here he is the transgressor. There is no indication that he is remorseful, nor that the quest is penitential. He comes upon the hag because he spies on some young girls dancing in a wood, and much less emphasis is put on the grotesque appearance of the hag than in other versions. The radical change, however, is that he walks into the bargain with the hag without knowing his part in advance. She accompanies him back to the court where the bargain is uttered in public. The quest is, therefore, manipulated so that instead of being morally enhanced, the hero is humiliated. He has no chance to demonstrate Florent's stoicism as all his opportunities for displaying bravery and chivalry are pre-empted by powerful and cynical women. The values of chivalry are transposed ironically into a lecture given by the transformed hag to her husband on their wedding night in bed. The relationship between Prologue and Tale is not so much the simple matter of the Tale being adapted as the wish-fulfilment of the invented narrator; rather the two sit in parallel, drawing attention through their internal juxtapositions of authorities and lived experiences, to the gap between official society and its mores, as enshrined in textual traditions, and the operation of other behaviours and performances.

MARGERY KEMPE

In The Wife of Bath's Prologue, anti-feminist exemplum is converted through the paradoxical discourse of a publicly performed confession, the open secret, into faux autobiography. *The Book of Margery Kempe* is the text from the Middle English period which presents itself seductively as a genuine autobiography in the voice of a real woman who chooses to make herself a public example.[46] It relates how a middle-class housewife, born around 1373, daughter of a one-time mayor of the Norfolk trading port of King's Lynn (then called Bishop's Lynn), goes through a conversion experience following a trauma, and adopts a life of religious vocation while continuing to live in the civic world. The third-person narrative opens with an account of how the illiterate protagonist struggled to have the book produced by an appropriate amanuensis. In terms of both process and product this remains one of the most problematic texts in the medieval English literary canon.

Critical approaches to autobiography begin from the premise that the protagonist is the author's former self or selves. Here, that relationship is further complicated by the acknowledged intervention of the scribe. The resultant text is a complex cultural performance in which, according to Derrida's classic opposition, the rigidity of *écriture* [writing] is superimposed on *parole vive* [living speech].[47] Humanist critics have tended to read the *Book* romantically, as a female voice struggling to be heard against its difficulties in being inscribed, and reflecting the protagonist's struggles to live her chosen life. There are, however, reasons for exercising caution before presuming that any individual voice can be excavated from the text. For example, much of the vocabulary in which spiritual experience is described is drawn from a particular literate, northern, mystical tradition to which an illiterate Margery Kempe would have no access. The narratives of her pilgrimages could also be constructed from written pilgrimage narratives rather than from lived experience. We cannot here attempt a systematic analysis of what is, incontrovertibly, a long book, running to some 8,536 lines in modern printed edition, but we can explore some of the ways in which, despite interpretative difficulties, it affords access to a particular mentality, albeit the product of a complex collusion.

The events in *The Book of Margery Kempe* are presented as dictated to a priest-confidant, and the text's relationship with the discourse of confession offers the reader a way in.[48] Until the realist novel offered autobiography an alternative model, confession provided the form for life-writing from St Augustine to Rousseau. Yet the pivotal crisis that goes on to prompt Margery's life choices is reported to have been a failed confession:

> aftyr that hir child was born, sche, not trostyng hir lyfe, sent for hir gostly fadyr, as iseyd beforn, in ful wyl to be chrevyn [shriven] of alle hir lyfetym, as ner as sche cowed. And whan sche cam to the point for to seyn that thing which sche had so long conselyd [concealed], hir confessowr was a lytyl to hastye and gan scharply to undyrnemyn [reprove] hir, er than sche had fully seyd hir entent, and so sche wold no mor seyn for nowt he mygth do. And anoon, for dreed sche had of dampnacyon on the to side, and hys scharp reprevyng on that other side, this creatur went owt of hir mende [out of her mind] . . . [49]

The remainder of the narrative is the account of the subject's recuperation of her selfhood from this experience.

The process of recovery is presented as an active and direct engagement with the deity which turns the tables on clerical intermediacy by claiming superior access to the central mysteries of the faith. The protagonist is shielded by third-person narrative, but God speaks in the first person, so that the reader experiences the subject's reality as a continuum which resists, and therefore challenges, divisions between the material and the metaphysical, the metaphorical and the 'real'. There is no formal distinction between the account of the protagonist's appearance before the Minster Chapter of York and her 'ghostly' marriage to Christ. Both involve a mixture of reported action and direct speech, both refer to her seemly apprehension, to the kindness of her supporters, and to the gathering of spectators. In the Chapter she is watched by a group of curious people, supported by 'frendys' who came to her and 'bodyn hir ben of good cher' (4044–5), and by a 'preste ful goodly' (4046). In the marriage 'in hir sowle' it is God the Father who leads her by the hand, and the event is witnessed by the Holy Ghost, the Virgin Mary, and a number of benignly disposed female saints and angels (2848–51). In terms of order, tone, and register, the two accounts are similar. Elsewhere, her compassion encompasses variously both the Virgin Mary at the base of the Cross, and her own elderly husband who falls from a ladder, becoming senile and incontinent. To criticise Margery Kempe, wherever she resides in the narrative, of somehow failing in her aspirations to mysticism because of the unrelentingly material nature of her relationship with the metaphysical is a category error akin to suggesting that Toni Morrison's *Beloved* is an instance of flawed realism. Demolishing the barriers set up by the medieval Church between the laywoman and her God is a social gesture, but as in *Beloved*, this book's social message is reinforced by a literary gesture, rendering it in discourse which bends and flouts common understandings of what is 'true'.

The inscription of witnesses into both the events described above is something which also characterises the narrative. Where the life of the female mystic approved by the medieval church was a life of withdrawal, and enclosure in an anchorage was the signature statement of spiritual soundness, Margery validates all her actions in the physical and metaphysical realms by performing them in public. Moreover, she is constantly portrayed in situations where, supported directly by the voice of God, she sets herself up in opposition to the crowd – of clerics, of fellow-pilgrims, of sceptical citizens of Lynn – thereby exposing the 'spiritual tepidity of the contemporary English'.[50] She is a social rebel, publicly resisting the multiply passive spiritual roles assigned to her as a sexually active laywoman. As the rebels of 1381 are available to us only through the reports of their performances inscribed in the resistant texts of conservative chroniclers, so too Kempe's representative role is dissipated by her scribe's project to confer a singularity upon a proto-mystic. That very singularity may set her up for canonisation, but in the same gesture it leeches away her power as a representative.

Taking a step back from *The Book of Margery Kempe's* formal complexities, we find within it the account of a remarkably self-confident woman. Her adoption of sexual continence within a burgess marriage which had already produced numerous children is performed by the defiantly public adoption of white clothing; her affective association with the events and personae of the New Testament is performed by extreme and noisy emotional demonstrations in church, and her devotional vocation is taken abroad on pilgrimages amongst strangers. Margery Kempe as a narrative construct signifies a new kind of noisy, publicly performed, social disruption, astutely shielded from gagging by its manipulation of establishment discourses and procedures. Historians see early modern social activism as a by-product of Protestantism, whose central tenet is a direct one-to-one relationship with God, but Margery's do-it-yourself religion is far from Protestant, fervently supporting the mystical and sacramental nature of medieval Catholicism. On the evidence of her *Book*, it is more likely that the one-to-one relationship with God is the *effect* of a greater valuing of the self rather than the cause, and that its cause lies in the economic conditions of late fourteenth-century England that constructed the daughter of a successful businessman as a social force for official society to reckon with. The *Book* is more interesting as a document of social than of theological change. The protagonist is 'this creature', not perhaps the enlightenment individual, but God's unique created thing, with social autonomy as her birthright.[51]

MYSTERY PLAYS

Whether it is the London of Winner, the Oxford of John the carpenter, or the Lynn of Margery Kempe, the city variously empowers the newly cash-rich middle orders in late medieval English society. Cities were opportunistic sites where those with some disposable income banded together to provide themselves with the amenities that the great landed aristocrat could enjoy on his estate. They provided protection, access to harbourage at sea or riverside, and a network of roads and bridges, facilitated the movement of people and of goods, which were lifted by city cranes into warehouses and ships for storage and onward movement. The city provided facilities for the care of body and soul by supplying a critical mass of populace to which the Church could easily minister in its parish churches, hospitals, maisons dieu, and schools. The benefits of city life covered, in short, all aspects of life from the spiritual to the economic, social, and physical.[52]

Civic life was organised around family, workplace, and parish. Craftsmen and traders, from the humblest cloth-worker to the grandest trader in luxury goods from the East, operated from small units based around the extended family of master craftsman, his wife, children, journeymen, and apprentices. The unit, in this nascent mercantile society, owned the means of production; industrial wage-labour was a thing of the future. In The Miller's Tale, as Absolon runs from John's fancy suburban house, he rubs his mouth with chips of wood he finds lying around, for John's workshop would be an integral part of the dwelling. Those engaged in the same occupation lived together, giving rise to street names like 'Coppergate' [Coopers' Street], and worshipped together in parish churches which enjoyed their benefaction, attended to their marriages and burials, and provided education in the functional literacy essential to trade. For urban medieval social life, however, the organisational structure was the confraternity or guild.

'Guild' – a semantic fusion between the Old Norse word for payment or tribute, and the Old English for sacrifice or reward – is the term commonly used to describe medieval occupational, charitable, and social associations. The blurring of the distinctions between different types of confraternal organisations is also the blurring between lay and clerical in the civic body, for although some guilds were purely occupational associations, others operated as burial clubs, friendly societies, and devotional organisations. Religious observation played a defining role in civic respectability, so guilds articulated their cultural activities by reference to the eternal, localising it and appropriating it as their own. They fostered local cults of saints, and sponsored dramas based on locally significant miracles or on the scriptural matter of religious worship. Guild activities also cut across class, gender, and lay/clerical fault lines, demonstrating the individual's exercise of free choice in relation to devotional predilections, all enabled by moveable wealth derived from manufacture and trade. Money was both the solution and the problem, as Chaucer and Langland knew. But respectable medieval citizens did not have to intellectualise the issue; they participated in a culture which managed it for them through an overarching rhetoric of ceremony, conspicuous display, and charity, all facilitated by the guild system.

Civic festivals offered a multi-media encoding of how their owning communities defined themselves. They took all manner of forms, of which the so-called mystery play is only one; what all have in common is that they constitute a civic theatre in which 'audience involvement' was fundamental. A great deal has been written about the production of medieval civic drama, about the manuscripts of plays that survive, and about the records of productions for which there are no extant scripts.[53] We shall look at some as devotional texts in Chapter 3, but we end here by considering how the great plays from York and Chester present elements of scriptural narrative in vernacular verse in ways that reflect their owning urban community.

The York Register, dating from around 1467, contains scripts of forty-seven pageants from the city's mystery cycle. It is a quality control document, maintained by the City Clerk to keep a check on what was performed, modified year on year, then abandoned with several items within it unresolved. Each pageant in it was owned by a guild, who arranged for its performance on its pageant wagon at a number of pre-determined 'stations' around the city's streets. Each is distinctive, suggesting a number of different authors working over a period of at least fifty years, so the Register was probably compiled by calling in the guilds' individual playbooks for copying. Performance took place on Corpus Christi Day, the great summer feast that celebrated the fact of transubstantiation, the appearance of the real presence of the body of Christ in the host at the Mass.

York was a priest-ridden city, centre of the Northern Province, and a major trading port with the Low Countries; Chester was a County Palatine and a military base for armies mustered in the North and on the western Marches with Wales. Chester's cycle was early in its history moved to Whitsun and spread out over three days. Although with Chester's play we are still securely looking at a cycle of scriptural drama as inclusive as York's, the character of the text is different. Chester's play is even in texture, divided differently at different periods to accommodate combinations of guilds, new texts, and balance across the days of performance. Moreover, while the Chester Play was suppressed by Protestant authorities in the 1570s, the earliest extant manuscript of the text is 1591. All the witnesses to what was performed in Chester are antiquarian exercises, recording something no longer performed. In both cities extra-textual records provide details about production methods and circumstances, including costumes and stage machinery. We know there was music in the performances, and that casts were probably all male, but we do not know who wrote them, nor whether performers were guild members. If *The Book of Margery Kempe* preserves an individual voice from medieval lay civic society, the only 'voice' performing in the plays from York and Chester is the consensual voice of the city itself.

The York Play reveals various ways in which the city validated itself through the culture's unifying Christian mythology. In the Skinners' pageant of Christ's Entry into Jerusalem, Christ arrives through the crowd at the threshold of the heavenly city, erected on the pageant wagon, to be met, greeted, and welcomed in by a group of burgesses. In ecclesiastical Palm Sunday rituals, this historical action was played out in a ceremony which took place at the west end of the Church, where processional movement into the church signified the entry into the holy city. In the pageant, Christ is greeted by those playing the burgesses, not at the threshold of the ecclesiastical space, but at a simulacrum of the gates of Jerusalem set up in the streets of York. The welcoming figures represent the high-ranking civic powers who managed the city space and its play, and who also formally greeted visiting dignitaries and royalty at the gates. By their embodiment within the city street, and the inevitable allusion to Palm Sunday processions, the civic domain uses the traditional threshold welcome ceremony to assert its own ownership of Christ.

A medieval city enjoyed certain autonomy and freedoms from direct Crown interference, yet just as there were churches within the civic space, so too there were officers and places there that asserted Crown authority. York's relationship with the Crown was uneasy after its archbishop, Richard Scrope, was executed for his part in a rebellion against Henry IV. The courtroom was the ritual embodiment of Crown authority, particularly the Court of Assize, where peripatetic judges of the King's Bench and crown-appointed justices administered the common law. In York, the assize court sat in the castle, also the location of the royal mint. In the Passion sequence, Christ is tried before Annas and Caiaphas, then Pilate, then Herod, and finally Pilate once more, in simulacra of courtrooms, where he refuses to acknowledge the authorities represented. Whereas poetry in the post-Black Death era tends to be hostile to, or to deride, the power of the urban middle class, in the York Play Christ himself is represented as belonging to that class, able to assert himself and challenge the rival authorities which existed within civic boundaries but subject to the higher authority of Crown and Church.

These dramas also evoke private civic space imaginatively. Christ is received in the houses of private citizens in marked contrast to his hostile reception by the first and second estates. In the Corvisers' pageant in the Chester Play, Simon, the cured leper, welcomes him thus: 'Well is me that I may see thy face / here in my house, this poore place' (XIV, 17–24), and the anointing of Christ's feet by the penitent Mary Magdalene is framed within an understanding of private hospitality. In the York Woolpackers and Woolbrokers' pageant of the Supper at Emmaeus, pilgrims share their supper with the risen Christ in a comparable imaginary situation. Private houses are places where Christ is warmly received; the representation of private interiors in these plays serves to emphasise the bourgeois homeliness of the most holy.

The city is also more than the sum of buildings, official, private, and domestic within it, however. If ecclesiastical and Crown spaces within the city are represented by civic drama as patrician, high-handed and dangerous, the public space is no anodyne alternative. The streets of a walled medieval city, which the plays both inhabited and represented, were teeming aggressive places, from which the private houses and gardens of the well-to-do provided refuge from unruliness. In particular, the city is a marketplace, a space of self-promotion and self-presentation. The excesses of the civic are represented in the specificity of the sins of the damned in pageants of the Last Judgement, those who failed to perform the Corporal Works of Mercy. Feeding the hungry, giving drink to the thirsty, clothing the naked, visiting prisoners and the sick, and taking in travellers (Matthew 25) were a byword for civic virtue, a code of practical Christianity for the busy man of affairs. York Mercer, Nicholas Blackburn, endowed a window in his parish church depicting a civic worthy, possibly himself, engaged in those very actions.[54] His guild, the Mercers, was responsible for York's Doomsday pageant. In the Chester Websters' Judgement pageant, the Second Demon grabs a passing merchant, well known for adulterating his goods to cheat his customers (XXIV, 669–76). Of all places that represent the down-side of civic life, however, perhaps the ale-house is foremost, becoming the objective correlative of all that is bad about evolved civic society. Memorably the only sinner left behind in hell in the Chester Harrowing of Hell pageant is an ale-wife who has been caught watering her ale.

These plays confidently demonstrate that the test of the autonomous power of the city is its ability to police and contain its unruly elements. More than that, however, the real validation of the city as a God-sanctioned place, is the plays' consistent presentation of Jesus Christ as a man in and of the streets. Born in a shed, spending his early years as a refugee from Herod the Great, finally he ends up on the streets of Jerusalem. Once he is there, the focus of all the represented activity from his ministry is the street, and he is in return treated to the kindness of strangers, both as a guest in their private houses, but also outside on his final journey through the city's streets to his place of execution, as Simon of Cyrene and Veronica step from the crowd to offer comfort. The retrievable traces of the York and Chester's scriptural cycles bear witness to English civic culture a century after the worst ravages of the Black Death impelled the social changes that are the preoccupation of all the texts considered in this chapter. In their ambition as cultural projects, they testify to the maturity of the civic communities that generated them, but also in their various celebrations of civic life they demonstrate that the old model of the three estates of medieval society – those who pray, those who fight, and those who till the soil – no longer provided adequate reference points for pre-modern England.

NOTES

1. All references are to Stephanie Trigg (ed.), *Wynnere and Wastoure*, Early English Text Society, OS 297 (Oxford: Oxford University Press, 1990).

2. Thorlac Turville-Petre, 'The Prologue of *Wynnere and Wastoure*', *Leeds Studies in English*, 18 (1987), 17–29.
3. There are numerous books on the Black Death; one of the best short accounts is James Bolton, 'The World Upside Down: Plague as an Agent of Economic and Social Change', in M. Ormrod, M. and P. Lindley (eds), *The Black Death in England* (Stanford: University of California Press, 1996), pp. 17–78.
4. Turville-Petre, 'Prologue', pp. 23–5.
5. Warren Ginsberg, 'Place and Dialectic in Dante's *Paradiso* and the Middle English *Pearl*', *English Literary History*, 55 (1989), 731–53 (735–6).
6. See further Nicholas Jacobs, 'The Typology of Debate and the Interpretation of *Wynnere and Wastoure*', *Review of English Studies*, 36 (1985), 481–500.
7. See Elizabeth Salter, 'The Timeliness of *Wynnere and Wastoure*', *Medium Aevum* 47 (1978), 40–65, in which she analyses the poem's heraldry, and contests the arguments in Israel Gollancz (ed.), *A Good Short Debate between Winner and Waster: An Alliterative Poem on Social and Economic Problems in England in the year 1352 With Modern English Rendering* (Oxford: Oxford University Press, 1921; reissued Cambridge: D. S. Brewer, Rowman and Littlefield, 1974).
8. Salter, 'Timeliness', pp. 53, 59; Turville-Petre, 'Prologue', p. 24.
9. See further Jacobs, 'Typology of Debate', pp. 490ff.
10. See John Spiers, *Medieval English Poetry: The Non-Chaucerian Tradition* (London: Faber and Faber, 1957), pp. 263–304, and Thomas Bestul, *Satire and Allegory in* Wynnere and Wastoure (Lincoln, NE: University of Nebraska Press, 1974), pp. 51–4.
11. Jacobs, 'Typology of Debate', pp. 486–7.
12. See 'The Canterbury Interlude and Merchant's Tale of Beryn', in John M. Bowers (ed.), *The Canterbury Tales: Fifteenth-Century Continuations and Additions* (Kalamazoo, MI: TEAMS Middle English Texts, 1992), pp. 55–196.
13. Paul Strohm, *Social Chaucer* (Cambridge, MA: Harvard University Press, 1989), pp. 64–6.
14. See, for example, the French poet Deguilleville's poems *Pélérinage de l'Âme* [Pilgrimage of the Soul] and *Pélérinage de*

la Vie Humaine [Pilgrimage of the Life of Man], both of which were translated into English by John Lydgate.

15. The persistent mass popularity of traditional devotional practices up to and through the period of the Reformation is the subject of Eamon Duffy, *The Stripping of the Altars: Traditional Religion in England, 1400–1580* (New Haven, CT and London: Yale University Press, 1992).
16. Jill Mann, *Chaucer and Medieval Estates Satire* (Cambridge: Cambridge University Press, 1973).
17. See W. J. Sedgefield (ed.), *King Alfred's Old English Version of Boethius De Consolatione Philosophiae* (Oxford: Clarendon Press, 1899), p. 40.
18. See further Strohm, *Social Chaucer*, p. 68.
19. The two earliest manuscripts of *The Canterbury Tales* are the 'Hengwrt' manuscript (Aberystwyth, National Library of Wales MS Peniarth 392D) and the 'Ellesmere' manuscript (San Marino, California, MS Huntingdon EL 26.C.9). Standard editions are generally based on the latter, but see also Norman F. Blake (ed.), *The Canterbury Tales: Edited from the Henwgrt Manuscript*, York Medieval Texts, second series (London: Edward Arnold, 1980).
20. Alexandra F. Johnston, '"What revels are in hand": Dramatic Activities Sponsored by the Parishes of the Thames Valley', in A. F. Johnston, and Wim Hüsken (eds), *English Parish Drama*, Ludus 1 (Atlanta, GA and Amsterdam: Rodopi, 1996), pp. 95–104 (pp. 98–9).
21. Derek A. Pearsall, *The Life of Geoffrey Chaucer* (Oxford: Blackwell, 1992), p. 217.
22. See further Pamela M. King, '"He pleyeth Herodes upon a scaffold hye"?', *Leeds Studies in English* n.s. 32, 212–28; P. H. Ditchfield, *The Parish Clerk* (London: Echo Library, 1907), p. 131.
23. Pearsall, *Life of Geoffrey Chaucer*, p. 212.
24. John M. Gamin, *Chaucerian Theatricality* (Princeton: Princeton University Press, 1996); Linda Lomperis, 'Bodies that Matter in the Court of Late Medieval England and in Chaucer's *Miller's Tale*', *Romanic Review*, 86 (1995), 243–64.

25. Nigel Saul, 'Richard II: Author of his Own Downfall', *History Today* (September 1999), pp. 36–41.
26. Margaret Hallisey, *Clean Maids, True Wives, Steadfast Widows: Chaucer's Women and Medieval Codes of Conduct* (London: Greenwood Press, 1993), pp. 59–74.
27. Anne Laykaska, *Chaucer's Approach to Gender in The Canterbury Tales* (Cambridge: D. S. Brewer, 1995).
28. Elaine Tuttle Hansen, *Chaucer and the Fictions of Gender* (Berkeley, Los Angeles, London: University of California Press, 1992), p. 228; Linda Lomperis, 'Bodies that Matter in the Court of late Medieval England and in Chaucer's *Miller's Tale*', *Romanic Review*, 86 (1995), 243–64.
29. John Gower, *Mirour de l'Omme* [The Mirror of Mankind], trans. William Burton Wilson (Kalamazoo, MI: Michigan State University Press, 1992).
30. See further Steven Justice, *Writing and Rebellion* (Berkeley and Los Angeles: University of California Press, 1994), pp. 208–19.
31. Ibid. 231–54.
32. Thomas Walsingham, *The St Albans Chronicle, Volume I, 1376–94: The Chronica Maiora of Thomas Walsingham*, ed. John Taylor, Wendy R. Childs, and Thomas Watkiss (Oxford: Oxford University Press, 2003), p. 547.
33. Justice, *Writing and Rebellion*; see also David Aers, *Community, Gender and Individual Identity* (London and New York: Routledge, 1988), pp. 20–72; and Kathryn Kerby-Fulton, *Reformist Apocalypticism and Piers Plowman* (Cambridge: Cambridge University Press, 1990), passim.
34. For contemporary sources, see R. B. Dobson, *The Peasants' Revolt of 1381* (London: Macmillan, 1970).
35. See R. H. Hilton, *Bond Men Made Free: Medieval Peasant Movements and the English Rising of* 1381 (London: Routledge, 1973); Christopher C. Dyer, 'The Social and Economic Background to the Rural Revolt of 1381', in R. H. Hilton and T. H. Aston (eds), *The English Rising of 1381* (Cambridge: Cambridge University Press, 1984), pp. 9–42; Herbert Eiden, 'Joint Action against "Bad" Lordship: The Peasants' Revolt in Essex and Norfolk', *History*, 83 (1998), 5–30.
36. Justice, *Writing and Rebellion*, pp. 13–66, reproduces and

discusses the letters, which are also printed in Dobson, *Peasants' Revolt*, pp. 380–3.
37. See Justice, *Writing and Rebellion*, p. 29.
38. Paul Strohm, *Hochon's Arrow* (Princeton, NJ: Princeton University Press, 1992), pp. 33–56.
39. Justice, *Writing and Rebellion*, p. 251.
40. The model set in G. L. Kittredge, 'Chaucer's Discussion of Marriage', *Modern Philology*, 9 (1912), 435–67, has now largely been superseded.
41. See Robert A. Pratt, 'Jankyn's Book of Wikked Wyves: Medieval Antimatrimonial Propaganda in the Universities', *Annuale Medievale*, 3 (1963), 5–27.
42. Geoffroy de la Tour Landry, *The Book of the Knight of the Tower*, ed. Rebecca Barnhouse (New York and Basingstoke: Palgrave Macmillan, 2006).
43. *The Goodman of Paris*, ed. and trans. Eileen Power (London: Routledge, 1928).
44. For extracts from Christine's work, and other medieval feminist and anti-feminist texts, see Alcuin Blamires (ed.), *Women Defamed and Women Defended* (Oxford: Clarendon Press, 1992).
45. Dyan Elliott, 'Women and Confession: From Empowerment to Pathology', in Mary C. Erler and Maryanne Kowaleski (eds), *Gendering the Master Narrative: Women and Power in the Middle Ages* (Ithaca and London: Cornell University Press, 2003), pp. 31–51.
46. All references are to Margery Kempe, *The Book of Margery Kempe*, ed. Barry Windeatt (Cambridge: D. S. Brewer, 2004).
47. Jacques Derrida, *Of Grammatology*, trans. G. C. Spivak (Baltimore: Johns Hopkins University Press, 1974), pp. 43–4.
48. Janette Dillon, 'Holy Women and their Confessors or Confessors and their Holy Women', in Rosalind Voaden (ed.), *Prophets Abroad: The Reception of Continental Holy Women in Late Medieval England* (Cambridge: D. S. Brewer, 1996), pp. 115–40.
49. Kempe, *The Book*, ed. Windeatt, lines 191–9.
50. Lynn Staley, *Margery Kempe's Dissenting Fictions* (University Park, PA: Pennsylvania State University Press, 1994), p. 35.

51. Ruth Evans, '*The Book of Margery Kempe*', in Peter Brown (ed.), *A Companion to Medieval English Literature and Culture, c.1350–c.1500* (Oxford: Blackwell, 2007), pp. 507–21 (p. 508).
52. See Gervase Rosser, 'Urban Culture and the Church, 1300–1540', in D. M. Palliser (ed.), *The Cambridge Urban History of Britain, Vol. 1, 600–1540* (Cambridge: Cambridge University Press, 2000), pp. 335–70.
53. A good starting point is Richard Beadle and Alan J. Fletcher (eds), *The Cambridge Companion to Medieval English Theatre* (Cambridge: Cambridge University Press, 2008 [1994]), which has a comprehensive bibliography. See also Pamela M. King, *The York Mystery Cycle and the Worship of the City* (Cambridge: D. S. Brewer, 2006); and D. A. Mills, *Recycling the Cycle: The City of Chester and its Whitsun Plays* (Toronto: University of Toronto Press, 1998).
54. The window is in the parish church of All Saints, North Street, York.

CHAPTER 3

Religion and Morality

THE CHURCH

By the fourteenth century, the medieval Church was a huge, complex institution with a sophisticated international administrative structure and economy, based, like that of the Crown, on land-holding. The psychological hold which the Church had over the populace may largely be attributed to the product it purveyed, eternal salvation, and to understandings of the geography of the afterlife, particularly the doctrine of purgatory. Pope Gregory X affirmed the doctrine at the Council of Lyons 1274, and in 1331 Pope John XXII pronounced that nobody went straight to heaven before the Last Judgement, and thereafter devotional activity focused on accelerating the passage through purgatory. The Church in England in the late Middle Ages taught the laity that good deeds were not sufficient for a swift passage to heaven because of Original Sin. It was necessary to go through a repeated cleansing process which was administered by the Church through its ordained priesthood in the form of the seven sacraments: baptism, confirmation, penance, the sacrament of the altar, marriage, the ordination of priests, and the last rites of extreme unction or viaticum. Thus the Church sanctified all rites of passage and ushered the individual soul in and out of this life. Penance and the Sacrament of the altar, that is Mass, were repeated processes by which sins were confessed and, provided the individual was adequately contrite, satisfaction was obtained and affirmed by ingesting the body and blood of Christ in the form of bread and wine, transformed in kind but not in substance during their consecration through the process known as transubstantiation.

In addition to the obligatory participation in the sacraments, there were a number of other ways of preparing for the afterlife. Saints administered a 'treasury of merits', a bank of surplus good deeds, and acted as intercessors for those who prayed to them. Purgatorial actions undertaken in life could also be banked against those anticipated in the next. The laity was also urged to undertake charitable actions, encoded in the six works of corporal mercy, as described by Christ in Matthew 25, the byword for pious living for the active lay-person. Prayers assisted those already dead on their passage through purgatory, and were also, therefore, charitable actions. The whole point of the medieval tomb, and the starting point of the medieval will, is as a focus to attract prayers for the soul of the departed. The tombs of the wealthy were lodged in chantry chapels, where priests were employed specially to perform such prayers. Sin had to be avoided at all costs, especially the seven deadly sins: pride and covetousness (sins of the devil), anger and envy (sins of the world), and gluttony, sloth and lechery (sins of the flesh).

The laity was also urged to copy the professionally religious by following their daily prayer cycle. Regular religious in monastic orders followed a pattern of daily prayer divided into the *horae* or 'hours': matins, lauds, prime, terce, sext, none, vespers, and compline. The liturgy for this daily round was enshrined in the Breviary. The day was also punctuated by Mass, a rite of worship of a different type, its liturgy in the missal. For those with leisure, wealth, and pious inclinations, these practices, and the written texts that supported them, were reduced to the primer. The basic texts of the primer were in their turn embellished and personalised into books of hours, devotional liturgies for the laity, focusing on a sequence, such as the popular Little Hours of the Virgin Mary, supplemented by fashionable prayers and meditations devoted to, for example, the five wounds Christ suffered at the Crucifixion, the holy name of Jesus, and individual saints amongst whom the Virgin Mary held pride of place. Books of hours and psalters are amongst the most lavishly illuminated luxury manuscripts of the later Middle Ages. The liturgical books of the regular religious, and the books of hours of the laity, all open with a calendar, charting the fixed feasts and fasts of the year – such as Christmas and various saints' days – and the moveable feasts which take their cue from Easter and include the great, late medieval, summer feast of Corpus Christi. Thus did the medieval Church permeate every aspect of life down to the marking of time itself.

The task in this and the following chapter is to consider how doctrinal and theological matter, and devotional practice, are reflected in vernacular writing in the later Middle English period. The simple version of this narrative relates that after the Black Death, the growth in lay affluence and literacy led to a proliferation of sophisticated works of vernacular theology, running alongside movements by the laity to take a more active and controlling part in their relationship with God. The growth in lay literacy supplied a receptive milieu for the more radical ideas emanating from the University of Oxford, particularly those attributed to John Wyclif and his followers, which eventually threatened the established doctrines and hierarchy of the Church to the point that there was a violent backlash against heresy. The radicals, dubbed 'Lollards' by their opponents, were persecuted, and the Archbishop of Canterbury issued a set of draconian Constitutions in 1407 which effectively withered the florescence of English vernacular theology until the Tudor Reformation. Like all convergent narratives, however, this one is no sooner formed than it is contested. Bearing that in mind, we shall in this chapter be considering some of the works of the whole late medieval period which seek to give aesthetic articulation to catechetical and theological ideas in the English vernacular. Then, in the next chapter, we shall explore how theological radicalism represents an extreme point on a trajectory which begins with social and political dissent, but also how some theologically conservative texts nonetheless sought to articulate dissatisfaction with the Church as an institution. Through all this we will bear in mind the probability that to divide these texts into the 'orthodox' as opposed to the 'heterodox' or heretical is to impose a tidy binarism on to a wide range of texts which are variously theologically nuanced.

The Fourth Lateran Council of the Church in 1215, convoked by Pope Innocent III, was the starting point for the production of treatises directed at reforming and shaping the life of the ordinary

Christian. The Council, called following a period of vigorous crusading, represented the major effort to assert the absolute primacy of the papacy, to stem the proliferation of religious orders, and to centralise doctrine. The fourteenth century saw a turbulent period for the papacy politically, as seven popes, all French, were sequentially based in Avignon, until, in 1378, the cardinals in Rome attempted to rectify the situation by electing Urban VI, thereby triggering the 'Great Schism' by which there were two, and briefly three, rival popes, until the matter was resolved by the Council of Constance in 1414–18.[1] Despite this, however, the work of pastoral direction of the laity continued unabated and moved from Latin into the vernacular, so that the fourteenth century has come to be seen as a 'golden age' of vernacular theology.[2] In England, the steer came from the Provincial Council called at Lambeth in 1281 by Archbishop John Pecham, instructing the clergy to teach the laity at least four times a year. The material listed – the articles of the faith, the Ten Commandments, the corporal works of mercy, the seven deadly sins, the seven virtues and the seven sacraments – set an agenda for lay catechesis that survived for the following two and a half centuries and addressed the ignorance of the laity and the clergy. Numerous catechetical treatises were produced during the period in question,[3] including the fourteenth-century work known as *The Lay Folks' Catechism*.[4]

While catechetical literature focused its audience's attention on the problem of sin and the nature of virtue, by mnemonically systematising and listing, the good sermon relied on vividly illustrated narrative examples. Two of the four poems in British Library MS Cotton Nero A. x, the sole witness to *Sir Gawain and the Green Knight*, combine the exemplary method of the medieval pulpit with the poet's signature skill in bringing together the extraordinary with the quotidian through the performance of an individual point of view, realised in a situation driven by one man's confrontation with the supernatural. In *Patience* and *Cleanness* the tester is not a laconically genial green knight, nor the authoritarian young woman we shall meet in *Pearl*, but a world-weary God.[5] The narratives are borrowed directly from the Bible, and each poem's exposition of its theme involves a vivid and dramatic elaboration of narrative detail, framed by the careful arrangement and rhetorical ordering of significant illustrative material.

The art of preaching was highly developed by the late fourteenth century, as we can see from the number of preaching manuals and collections of model sermons that survive. The most widely circulated of the latter is the *Festial*, a collection aimed at uneducated rural populations written by the Shropshire cleric, John Mirk.[6] Earlier in the fourteenth century, the Dominican John Bromyard, also from the Welsh border, wrote his *Summa Praedicantium*, drawing on a range of European and Arabic sources for suitable exempla, and theorising the organisation of information, both spoken and written.[7] The detail of sermon methodology is most succinctly described, however, by the anonymous author of the *Tractatus de forma sermonem*, preserved in British Library Additional Manuscript 21202: 'Preaching involves the taking up of a theme, the division of the same theme, the sub-division of the theme, the appropriate citing of concordant points, and the clear and devout explanation of the authorities brought forward'.[8] The choice of the theme involved the selection of a moral lesson from the New Testament reading for the day, as set down in the missal. The subdivision and all that follows bring in supporting commentary, typically from the Old Testament and the Church Fathers, and also draw directly on lived experience and the characteristics of material objects. The highly wrought structures of the two poems mimic the textbooks, while the machinery of the sermon is, at the same time, transformed into performances in which that intricacy becomes a source of aesthetic pleasure.

PATIENCE AND *CLEANNESS*

Patience is memorable as a vivid retelling of the story of Jonah, but in fact that story is the embedded exemplum within an intricate sermon structure. The story – of Jonah's flight from God, his sojourn in the whale's belly, his reluctant visit to admonish the Ninevites, and the loss of his woodbine bower – supplants the account of Job, the standard example of patience as a virtue, and is carefully set up and internally adapted for the purpose. The original audience would doubtless have recognised the sermon structure, and been alert to how the prefatory material functions, establishing the homilist's central theme:

Pacience is a point, þaȝ hit displese ofte.
When heuy herttes ben hurt with heþyng oþer elles,
Suffraunce may aswagen hem and þe swelme leþe,
For ho quelles vche a qued and quenches malyce.
For quoso suffer cowþe syt, sele wolde folȝe,
And quo for þro may noȝt þole, þe þikker he sufferes.
Þen is better to abyde þe bur vmbestoundes
Þen ay þrow forth my þro, þa me þynk ylle. (1–8)

[Patience is a virtue, though it may often displease. When sorrowful hearts are hurt by scorn or something else, long-suffering can ease them and assuage the heat, for she (patience) kills everything bad and extinguishes malice. For if anyone could endure sorrow, happiness would follow; and anyone who, through resentment, cannot endure, suffers the more intensely. So it is better (for me) to put up with the onslaught from time to time, though this may be distasteful to me, than to give vent continually to my resentment.]

The poem's opening establishes the theme in the abstract, but also introduces a sophisticated pun or paronomasia: 'suffering' is used in the sense of both discomfort and forbearance ('sufferance'). This pun will sustain the whole of what follows, as the story is subjected to a rhetorical amplification in which Jonah comes to accept his discomforts as he learns to bow to the will of a long-suffering God.

It is through this witty opposition between man's adversity and God's forbearance that the poet then approaches his Gospel text, taken from the Beatitudes, the catalogue of blessings set out in the Sermon on the Mount (Matthew 5: 3–12). He fixes on the first and the last: blessed are the poor, and blessed are they 'that con her hert stere' (27), the patient. The preacher-poet claims direct experience of suffering material poverty, thereby engaging in a complex bridging exercise between himself, his audience, and Jonah the protagonist. The manuscript-owning audience for this poem is unlikely to need advice on how to endure material poverty, but has some control over the poet's income, which opens up the possibility that his references to his own condition are mildly ironic. Jonah, the reluctant prophet, is not materially poor either, but exemplifies the kind of poverty intended by the Beatitude's 'poor in heart', that is mean-spirited, which is the real burden of the message. The poet sums up:

> Thus pouerté and pacyence are nedes playferes.
> Syþen I am sette with hem samen, suffer me byhoues.
> Þenne is me lyȝtloker hit lyke and her lotes prayse
> Þenne wyþer wyth and be wroth and þe wers haue. (45–8)
>
> [Thus poverty and patience are necessarily playmates. Since I am beset by them both together, it behoves me to suffer. Then is it easier for me to like it and to praise their manners than to complain about them and endure worse.]

Since he is materially impoverished he suffers, so he must make the best of it, by striving not to be poor of heart, and that is best achieved through the exercise of forbearance, or sufferance.

The first sixty lines of the poem establish the theme by careful weaving of etymology, a patterning of verbal abstractions drawn from the Gospel text, for which the Old Testament story of Jonah will be the illustration. The theme is sustained through that retelling by the elaboration of significant actions as well as by interventions from a narrator whose personal credentials have been established. Jonah stands as a negative example of the virtues the narrator promotes, poverty of heart and patience, while the positive example is given by the animated personality of God himself and his exercise of patient forbearance when confronted by Jonah who 'wrathed in his wit' (74). There is no need for the preacher to analyse or explicate any hidden meanings, for the story is a plain and literal demonstration of his theme in action.

Cleanness takes the project further, and makes an ambitious attempt to link four quite disparate Bible stories in an illustrative and expository network, as 'cleanness' is expounded as everything from physical to moral purity. The gospel text is again taken from the Beatitudes where the pure – or clean – of heart are blessed. The theme is first illustrated by the parable of the wedding feast at which a guest who turns up in his soiled working clothes is turned away

(Matthew 22: 2–14). This account, which seems rather harsh when read literally, does require an allegorical reading, but that is already supplied in its biblical context: human beings should bear in mind that 'many are called but few are chosen' (22: 14), so make sure they are fittingly arrayed in spirit for their invitation to God's banquet. The explorations of uncleanness in the poem stretch ingenuity to its limits. They are hung around three extended examples: Noah's Flood is presented as punishment for sexual promiscuity. God's fury then escalates over the excesses of Sodom and Gomorrah, reaching its climax over the defilement of communion vessels at Belshazzar's feast. A case can be made for the poet moving from examples of sexual excess, to sexual perversions, to the symbolic defilement of holy vessels, the body being the vessel of the spirit, and certainly there is a pleasing symmetry in the movement between the two feasts, but this broad pattern cannot account for all the other minor examples of filth and the transitional stories that the poet also works in. Where there is order, however, amidst the teeming chaos of the examples of the unclean, is in the poem's central section (1049–148) where the poet turns from uncleanness to its contrary. Here the technique is comparable with *Pearl*, where cumulative linked imagery converges on the image of Christ as the epitome of all that is pure, born of a clean maid, wrapped in clean swaddling clothes, laid in a clean manger, serenaded by pure angelic song. Christ begins as a recipient of all that is clean then, in his ministry, becomes an agent of cleanliness, curing lepers, the blind, and the lame. Christ in heaven is compared to the perfect pearl, and finally the audience is exhorted to cleanse themselves through the sacrament of penance in order to emulate Christ and receive his grace, thereby reprising the message of the parable of the wedding guest. This section is so uncluttered and intellectually well formed, that it stands as an island of poetic order amidst the teeming examples of the contrary. The force of the multiple examples of uncleanness is that everything that is not clean, that is converging on Christ, is unclean, and the eclectic range of exempla stands as a warning about the dangers of vice.

What both poems have in common within the adapted homiletic framework is the expression of virtue as a theme, elaborated syllogistically and allegorically according to the preacher's art. Contrasted with this is the vivid dramatic narrative poetry which demonstrates the contrary vices, contrived so as to provoke ridicule and revulsion. The stories the poet chooses all contain latent dramatic narrative that is undeveloped in the source. In *Patience* for example, Jonah's conversation with God projects backwards, motivating all the preceding action because it characterises Jonah as an impatient man, lacking in humility. Similarly in *Cleanness*, when Lot offers his daughters to his sexually incontinent neighbours in place of the visiting angels they have been propositioning, the poet imagines the account for his audience as a socially awkward situation. Lot's wife's hospitality is less fulsome than her husband's, and she resentfully slips unwanted salt into her angelic visitors' food, thereby poetically justifying her later fate. Her muttering, the commotion around the house, the anxious Lot, and the beautiful supernatural guests, all lend immediacy to the scene of chaos, of social and moral depravity, that the biblical account only hints at. In both poems too, the creation of dialogue, and of presenting thoughts as if spoken aloud, creates the illusion of entering into the consciousness of mythical biblical personae. The wrath of this poet's God is motivated by exasperation, making him humanly accessible, as he appeals to Jonah's better nature, and asks him to empathise with the burdens of godhead:

> 'Þenne byþenk þe, mon, if þe forþynk sore,
> If I wolde help My hondewerk, haf þou no wonder;
> Þou art waxen so wroth for þy wodbynde,
> And trauayledez neuer to tent hit þe tyme of an howre,
> Bot at a wap hit here wax and away in an oþer:
> And ȝet likez þe so luþer, thi lyf woldez þou tyne.' (497–500)

> ['Then think about it, man, if you think hard, and don't be surprised if I want to help my handiwork. You have grown so angry about your woodbind, and yet you worked not even the space of an hour to tend it, but at a stroke it grew and went in another; and yet it pleased you so ill that you want to give up your life.']

If Jonah can be so upset by the loss of a plant that he did little to tend, is God not entitled to be upset when his work of ages threatens to destroy itself through sin?

At the same time, God's anger once provoked is wreaked on a frighteningly cosmic scale, which in turn lends poignancy to the suffering of earthly transgressors. In *Cleanness* the plight of the commonly unregarded multitude for whom there is no room on the ark is just one instance of how this poet uses alliterative verse's potential for affect, reinforcing what he has expounded intellectually by creating scenes of epic pathos encompassing imaginatively the panic of drowning animals (389–93), and of parting lovers, soon obliterated (401–4). He evokes what it would be like sitting in a whale's belly listening to the sea pounding on its sides, or, more extraordinarily, what it would feel like to be God trying to handle one of his more petulant creations. The substitutions of the allegorical method are supplanted by arrestingly novel poetic imagery, such as the simile which perfectly demonstrates the insignificance of humanity in the presence of God, as Jonah is swallowed by his Leviathan, 'as mote in at a munster dor' [like a speck in at a cathedral door] (268), or the falling angels in *Cleanness* who are compared first to snowflakes, then to a swarm of bees, and finally 'as smylt mele vnder smal siue smokez for þike' [as fine meal under a fine sieve smokes thickly] (226). By imaginatively extrapolating details from the original story, this poet contrives to essentialise his mythic narrative in all its latent concrete detail, transforming sermon into poetry.

CONFESSIO AMANTIS

Around 1303, long before the anonymous author of *Patience* and *Cleanness* drew his inspiration from sermon techniques, Robert Mannyng of Brunne (Bourne near Sempringham in Lincolnshire) wrote his lively 12,658-line devotional poem, *Handlyng Synne*, a free translation of William of Waddington's Anglo-Norman *Manuel des Peches*. His poem is in the vanguard of Middle English moral writings, written in English, he claims, to entice men away from secular 'talys and rymys' (46), and to make his instructional material accessible to ordinary people. A near contemporary of Mannyng's work is the 24,000-line northern poem, *Cursor Mundi*, the source already cited for the division of romance writing into 'matters'. This work presents itself as a moralised history of the world, based on the *Historia Scholastica* of Peter Comestor, but again written in English to edify the common people and again in overt rejection of French.[9] The popularity of these two early vernacular compendia of exemplary material of spiritual edification pales into insignificance when set alongside the 117 manuscripts that survive of the mid-fourteenth-century poem *The Pricke of Conscience.* The poem, more theologically ambitious, and running to almost 10,000 lines in its various versions, did not deter contemporaries as much as it has modern editors,[10] and was clearly popular across the length and breadth of England as bequests testify. Relentless and sometimes stuttering rhymed couplets, and apocalyptic threats, cause *The Pricke of Conscience,* and the dialectically near-impenetrable Kentish sister text by Dan Michel, the *Ayenbite of Inwit*, to be left on the shelf along with the other rhymed vernacular catechetical enterprises of the early to mid-fourteenth century, but their urgings towards introspection also presage some of the more urbane and literary works of moral and theological reflection which characterise the Chaucerian period and beyond.[11]

These texts may be more notable for their prodigious length, and their authors' stamina for their projects, than for any real theological speculation, but almost a century later the far more urbane London layman, John Gower, wrote his long English poem *Confessio Amantis* according to a similar model.[12] Chaucer described his old friend as 'moral Gower', and the appellation stuck. Gower is celebrated these days as 'quintessentially medieval', because his massive output is trilingual, his three major works being the French *Mirour de l'Omme* ('A Mirror of Mankind'), the Latin *Vox Clamantis* ('A Voice Crying Out'), and the English *Confessio Amantis* ('A Lover's Confession'), all concerned with a particular brand of genteel didacticism directed at achieving his ambitions to be principal poet recognised during his long life successively in the courts of Edward III, Richard II, and Henry IV.[13] The *Confessio Amantis* is, like *Handlyng Synne*, an encomium of moral tales. It is also, like *The Pricke of Conscience*, a poem which promotes self-examination as the path to spiritual wisdom. Gower also employs the commonplace of medieval instructional writing that the way to capture an audience and convert them to virtuous living lies through entertainment. At around 30,000 lines, Gower's poem is another blockbuster, but the *Confessio Amantis* is also a poem that utterly transforms the tradition of multiple exemplary narrative from the cumulative scare-mongering of its antecedents. The imagined audience for the *Confessio,* as with Gower's other work, is a learned and sophisticated elite, designed around an ideal, 'himself well read' in Robert Yeager's words, its status part and parcel of the poet's own social and intellectual aspirations.[14]

The poem is, unlike *The Canterbury Tales*, highly finished, and bears signs in the manuscript tradition that the poet intervened in its reproduction to ensure that it was as he designed in every detail.[15] Like *The Canterbury Tales* it has an ambitious frame-tale structure, and, as with *Patience* and *Cleanness*, it is the careful fashioning of the frame that makes this a more highly wrought intellectual endeavour than its precursors in exemplary moralised narrative. Each of the books is devoted to the exploration of one of the seven deadly sins, its parts and its remedies. The frame is itself influenced by manuals of confession, however, and concerns the evolving relationship between the protagonist Amans, and his father-confessor, Genius. English, the language in which Gower actually communicated conversationally, as opposed to the Latin or French of his other major works, inspires him to exploit the performative act of confession as dramatic narrative, and to replicate in the frame a human relationship. The reader witnesses the inductive process by which a patient and benign confessor brings his slow-learning subject to the understanding that he can assert rational control over the appetitive urges that he encounters in the world. Moreover the personae, Amans and Genius, whose developing relationship constitutes the overarching plot of the poem, are together dimensions of a composite protagonist. They perform in sequential dramatic narrative the introspective psychological process of anatomising a philosophical problem, sin, and mimic a range of real human responses to the range of *exempla* which are adduced in the course of their encounter. Finally, in the eighth book, Amans directly considers his inappropriateness as a lover, not least because of his old age, and becomes in the process the figure whom Venus expels from the garden at the end of his confession by his name, 'John Gower' (VIII. 2321).

Genius, the confessor, is derived from the secular *Roman de la Rose*, and the confession of Amans, the 'lover', is partly about courtesy and partly about Christian doctrine. The poem's focus on love is explained in the Latin headnote to the first book: love is contrived by nature and affects all men alike, but incites wildness in the harmonious (or harmony in the wild), and, like fortune, blindly entraps people. The ultimate oxymoron, love is the most enigmatic of the forces the human being experiences. Taking its cue from this, the poem is able to temper its didacticism and explore humanely, even sentimentally, the underlying reasons for examples of disastrous human choice and moral crisis. Gower perceives 'discord' as lying behind all problems, and applies this theory both introspectively and, equally, in adopting the mantle of royal poet-counsellor, as advice to a rational monarch.[16] The poem explores the great taboos of Christian society then and now, such as incest and cannibalism, with a delicacy born of 'true justice . . . administered by the divine attribute of mercy towards the human tendency to act lawlessly under the influence of passion'.[17] Gower's achievement lies in his control of the transitions between statements about the moral nature of the human condition, to and from illustrations of particular instances of that nature in action. Thus the poem's overarching pressure to understand universal truths drawn from natural law is balanced by its illustrations of the real difficulties of moral discrimination.

There is space here to look in detail at only one of the sets of exempla in the *Confessio,* following the pattern of how the story is prepared, internally customised as a particular moment of crisis, then how the reasons for, and responses to, the embodied action are explored. Book IV, at the poem's centre, deals with sloth, which it divides into more component parts than any of the other sins. Sloth is made up of 'lachesce' – that is procrastination – pusillanimity, forgetfulness, negligence, idleness, somnolence, and despondency. Its component parts are predominantly illustrated by tales drawn from Ovid. There is also a major digression in this Book, as Genius delivers a sermon on love, labour, and invention, marking a move in the poem overall from Genius's inductive role in relation to Amans, towards a more expository function, directly supplying the audience with improving materials.

Procrastination has a special significance for Amans, as he readily confesses at the outset. He characterises himself in dialogue with this vice who tempts him not to declare his love:

He seide, 'Another time is bettre;
Thou schalt mowe senden hire a lettre,
And per cas wryte more plein
Than thou be mowthe durstest sein.' (37–40)

Although his heart is keen, diffidence keeps him from declaring his love. The reader is sympathetically drawn into this characteristic lover's plight only to have it abruptly countered by Genius's recounting of the tales of Aeneas and Dido, and Ulysses and Penelope, both of which mirror Amans's indolence in love. In the first case, both lovers are presented as hopelessly slow off the mark. They fall in love, but Aeneas eventually has to go on his way. Dido sees him off, then 'withinne a litel throwe' decides that she cannot bear to be parted from him, so writes to tell him that if he postpones coming home she will kill herself. By the time the letter reaches him, he is too preoccupied with the affairs of war to deal with his lover, so does nothing about it. The sharp lesson is that, while the situation resembles the commonplace of love affairs that have petered out for lack of decisive action, in this instance,

A naked swerd anon sche threste,
And thus sche gat hireselve reste
In remembrance of alle slowe. (135–7)

The whole epic story is thus reduced to a short and dismal tale of two lovers whose failure to cement their relationship has disastrous consequences. By contrast, Penelope, in the immediately following example, by persistent industry with her letter-writing to her husband, eventually induces in him a state so impatient that he rushes home to her side. The slothful are compared to the foolish virgins in Matthew 25: 1–13, who are not invited to the lord's wedding as they were unprepared with oil for their lamps. As Genius is finally pressing the point home, however, Amans appears to turn the tables, by protesting that he is not guilty quite of sloth, lacking not so much the motivation as the opportunity to press his suit:

I seche that I mai noght finde,
I haste, and evere I am behinde. (289–90)

Amans is urged to change his ways, but will return to his wistful longings later in the book, embellishing the picture of an attentive suitor who fails to progress because he is, simply, ignored; protesting that the 'idle' outcomes of his efforts are not a consequence of his idleness.[18] Faced with classical exempla of men who go away to war, thereby attracting the attentions of their ladies, he wistfully asks what use it would be for him to go and waste men's lives abroad, when he cannot even keep her interested in him at home (1656–65). His wry intransigence in asserting that his lack of activity is not slothful in intent, but a justifiable tactic in a near-hopeless suit, is then supported by the example of Achilles who actually 'lefte hise armes' (1694) for Polixena, refusing to fight further against Troy, her home. Why, he asks, should he go into strange lands and leave his love at home? Though if he thought it would do any good he would 'fle thurghout the sky, / and go thurghout the depe se' (1714–15). He describes such efforts, which he believes fruitless, three times as 'travaile' (1713, 1721, 1723), reinforcing his defence against accusations of slothfulness. Amans's sturdy defence draws the reader further in, as he debates with his confessor about the value of pointless activity. This also then triggers Genius's disquisition on all the uses of labour, without which no discoveries would have been made, no inventions achieved. The message is that the outcome of activity good or bad cannot be predicted, but that activity is, of itself, a good thing.

The concentration on exempla drawn from Ovid, specialist in transformations and changes, in Book IV serves to underscore the larger message of the poem. Outcomes are unpredictable, and whether procrastination elicits the response of a Dido or a Penelope is contingent upon the will of each as an individual. Within the larger structure, Genius can only lay his arguments before Amans and hope to elicit the right response from his pupil. This pivotal Book, with its shift to laying wisdom or 'lore' before the protagonist and reader, rather than simply attempting to correct through examples of the negative, is part of the larger movement in the *Confessio* to offer up the lesson that, through reason and grace, the sensual appetites may be controlled, and even love, which generates the most urgent impulses experienced by human beings, can be managed. The long journey to this message marks the compassion with which the overall project is treated.

MORALL FABILLIS

If *The Canterbury Tales* is a competition in which some of the stories told are incidentally dedicated to moral and theological topics, Gower's *Confessio* presents a unified persuasive moral lesson built from the sequence of narratives whose ability to stand alone is incidental. The later Scots monk-poet, Robert Henryson, took a ready-made sequence of moralised stories that were the commonplace of the medieval schoolroom and rewrote them as *The Morall Fabillis of Esope the Phrygian.*[19] Aesop had legendary status for the Middle Ages as a wise slave who wrote fables for King Croesus, but the immediate source for the fables themselves was a compilation from two late Latin sources written around 1200 and attributed to 'Walter the Englishman'. There were numerous reworkings, from Alexander Neckham's scholarly *Novus Aesopus* to Marie de France's playful *Fables*, and 'Aesopian' material also turned up in countless ephemeral contexts, in bestiaries, wood carving, manuscript illumination, and in the school books used by those like Henryson whose duties included teaching young boys to read.[20] The poet engages in dialogue with 'Aesop' his master, but the pose of inadequacy he adopts is the vehicle for a broad ironic shift through which the conservative black-and-white messages of the sources are exposed as simplistic by Henryson the faulty moralist who is too sympathetic, and too pessimistic, to accept their brutalities.

The Prologue to the *Fabillis* opens with the assertion that 'morall sweit sentence' can be gained from 'the subtell dyte of poetry' (12–13), a relationship arising from mixing 'ernist' with 'merie sport' (20), suggesting again the truism of the sugared pill, the unpalatable lesson dressed up in an entertaining story. In Henryson's most aesthetically successful fable, however, the message about human limitations and God's limitless providence, which is the source of humour in many of the other retellings, is conveyed through a moving mini-tragedy. 'The Preiching of the Swallow' opens with an extended universal vision celebrating the creative goodness of God set against the destructive powers of his creatures. Although the human soul is tragically trapped in a sensual body, the evidence of God's works is there to be seen all around. Six philosophical opening stanzas are followed by a description of the passage of the seasons, a lyrical signification of the perfect world that is there to be observed, balancing self-conscious poetic convention with realism in a way comparable perhaps only with *Sir Gawain and the Green Knight*. Then, as the narrator places himself and a gathering of birds into this landscape, the passage of time becomes the agent of pessimism and, as the seasons pass again, the focus is less on nature's renewal than on how time runs out for the birds who, ignoring the swallow's warning, refuse to destroy the flax seed which will provide the material from which the fowler will make his nets. Looking back from this later perspective, the initial description of winter takes on proleptic meaning:

> Syne wynter wan quhen austerne Eolus,
> God off the wynd, with blastis boreal [northern]
> The grene garment off somer glorious
> Hes all to-rent and revin [torn] in pecis small;
> Than flouris fair faidit with froist man fall,
> And birdis blyith changit their noitis sweit
> In styll murning, neir slane with snaw and sleit. (1692–98)

The birds who enter the bountiful landscape begin as speaking *fabula* birds, but when the winter comes, in which they are killed by the fowler, they are only starving birds, devoid of speech, fatally landing on the 'calf' (chaff) in the trap, so that 'this churl over thame his nettis drew' (1873).

The fable's focus on the inexorable march of time subverts the usual pattern in which the moral depends on the possibility of alternative outcomes. Tragedy grows from the certainty that the birds are not free to choose their fate, and winter's significatory range expands to represent the presence of real and unaccountable evil in the world. In other versions, the knowing swallow exchanges her silence for a warm lodging in the fowler's roof; here that ending is omitted, and Henryson refuses to scorn the actions of the birds, rather expressing pity and horror in the face of the real unlikelihood that humanity can change.

For the modern reader, fables in the Aesopian tradition are moralised animal tales; to Henryson's contemporaries, the salient characteristic of the fable is that it is a rhetorically constructed invention, a fiction, and the presence of speaking animals is a sign of that fictionality:

> Thocht feinyeit [invented] fabils of ald poetre
> Be not al grunded upon truth, yit than
> Their polite [stylised] termes of sweit rhetore
> Richt plesand ar unto the eir of man;
> And als the caus that thay first began
> Wes to repreif [reprove] the haill misleving [wrong living]
> Off man be figure of ane uther thing. (1–7)

Henryson begins the *Fabillis* by reflecting on the moral utility of fiction. He considers how fictions are entertaining, and how figural fictions, or allegories, simultaneously can have moral worth. He also inverts the common underlying assumption in beast fable that animals are like people by promoting a morally self-conscious reminder of difference: human beings can behave like animals, but, uniquely endowed with reason, should not. The apparent accessibility of the animal fable allows Henryson to develop dry social satires which depend on images of cruelty. Like *The Canterbury Tales*, *The Morall Fabillis of Esope the Phrygian* is an unfinished experiment, full of unevennesses, whose overarching project can be determined only from its Prologue:

> The nuttis schell, thocht it be hard and teuch,
> Haldis the kirnill and is delectabill;
> Sa lyis their ane doctrine wyse aneuch
> And full of frute under ane fenyeit fable . . . (15–18)

The rhetorical construct forms the shell which has to be cracked in order to extract the delectable kernel. That shell is hard and tough, not because the connotations of the fiction are difficult to decode – in fact the use of moral tales for children illustrates precisely the opposite – but the pessimistic revelations within them of the unpalatable, inhuman cruelty and stupidity abroad in the world and recognised from experience, are, when confronted through the vivid immediacy of fiction, hard to take.

RELIGIOUS LYRICS

This chapter so far has explored the literary inspiration that Middle English authors drew from the Church's use of exemplary narrative, and it has looked at the various characterisations of the mentor and pupil relationship in devotional writing. A related type of exemplary narrative model is offered by devotional biography, in which the performance of an exemplary life is rehearsed as a model for the devout. Again, the pressure on the reader is for penitential self-examination, but exemplary lives are also selectively held up as models for emulation. The lives of Christ and of the Virgin Mary offer obvious examples, but a whole industry in hagiography puts exemplary religious biography up there with the secular romance, to which it can be a remarkably close cousin, as one of the most pervasively popular modes of medieval narrative.

Saints' cults played a vital role not only in the search for salvation, but as an agent of social cohesion in the Middle English period. Figures of individual saints met the eye everywhere it travelled in the medieval church. Although represented as a living human figure, the representation of the saint is a sign for the 'real' saint who looks benignly on the devotee from heaven. The critical attribute shared by all saints is that they are dead. The other encounter the medieval Christian had with a saint was with his or her relics, but the affective interaction between onlooker and the saint – represented metaphorically by an image, or metonymically by some bones in a reliquary – depended on an imaginative interaction with that saint's back history. Representations of saints invariably include their attributes – St Andrew's cross, St Catherine's wheel, St Lawrence's grid-iron. Saints' attributes function as identifiers, much in the way that coats of arms act as ciphers validating lay aristocratic identity.[21] The attribute is associated with the climax of the saint's life, which is, almost always, his or her death. Christ's death was the ultimate exemplum; the success of the individual saint's death being marked by protracted suffering borne stoically, and by conduct that consciously copied that model. The representation of saints in the visual arts may be divided into two main types: the static attribute-bearing image, and the cartoon-strip representation of scenes from the life in which the moment of climax from which the attribute is derived becomes a particularly rich node of meaning. The literary correlative of the static image is, broadly speaking, represented by the lyric mode, whereas the life history is clearly narrative, but the division is not tidy. Both forms are offered up as material for pious reflection.

Medieval lyric is a permissive literary category, used to gather up all poems which are short. The corpus of surviving short religious verses in Middle English comes from a variety of physical contexts: embedded in sermons, written on flyleaves, and engraved on funerary monuments, usually anonymous and hard to date. Most devotional lyrics focus on Christ and the Virgin Mary. A well-known example is the lyric beginning 'Wofully araide', which survives in British Library manuscript Harley 4012 (f. 109r), a devotional compendium compiled in the mid-sixteenth century for a pious gentlewoman, but certainly of earlier date.[22] It draws attention to a number of features of the devotional lyric which focuses on Christ. Christ addresses the reader directly, alternating descriptions of what he endured during his Passion with reproaches and exhortations to reciprocal action. The compressed narrative evokes standard iconic images of Christ's suffering – the crown of thorns, the scourging, and the nailing to the Cross. The reader is finally reminded of what is at stake: hell or heaven, where a place is prepared for the reader, provided she emulates not Christ's suffering, but the emotional motivation for that suffering, love. The lyric draws on the heritage of Franciscan piety, which designated the relationship between Christ and humanity as bound by reciprocal loving self-sacrifice.[23] Reader is more properly listener, for whereas the listener is urged to love Christ in order to join him in Heaven, the reader is given a much more specific bargain that takes us back to the catechetical agenda. Saying this lyric devoutly buys her a portion of a chantry when she dies that will in turn speed her passage through purgatory by 600 days.

In a number of comparable lyrics, Christ speaks directly from the Cross, describing his wounds and recollecting the events of the Passion. The reader is set up as addressee in many of these, such as the lyric beginning 'Jesus doth him bymene',[24] in which details of the luxuries of courtly life that the reader is imagined as enjoying are contrasted with the details of Christ's privations and agonies.

Sometimes the voice of the lyric is non-specific and presumed authorial, the addressee either the reader, or in an alternate dramatic orientation, Christ. The lyric beginning 'In the vaile of restles mynd' has it both ways, addressing the reader directly, but switching to an imagined account of the Passion so vivid that Christ's voice is represented in direct speech within the lyric. Sometimes the dramatic orientation of the lyric excludes the reader's direct dramatic engagement altogether, casting him or her as eavesdropper, and the addressee becomes instead, for example, the Virgin Mary at the base of the Cross. 'Stond wel, moder, under rode' is a vernacular rendering of the liturgical hymn *Stabat mater*, a trope embedded in some liturgies for Good Friday in which Christ admonishes Mary for mourning his death, reminding her of the salvific purpose of that death, and the reader of some basic theology. The classic affective lyric, a liturgical trope appropriated to a variety of vernacular contexts, is in the voice of the Virgin Mary herself. The *planctus Mariae* [Mary's complaint] is a stylised but direct outpouring of grief for the death of her son. In the lyric 'O alle women that ever were borne', a similar technique is employed to that in 'Jesus doth him bymene', as the speaker, cast as the Virgin Mary of the typical *pieta* scene, holding the dead Christ across her lap, compares her lot with that of young mothers with their healthy babies dancing on their knees. In the last stanza, the performative nature of the text is foregrounded as the speaker declares that she 'may no more / For drede of deth reherse his payne', moving on to offer her loving protection and intercession on behalf of the reader's imagined child in return for the reader's love of her child, Christ, as the devotional bargain with which the poem closes.

The Virgin Mary is chief of all the saints who offer intercession on behalf of the devout, and medieval Mariology is the subject of a number of studies. As well as being represented as young wife and mother, and then as bereaved mother, she, like Christ, has her position at the head of the company of heaven, where she is the embodiment of idealised womanhood designed by a patriarchal Church, both virgin and mother. Like the heroines of medieval romance, she is the subject of male desire, morally, and therefore, temperamentally and physically perfect. The crossover between the adoration of the idealised courtly lady and of the Virgin Mary, each referencing the other, is found in one of the most widely known lyrics focusing on the Nativity. 'I syng of a mayden that is makeles' celebrates the Virgin Mary as mother and maiden through images of April dew. The lyric revolves around two conceits, the first a pun on 'makeles', meaning 'matchless', like the superlative courtly lady, but also 'mate-less' that is unmarried, so, by extension, virginal, and 'immaculate', that is unmarked. The second is the image of the dew drop, a figure of Mary's conception of Jesus drawing on the medieval natural lore found in *Pearl*, whereby the pearl, connoting perfection in its various facets, was believed to arrive within the oyster by the miraculous coagulation of dew drops.

The homeliness and courtliness of the connotative range of these lyrics to the Virgin should not, however, distract us from their denotative purpose as signalled by the ending of 'Wofully araide': the reference point of all is the practice of the ritualised recreation of those events in the practices of worship of the medieval Church, and many lyrics macaronically switch between lines in the vernacular and direct Latin quotations from the liturgy as a reminder of this. What is arguably conjured in the mind's eye in lyrics evoking moments of the Passion, or indeed of the Nativity, are not so much the 'real' events in Bethlehem or on Calvary, but, by an implicitly ekphrastic process, the visual images set up in their turn for contemplation in churches up and down the land.

THE DRAMA OF FRANCISCAN PIETY

Just as the lyric verse is the verbal equivalent of the painted or carved image of Christ Crucified, or of the Virgin at the base of the Cross, lives of Christ and of the Virgin in the vernacular are the literary equivalent of the large altarpieces or sequences in stained glass which synthesise the accounts in the Gospels and apocrypha to fashion episodic narratives designed to renew well-worn stories for the reader to follow in his or her mind's eye. Particularly arresting are those devotional biographies based on the methodology attributed to St Bonaventure (1221–74). Bonaventure was Minister General of the Franciscan order of friars from whom what is commonly referred to as 'Franciscan piety' effectively originates. His particular brand of scholastic teaching is marked by strategies designed to arouse devotion by appealing to an intelligence of the heart as well as of the mind. The particular characteristics of his theological writings led a number of other Franciscan texts, which bore his hallmark in being practical, moving and accessible, to be erroneously ascribed to him. Amongst these 'pseudo-Bonaventuran' writings, the single most influential was the *Meditationes de Vita Christi* [Meditations on the Life of Christ], written by an anonymous Franciscan for the instruction of nuns in the order of the Poor Clares, of which over 200 manuscripts survive. This Latin text attracted the attention of a number of Middle English writers of works of vernacular devotion, including the Yorkshire Carthusian, Nicholas Love, whose prose work, *The Mirror of the Blessed Life of Jesus Christ*, is a life of Christ based on the *Meditationes* written in English at a peculiarly sensitive theological moment.

Love's *Mirror* was one of the first theological works in the vernacular to be licensed by Archbishop Thomas Arundel after the promulgation of the Constitutions of 1407, designed to control the proliferation of theologically diverse writings in English. In some respects, therefore, we are getting ahead of ourselves in looking at Love's work here, before we have explored the 'dissenting' positions for which it was seen as a counter. The current scholarly climate is, however, one in which binaries such as 'heterodox' and 'orthodox', 'radical' and 'conservative' as descriptors for individual theological positions in the period are being subjected to close and sceptical scrutiny.[25] It is likely that both the expectation of a wider audience and the dedication to *The Mirror* may have been conceived by the Church as fulfilling a particular purpose – written 'for the edification of the faithful, and the confusion of heretics and Lollards'[26] – but it also found a market characterised more by social than doctrinal considerations. Written originally for an audience of enclosed female religious, it is nonetheless dedicated to 'lewed men and wommen and hem that ben of symple understonding' (Proheme, 6). It adds to the material drawn from the pseudo-Bonaventuran text, material from the English translation of another devotional work, Henry Suso's *The Seven Poyntes of Trewe Love and Everlastynge Wisdome*, to give it a particular focus on Eucharistic worship. This reinforcement of sacramentalism fulfils the Church's formal agenda to re-assert the importance of the ecclesiastically administered sacraments as central to lay devotion. It also, and in some respects paradoxically, plays to lay devotional tastes which were leading to the foundation of confraternities devoted to Corpus Christi within, and controlled by, secular civic communities.

Love's narrative methodology provided inspiration to the anonymous, probably clerical, authors who were at the same time engaged in supplying those same civic communities with material for performance in celebration of Corpus Christi. Both the York Play, and the East Anglian compilation known as the 'N. Town Play' draw on his text, and show the impact more generally of Bonaventuran techniques in affective theological writing. The later manuscripts of the Chester Whitsun Play, once also a Corpus Christi Cycle, on the other hand show the heavy influence of the fourteenth-century text known as *The Stanzaic Life of Christ*, and the Play is much more dogmatic in its organisation of content. The N. Town Play is so called because the text opens with 'banns', an announcement designed to advertise a touring performance. Scholars now agree that the manuscript is a collection of individual plays, short sequences, and significant stand-alone plays strung together to create a manuscript logically organised by a scribe to tell a sequential story of salvation history, and probably used for private reading. Two long plays have been excavated from it which the scribe seems to have had to hand when making the compilation, a play of the early life of the Virgin Mary and a long Passion Play. Scholars of French medieval drama are familiar with the great *Passions,* such as those from Grebain and Valenciennes, but it seems that the only surviving comparable English Passion Play has been buried in the N. Town manuscript, although another English example, the lost New Romney Passion Play, has emerged from archival research.[27] The other embedded play in the N. Town manuscript, edited as *The Mary Play*, takes its place alongside the numerous records of local saints' plays, performed hagiographic narratives, which emerge from the shadows in parish archives up and down the country.[28] In the hands of a highly competent dramatist, *The Mary Play* adapts Love's affective prose into theatre in which spoken text and staging carefully guide the audience's gaze to iconic images, such as the Virgin and child, or Christ on the Cross, and these images speak to them directly, reminding them through words and images what their significance is here, now and perpetually.[29]

In his passage on the Annunciation, for example, Nicholas Love offers a meditation on how, at a particular moment in sacred history, the fate of all Creation waited upon the consent of a young innocent girl to agree to bear a child by the Holy Ghost (Love 2005: 26: 29–36). Both Love's content and its homely style are imported by the dramatist, but *The Mary Play*'s Gabriel, who urges Mary to 'come of and haste the' (1324), is more impatient. Out of Love's accessible middle style is fashioned a particular tone of voice for the angel, and a dramatic character is born. Moreover Gabriel reminds Mary that everyone in heaven, earth, and hell awaits her decision on whether to bear the son of God, including 'all þe gode levers and trew / that arre here in þis erthely place' (1335–6), neatly engaging the audience's understanding of the direct implications of a moment in sacred history for them.

The playwright of *The Mary Play* is a particularly accomplished proponent of the techniques by which the inner drama prompted by affective prose meditation, combined with the public procedures of worship, itself highly dramatic, could be exploited to create theatrical dialogue and action which is at once formally demonstrative and richly connotative. Again, at the culmination of the Virgin's visit to Elizabeth, the playwright draws on the core materials of the catechetical agenda in another affecting scene when the two women recite together the *Magnificat*, Mary in Latin, and Elizabeth interpolating an English verse translation. The macaronic text is in direct contravention of Arundel's seventh Constitution, which forbade the translation of biblical material into English. Its effect is, however, arguably not primarily dogmatic. Sound patterns dominate, reminiscent of antiphonal chant moving recursively to its conclusion. The resonance of liturgical Latin has a familiar formality so that the scene in its entirety performs the paradox of the awesome and the homely that is central to the theological message of the text.

In the York Play, similar techniques can be observed controlling the pace and register of the action, switching between narrative action and moments of lyric contemplation. This can be illustrated from the two pageants which deal with the climax of Christ's Passion, the Pinners' *Crucifixio Christi* [Crucifixion of Christ], and the Butchers' *Mortificacio Christi* [Death of Christ].[30] The former is a relatively simple piece of dramatic action involving only Christ and 'soldiers', the workmen who have to fix him to the cross. The dramatist's conceit is to depict the soldiers as local workmen, absorbed by a difficult job and at odds with one another. This is conveyed through rapid low-style exchange, while the actor playing Christ lies silent on the cross, horizontally laid out on the bed of the pageant wagon. When the cross is raised, Christ speaks, and the deixis of his speech, like that of Gabriel in the N. Town Annunciation, includes the audience as he addresses 'Al men that walkis by waye or strete' (253), urging them to pay attention to the wounds in his head, hands and feet, and 'fully feele' whether anything equals his suffering (253–7). His words are a free translation of the Latin *improprreria*, literally 'reproaches', which form part of the special liturgical office for Good Friday. The following pageant is more elaborate, including the full narrative sequence of events on Calvary, from the gathering of spectators around the base of the Cross, through the death, deposition, and burial of Christ. The action, therefore, involves a number of iconic moments and characters, and the dramatist has accordingly punctuated its forward narrative movement with moments of stillness accompanied by lyrical dialogue. Central among these is the *planctus Mariae*, the lament of the Virgin Mary at the base of the Cross. In this pageant it is set up to intersperse the narrative action with nodes of meditative reflection that are built as a dialogue between Mary and her son on the Cross (131–60). This brief sequence is drawn out to almost intolerable length in the non-cycle play known simply as the Bodley *Burial of Christ*, written to be played on Good Friday with its counterpart for Easter Sunday performance, *Christ's Resurrection.*[31] Here Mary delivers eighty lines of lament, all exclamation and question, a veritable barrage of incitement to emotion that comes dangerously close to backfiring, for the modern reader at any rate, on grounds of its excessive hysterical sentimentality of tone.

THE PRIORESS'S TALE

The boundaries between affective piety and religious sentimentality are explored in a more urbane and knowing way by Chaucer in

The Canterbury Tales in the person and Tale of the Prioress. The Prioress's Prologue is an extended invocation to the Virgin Mary, and precedes a brief saint's life – brief because the saint is affectingly martyred in his infancy. The Prioress's Tale is also an account of a miracle performed by the Virgin Mary, thereby combining two popular story types from the less challenging end of the spectrum of vernacular theological writing. The account concerns a little 'clergeon' who is so enchanted by the words of the *Alma redemptoris*, an antiphon sung in honour of the Virgin Mary at compline during the Christmas season, that he determines to learn it off by heart, so sings it on his way to and from school. Unfortunately his path takes him through a Jewish quarter, where his singing causes such offence that his throat is cut and he is tossed in a privy. As his widowed mother searches for him, he miraculously sings, attracting attention to his plight. An abbot is summoned, and the child reveals that he is able to sing because of a grain placed on his tongue by the Virgin. The grain is removed, the child falls dead, and is buried in a shrine.

In The Prioress's Tale, Chaucer constructs a narrative about pure innocence. Moreover, the constructed narrative voice is a performance in all its details designed to promote an impression of the teller as a pure innocent herself. Thus the Tale develops 'infant ventriloquism' as a theme, as not only the child within the Tale, but the narrator herself, like a young choirboy, mimics devotional material with feeling but without understanding.[32] The whole verbal texture of the account resonates with anglicised liturgy, performed as a sign of purity of utterance, but laced also with a number of flat spots created by clichés and inappropriate domestic details. An underlying satirical reading is thus developed by applying a relatively vacuous presentational surface to narrative content which, with its violent anti-Semitism and its image of the loudly singing living corpse, has considerable latent, but largely unrealised, potential to unsettle.

The Prioress's Tale, by dramatising limitation, thus offers rich potential readings which inform understandings of hagiography as a vehicle for medieval anti-Semitism and anti-feminism.[33] Hagiography, with its focus on martyrdom, needs to dramatise a hostile other, and the Jews, expelled, ghetto-ised, and persecuted, offered a convenient stereotype. The construction of the Jews as

Christ's tormentors in particular, extended to an understanding that, as the Christian's other, they were in league with the devil. This is explicitly presented in The Prioress's Tale. The Tale draws on two other stock concentrations of anti-Semitism, the first deriving from the belief that Jews murdered Christian infants, the second that located particular anti-Semitic diatribes in accounts of miracles of the Virgin, where a standard component involves inveighing against those who refuse to venerate her. More broadly medieval Christian anti-Semitism exemplifies unbelief through a variety of accounts which position the Jew as miracle-denier. A particular sub-set of the Jews' reported refusal to acknowledge the transformational power of Christianity is the rich seam of legends about transubstantiation-denial which is dramatised in English in the *Croxton Play of the Sacrament*.[34] There the represented unbelieving Jews subject a Mass-wafer to a series of trials that mirror the Passion of Christ, bringing on a startling theatrical denouement when Christ in the flesh bursts from the oven in which the Host was being roasted.

Women, and particularly the female religious, provided a particular market for hagiographical narrative, being excluded from reading devotional material in Latin. Tales of virgin martyrs encouraged female readers to internalise and perpetuate their own subjugation to the Latin over-culture. Tales of equally virginal child saints of either gender, almost invariably the victims of ritual murder by Jews, provided an unedifying variant within the category that Jocelyn Wogan-Browne aptly dubs 'body-ripping' literature.[35] In The Prioress's Tale, according to a strategy typical of *The Canterbury Tales*, the whole nexus of misogyny and xenophobia which typifies hagiographic narratives written for women is undercut by the Tale's foregrounding of the inadequacies of a narrator who is herself fashioned from the stuff of her library. The portrait of the Prioress in The General Prologue takes this strategy a step further, objectifying her literary inadequacies in her limited mastery of French, and using her as a vehicle to expose the blurring in a particular female sub-culture of the models presented to them in their devotional reading with those of secular romance. The focus for this is the wonderfully bathetic sequence of transpositions and elisions surrounding 'love' embodied in the psyche of the Prioress: the love of God and the Virgin represented by her vocation, becomes in the Tale the sentimental attachment to a small child, which, in The General Prologue portrait, is actually transferred on to her spoilt and overfed lapdogs. Her brooch with its legend *Amor vincit omnia* [love conquers all] takes on particular satirical resonance. Although ephemeral detail has proved a temptation for some to find a real-life model for the Prioress, this is surely a distraction, for, like the Wife of Bath, the Prioress is another textual construct. Again, what leads to the illusion that she is a dramatic character, or even a real woman, is the Tale's performance of a constructed point of view and manner of delivery.

Blurring the distinction between hagiography and romance is not simply a matter of flawed reception, however. Ad Putter refers to the 'direct line of descent from saints' lives to tail-rhyme romance',[36] citing the shared motifs in *Sir Isumbras* and the *Life of St Eustace*, and observing that *Guy of Warwick* changes to tail-rhyme when the romance comes to deal with the protagonist's life of penance (see Chapter 1). The connection clearly is metrical, a product of coincidental earlier contexts of aural reception, but it is also structural, as both popular romance and hagiography share similar linear patterns of achievement and setback until brought to their often arbitrary end by a resolution involving union by marriage in the romance, or with God in the saint's life. *Emaré* is one of the more striking examples, sitting so precisely on the cusp as to absolve the Prioress of any category error.[37] Its protagonist is as saint-*like* as all the Griseldas, Constances, Virginias, and others who find their way into the writings of Chaucer, Gower, Lydgate, John Capgrave, and Osbern Bokenham, an unhelpful female role model, and a martyr in life as much as in death in her complete subjugation to Christian patriarchy.

ST ERKENWALD

A further type of hagiographic narrative concerns the afterlife or relics of the saintly body. These accounts also have their structural conformities, as the saint is invariably discovered as a result of revelation, often to someone low-born. A high-ranking Church official is informed and the exhumation of the remains authorised. Those remains demonstrate sanctity by being incorrupt and emitting a ravishingly sweet smell, a motif transferred audaciously by Malory to the dead Lancelot. A new shrine is erected and reports of miracles turn it into a pilgrimage destination. Translations of saints' remains were, for the late medieval period, familiar religious events, particularly in England where a comparatively large number of secular persons were canonised.

Stories of miraculous exhumations and speaking incorrupt tongues are manipulated in the 352-line late fourteenth-century northern alliterative poem *St Erkenwald*.[38] The poem is a narrative account of how, during the rebuilding of St Paul's Cathedral in London, masons uncover an elaborate old tomb. Puzzled by the discovery, they decide to lift the lid. The description of the body that lies within draws on the hagiographical tradition, possibly deriving some detail from Bede's story of St Cuthbert's exhumation:

> Als wemles were his wedes, with-outes any tecche,
> Oþer of moulynge, oþer of motes, oþir moght-freten,
> & as bryȝt of hor blee in blysnande hewes,
> As þai hade ȝepely in þat ȝerde bene ȝisturday shapen;
> & as freshe hym þe face & the fleshe nakyde
> Bi his eres & bi his hondes þat openly shewid,
> With ronke rode as þe rose, & two rede lippes,
> As he in sounde sodanly were slippide opon slepe. (85–92)
>
> [As spotless were his clothes, without any mark, either of mould, or of specks, or of moth-eating, and as bright in their beautiful colours, as if they had just been made yesterday in that place; and his face was fresh, as was the naked flesh of his ears and his hands where it was on display, rose pink all over, with two red lips, just as if he had, in full health, slipped suddenly into sleep.]

This is not, however, a saint, but a pagan judge. He was a paragon of truth and justice, but was excluded from heaven and left in limbo when hell was harrowed, because he did not know Christ. Yet this is still the account of a saint's miracle. Erkenwald, bishop of London, is out of town when the discovery is made, and returns to confusion and hubbub because of the discovery of the as-yet unidentified corpse. After a night of solitary prayer, he conjures the corpse to reveal its identity, and it speaks eerily, telling its history. Erkenwald, like all the bystanders, is so overcome that he is unable to speak further. He weeps over the corpse, and one tear falls onto its face (323), at which it emits a sigh. It speaks again, and the vigour of these lines, contrasted with the mournfulness of its earlier speech, reflects the moment of its admission into heaven (329–32). The source of the story is the widely retold legend of Trajan, and focuses on the merits of relinquishing human agency to God found in Bonaventuran spiritual counsel.

The poet also extends the lesson about good works and grace into more specifically English ecclesiological territory, adapting the legend to affirm the importance of the Church's sacramental intervention as the means to God's grace.[39] The action of the poem is set precisely in place, 'London in Englonde' (1). Erkenwald is presented as the heritor of St Augustine's mission to the Anglo-Saxons, thereby foregrounding by implication the danger that a nation without an effective Church can relapse into error. Erkenwald himself tests the contrary when he enquires after the health of the judge's soul, suggesting that there is something wrong with royal reward on earth if it does not anticipate royal reward in heaven (278). The speaking corpse does not reply directly to him but hums, wags its head, groans, and prays for mercy (281–4). Hence the agency of even Erkenwald's reason is compromised, and the resolution of the corpse's predicament is left to 'þe riche kynge of reson' (267), Christ, the ultimate just judge. The concluding action makes clear not only that the sacraments of the Church are the mechanism by which the soul will be released from limbo, but that the priest is simply a conduit for divine grace through his compassionate tears.

The narrative of well-meaning but futile human actions – the burial of the corpse in its finery, its exhumation, and attempts to relieve it – expose their own limitations. They are contrasted with the submissive silence of the bystanders while the single tear of the holy Erkenwald, inadvertently dropped on the corpse's head, performs the only productive act. The corpse then goes through a paradoxical transformation, as the soul rises to bliss and the body turns into vile-smelling carrion before the onlookers' eyes (345–46). The paradox is reflected by the departing crowds in whom 'meche mournynge & merthe was mellyd [mingled] to-geder' (349) as they process from the church, and all the church bells in the city are rung at once, sound released into the air to accompany the soul departing for heaven. *St Erkenwald* offers a clear endorsement of the efficacy of the intercession of the saints, and of the centrality of the sacraments of the Church. Too much focus on its theological 'orthodoxy', however, generates instrumental readings which are reductive of its aesthetic qualities. The poem's evident stylistic similarities with the poems in the '*Gawain* manuscript', particularly with *Pearl* to which we turn next, have also attracted attention. The argument for common authorship has, however, rested on an obscure anagrammatic signature, and is probably another critical cul-de-sac.[40]

PEARL

Pearl accompanies *Sir Gawain and the Green Knight*, *Patience*, and *Cleanness* in British Library MS Cotton Nero A. x. It is another highly wrought alliterative poem, sharing many formal and stylistic features with *Sir Gawain. Sir Gawain* is 2,525 lines long and focuses on patterns of five, radiating out from the pentangle on Gawain's shield which is presented as a diagrammatic embodiment of his value system; *Pearl* is 1,212 lines long and is made up of concatenated stanzas, where the first line of each contains a cognate of a word in the last line of the preceding one, repeated with variation as a refrain through each of the 'fitts' into which it is divided, so that it forms a linked chain, or string of pearls. Both poems return to their beginnings, as the first and last long lines are similar, mirroring the pentangle's 'endless knot', the circularity of a single pearl, or of a rosary of individual pearls. In other respects, the poems diverge: the relationship between production and reception in *Sir Gawain* is built around puzzle and suspense, whereas *Pearl*, as a work of devotional didacticism, is built around exposition and revelation, more like *Patience*, *Cleanness*, and, indeed, their anomalous poetic cousin, *St Erkenwald.* All are poems that ask difficult theological questions and enact their novel exegeses aesthetically.[41]

The circular form of *Pearl* celebrates the poem's involuted self-sufficiency, despite its deployment of a number of familiar medieval literary conventions. It is a dream-vision which opens and closes in a garden arbour, but one in which the vegetation whose sweet smells lull the dreamer to sleep is drawn not from secular love poetry but from the Bible's own poem of love-longing, the Song of Songs. This mutable earthly paradise is quickly replaced by a heavenly one constructed of precious stones that will later open up to reveal the gem-encrusted new Jerusalem, mimicking in content and method the vision of St John in Revelations 22. The poem tells of a quest for a lost loved one, the object of 'luf-daungere'(11), which the narrator pre-emptively calls his 'pryuy' [secret/personal] or 'precios perle wythouten spot' (12, 24, 36, 48, 60). She has been lost to the ground by a 'jeweller' to whom she was nearer than aunt or niece (233), when she was less than two years old (483). So this is not a poem about unrequited erotic love, but seems to be about the death of a little girl. The potential for sentimentality, is, therefore, comparable with that exploited in The Prioress's Tale; yet those expectations are to be artfully thwarted when, in his dream, the narrator meets the object of his mourning. The initial connotations of his description, poised between, or eliding, the secular 'rose' and the Virgin Mary, are not so much set aside as set within a larger cognitive hierarchy:

> . . . þat þou lesteȝ [lost] was bot a rose
> Þat flowred and fayled as kynde hyt gef [nature granted it]. (269–70)

She was a flower, is now a pearl, and, like the Virgin Mary, is also now a queen in heaven. She also wears 'the pearl of great price' (Matthew 13: 45–6) that is personal salvation. Moreover, in direct inversion of the female and/or infantilised vehicle of devotional feeling without understanding, she develops a voice of spiritual authority that dominates the centre of the poem, and one so uncompromisingly severe that the affective object remains the narrator, whose earnest spiritual fumblings lead to the particular type of active spiritual enquiry that the poem promotes to its readership.

The maiden's animation, which transforms her from complex signifier to pedagogic voice, carries the poem's theological burden. Its central focus is a particular reading of the parable of the Labourers in the Vineyard (Matthew 20: 1–16). The jeweller questions his pearl from the point of view of ignorance about the geography of his vision and, in particular, about her place in heaven. Her replies are oblique, but probe his misunderstandings, demonstrating, for example, the difference between exclusive earthly hierarchies, and heavenly hierarchy which is based on altruism (458). As she guides him towards asking the right questions, the jeweller's voice shifts to a more informed, but heretical, understanding. The Pelagian heresy which he enacts claims that a place in heaven can be earned. She refutes it, drawing on the parable which is the poem's chief dogmatic tool. The standard interpretation of the parable of the Labourers puts it alongside the parable of the Prodigal Son, as a metaphorical exemplum of the infinite nature of mercy available through Christ. Accordingly, the last-minute penitent may be admitted to heaven by the grace of God on the same basis as those who lead their whole lives in the avoidance of sin. The Pearl maiden's exegesis has a different emphasis, as she presents the labourer who comes late to the vineyard as the newly baptised infant, born near to her death-day. The theological debate about the relative value of good works and grace, connoted in the action of *St Erkenwald*, is brought together in the poem's dead centre. The jeweller summarises his position, citing the Psalms as his authority, that everyone is rewarded according to their deserts (590–600). The maiden refutes his Old Testament authority by assuring him that 'þe gentyl Cheuentayn is no chyche' (605), that is Christ is not so niggardly.

As the Pearl maiden, ventiloquising the poet's didactic message, pushes her case, the reader's attention is drawn, again as in *St Erkenwald*, to the sacraments of the Church as the specific ritual manifestations of the bestowal of grace. Here initial emphasis is placed on infant baptism, which gives infants 'innoghe of grace' (625), so that if the day or life inclines immediately to the night of death, they are rewarded because they 'wroȝt neuer wrang er þenne þay wente' (631), and the Lord pays his servants accordingly. In her following exposition, however, the emphasis shifts from the position of the newly baptised infant to the barriers to salvation faced by the adult. The river at the centre of the visionary landscape, separating the jeweller from the Pearl, was initially understood to represent death, but now comes to connote the water of baptism and of eternal life. More particularly the landscape is transformed by analogy to God's body, which flowed blood and water (650), and the water of baptism unites with the blood of the Eucharist through images of lavage.

The debate's movement to a conclusion is signalled by the jeweller's asking the critical question, 'Quo formed þe þy fayre fygure?' (745–7). Who made you? The answer is Christ the Lamb, introduced as the Pearl's lover, in a landscape which is now finally transformed to a vision of the heavenly Jerusalem. The Lamb himself becomes too the revised and perfected exemplum and source of whiteness, purity, and innocence, from whom the blood of the Passion flowed to make grace possible for those for whom baptism was inadequate because of their sins in the world. The narrator's vision of the heavenly city is explored and explained, then experienced, as the Pearl maiden recedes to take her place in the procession of brides of the Lamb. The dreamer awakes in his arbour, and re-awakes to the knowledge of his loss, which he is now prepared to confront with patient spiritual understanding. For him the purifying potential of the blood of the Lamb is finally understood as 'þe forme of bred and wyn' (1209), as the Eucharist is promoted as the means to eventual participation in that ravishing vision.

The poem's structural method owes much to the metaphorical and connotative orderings of narrative material employed by the Church in the patristic tradition of biblical exegesis. The ordering of images submits readily to analysis according to the fourfold method of decoding scriptural allegory, and thereby appears to strive to mimic and model the properties of holy writ itself as received by the western medieval Church. It tells a literal story, set in concretely realised landscapes, of a dreamer who falls asleep and has an encounter with his dead child in heaven. Tropologically, or morally, it maps the progress of an individual Christian from a position of ignorance and misbelief on the nature of salvation, to a state of spiritual understanding of grace through the Redemption. It alludes centrally to Christ's teaching and his Passion as recounted in the Gospels, and anagogically, or mystically, it ends with a vision of the heavenly city and the perpetual nature of Christ's sacrifice, as the wine and bread of the Eucharist were understood to be transubstantiated by the action of the Holy Ghost. It thus accretes meaning cumulatively and obliquely but in a manner that would have been recognisable to an audience familiar with the methodology of biblical exegesis. Furthermore, the progress of the narrative voice in *Pearl* enacts a process analogous to, and in parallel with, the way in which the poem's images incrementally accrue meaning. The narrator moves from spiritual ignorance to spiritual knowledge through a process that begins with sensory surfeit, goes through intellectual challenge, and is rewarded by a higher inspirational vision. It owes much to Bonaventuran teaching and is comparable with some of the more directly mystical prose of the period.

JULIAN OF NORWICH

Foremost amongst those mystical prose writers in English must be Julian of Norwich. In the last chapter we considered Margery Kempe – who allegedly met Julian – and her *Book* as witnesses to social change. Placing her there acknowledged Margery's anomalous standing as witness to any particular theology; her radicalism inheres in her practice, and she contributes little in the way of new and probing insight into the fundamental truths of her faith. Standing behind her, however, is Julian, anchoress of Norwich, the other remarkable East Anglian woman whose testimony has survived. Julian's *Vision* and *Revelation*, properly two books, is an account of, and reflection on, a series of visions which qualify their author as a mystic squarely within the Franciscan tradition.

Julian's short text, *A Vision Showed to a Devout Woman*, was written in the mid 1380s, and gives an account of a visionary experience, or 'showings' during a serious illness which she suffered at the age of thirty, on 8 May 1373.[42] Believing, as she did, that she was likely to die, a priest held a carved crucifix before her face, which had on it a figure of Christ. As the sick woman looked at it, Christ's head began to bleed. There then appeared around the central image a series of scenes from the Passion of Christ which became more and more terrible to witness so that she was moved to extreme compassion. At the conclusion of the vision, Christ came to life on the sculpted cross and assured her that despite all she had witnessed, 'alle shalle be welle, and alle maner of thinge shalle be wele' (93). He also tells her that sin is 'behovelye' (91) – that is, necessary or even fortunate – reflecting the central paradox of Christian faith, that had Adam not sinned, God would not have become man in Christ. Julian's account of her visions is peculiarly vivid because she presents herself as a participating actor, rather than a meditative bystander, in the events she describes.

The long text, *A Revelation of Love*, is a reflective interpretation of her earlier narrative, and was written at least ten years later. In the intervening period she had experienced two further visions. The theological positioning of this text is subtle and optimistic. Julian understands that sin is necessary, but does not penetrate the whole soul. The soul retains a component which is unfallen and remains with God, an understanding which, like Bonaventuran meditative writing, resonates with a kind of Christian Platonism in which all humanity inheres in God and is potentially saved. Characteristic of her theology also is its refusal of the scholastic dogma in which body and soul are distinct or opposed. She argues that it is Christ's humanity, his taking on of the flesh, that made possible the redemption of humanity. That flesh was taken from the Virgin Mary, but because Mary in turn derived that flesh from he who gave everyone humanity by taking on humanity himself, the true mother of all body and soul is Christ.[43] This convergent, holistic impulse that characterises Julian's thought derives from the Franciscan tradition, but it is still, as her recent editors put it, 'outstanding even in this company for the intensity of its determination to re-imagine Christian thought in its entirety, not as a system of ideas, but as an answer to human need'.[44] Where Margery Kempe's *Book* is full of references to her life in the world, Julian tells us little about herself beyond the circumstances in which she had her visionary experiences. There is, therefore, no reliable information about her as author, and there is no autograph manuscript. We can surmise from her level of education that she came from an affluent background, and recent work on the sources of much of her theological thought has convincingly tracked them down in the numerous compilations of devotional writing in English to which she appears to have had access.[45]

It is simply impossible here to do justice to the subtleties of

Julian's theology, let alone the whole English mystical tradition, which accounts for a significant proportion of the prose output in English from the mid-fourteenth century.[46] It includes the works of Richard Rolle, who, like Julian, chose the hermitical life, living in a cell in Hampole in Yorkshire. Many of Rolle's English writings were directed at Margaret Kirkby, a nun for whom he acted as spiritual advisor, but his most famous work is probably the Latin *Incendium Amoris*, a tract focusing on what became Rolle's signature message in all his writings, advising his reader to turn from the concerns of the world to burn in the 'fire of love' for Christ. The majority of devotional texts with a contemplative focus are, however, anonymous, either by accident or design. *The Abbey of the Holy Ghost*, *The Orchard of Sion*, *Pore Caitif*, and *The Chastizing of God's Children* are a handful of examples of the devotional diet in the vernacular that turn up alongside Latin works in devotional compilations. They are the output largely of regular religious who, by virtue of their vocation, 'seek to articulate a truth that is above time, place, and individual circumstances'.[47] One anonymous text conventionally attracts attention for the detailed level of instruction it offers on the meditative technique: *The Cloud of Unknowing* is founded on the pseudo-Dionysian premise that because God is different, only negative statements can be made about him. The self-effacement that is central to the deconstructive agenda of all these texts translates into authorial self-deprecation that urges the imaginative empowerment of the reader in connecting with metaphysical realities.

MORALITY PLAYS

Throughout this chapter we have encountered various connotative means by which moral and theological instruction and reflection were given expression, including mystical methods for affectively expressing the ineffable. In all this, it has been important to resist too instrumental a reading of religious literature, even when, as is often the case, there is an expressed intention to instruct the target audience. Allegorical writing of the kind adapted to imaginative ends in *Pearl* was a highly constructed method beloved of preachers, whereby entities and narratives stood as figures for other entities, narratives, or abstract ideas. It is not primarily a literary technique, but a theological method for organising and systematising scriptural material, which medieval devotional literature draws on widely and permissively for the fashioning of oblique modes of expression and multiple significations. The Prologue to Henryson's *Morall Fabillis*, as we have seen, is, among other things, a commentary on the utility of narrative methods drawn from allegory in the construction of didactic fictions.

The action of medieval morality plays is frequently described as 'allegorical', where the term is used loosely to describe the rhetorical separation between the play world and the 'real' world, as on stage abstract qualities, human categories, and attributes are embodied in individual players. The genre is largely defined retrospectively by the moral interlude, strictly speaking a Tudor phenomenon, which extends the allegorical method into examinations of political principle, and often occluded satire. The action of the medieval examples centres on the temptation, fall into sin, and restitution of a protagonist representing all humanity. Personifications of vicious and virtuous agency make up the remainder of the casts of characters in actions designed to explore the degree to which human beings control their own access to salvation. In their cross-over from matters strictly theological to issues concerning contemporary ecclesiastical organisation, they too can offer rich opportunities for satirical asides.

Before accepting that the morality play takes allegorical discourse to the stage, it is important to stop to consider what the concept of 'reality' was for the intellect raised on scholastic thought. In a way that reverses modern empirical understandings about the world, to a medieval theologian the observable phenomena of this world were ephemeral and provisional reflections of underlying metaphysical realities. Hence the action of a morality play is better viewed as a dramatised instance of an underlying eternal verity. The matter of the plot of each play, though thematic and couched in generalised terms, is played out as a narrative demonstration of the manifestations of a particular sin and the armament available to overcome it.[48] The three securely datable medieval morality plays all survive in one manuscript of East Anglian provenance: manuscript V. a. 354 in the Folger Library, Washington DC, formerly the property of a Suffolk antiquarian called Cox Macro, so that *The Castle of Perseverance*, *Mankind*, and *Wisdom* are known collectively as the Macro Plays.[49]

The Castle of Perseverance is designed for large-scale outdoor production in an amphitheatre on a set whose design is appended in the manuscript. The life of the protagonist, Humanum Genus, is played out as a journey through time from birth to death. The sin which dogs him is Covetousness, signalled by the fact that the actor embodying that sin occupies a scaffold all of his own on the perimeter of the set. Its location destroys the symmetry of that set, which otherwise has God, the Devil, the World and the Flesh located in the east, north, west and south respectively. Humanum Genus falls prey to Covetousness at the point in his journey that represents middle age, but Covetousness's aberrant positioning also performs a perpetual truth for the whole assembled company, for the set design is such that the audience is also contained within it, and it is a moralised sign of their universe. Thus the protagonist performs as their delegate in a time-bound sequence whose climax is a battle between the forces of good and evil for the eponymous Castle in the centre of the playing space, but this represents for the audience a model of a shared and continuing metaphysical reality. In *Mankind* the moralising dramatic strategy is remarkably similar, although the theatrical auspices of the play are very different, as it is written for performance by a small cast on a non-specific set. In place of the journey and battle metaphors which unify the *Castle*, this play uses work, specifically hard agricultural work, to represent virtuous living, and armament against the focal sin, which is Sloth in this instance. Sloth is neither a place nor an embodied person here, but is exemplified in the behaviour of three vice figures, Newgyse, Nowadays, and Nought, who try to distract Mankind to give up his labour. Commentators on the play have recognised that the dialogue in the play is contrived as a sign, exemplifying the contrast between virtuous and slothful discourse.[50] Hence Mankind successfully resists the efforts of the vices to corrupt him, but not so the audience, who are forced at one point into singing a rude song before the play will continue. The vices then also force them to pay to see a devil, Tutyvillus, who finally succeeds in bringing Mankind's labours to an end by putting a board under the soil which makes it impossible to dig, and sending an urgent call of nature. Tutyvillus in popular tradition is the minor devil believed to specialise in gathering all the language that idle priests missed out of the liturgy, and all the gossip spoken in church, in his bag.[51] Accordingly, where the *Castle* manipulates its audience into a subjective understanding of the moral realities it represents through their positioning in the theatrical space, *Mankind* constructs a similar understanding by entrapping the audience into actions – and speech acts – against their 'better' moral judgement without which the play they have come to see cannot proceed.

Wisdom is a more intellectually challenging play whose process represents the individual's movement towards mystical union with Christ. Apart from Wisdom, who represents Christ, and Lucifer, who represents himself, all the other characters, including a number of non-speaking parts, are elements of a composite protagonist, Anima, the soul. Here the metaphysical reality which the play's action embodies involves a lesson on the internal workings of the moral psyche. The soul is constituted of three 'mights', Mind, Will, and Understanding, and is disfigured as they are corrupted, then is restored by penance. The play also incidentally enacts contemporary understandings of the relationship between gender, piety, and power, as the soul is feminised and seeks fulfilment through marriage to Wisdom, represented as a male authority figure. It uses elaborate costume emblematically, including the device of having characters signal changes in their moral identities through name-change and disguise. The play's understanding of sin is commensurately sophisticated, drawing not on the conventional absolutes of deadly sins, but on contemporary debates about the relative virtues of different ways of life. In particular it takes us back to the mystical prose writings in which East Anglia was particularly prolific in the late fourteenth century, and shows the influence of Walter Hilton's *Treatise on the Mixed Life* and *The Scale of Perfection*, as well as possibly Richard Rolle's *Novem Virtutes*, and the German Henry Suso's *Orologium Sapientia*.[52] Lucifer's specious argument promotes what he calls the mixed life over the monastic ideal of pure contemplation. His designation of what constitutes the mixed life is, however, wholly secular, and thus the play develops an object lesson on the difficulty of internalising a balance between asceticism and worldly engagement that is pleasing to God. Like its two companion plays,

Wisdom is rhetorically unambivalent, confirming and celebrating a dimension of eternal verity. Verbal and visual signs conspire to place character and action at any given moment on a clearly articulated moral scale. There is plenty of theatrical inventiveness in all three, but no internal conflict, as all the pressure is directed at bringing the audience not only to recognise, but to submit to, specific moralised behavioural patterns.

We have seen in earlier chapters how 'secular' literature in the Middle English period is performative insofar as it engages with the process of image-building and manipulation, earnest posturings from a variety of different political and ideological points of view, some of which involve display, others occlusions which are, in their own way, the paradoxical openings of vital secrets. The literature of vernacular theology in the late Middle Ages involves a related kind of performativity, enactments driven by the exemplificatory method which perform central theological understandings about different orders of reality. The stories in the *Confessio Amantis*, the account of Jonah's sojourn in the whale, the fable of the Swallow, or the dilemma faced by Mankind when the ground proves too hard to break, are all dramatised instances of larger truths. They operate according to different related metaphorical decora which we can label 'allegory' or 'fable', but what they share is that they are signs of larger metaphysical truths. Dramatised instances drawn from the Bible itself, such as the encounter between Gabriel and Mary, or between Mary and Elizabeth in the N. Town Play, conform to the same decorum, their mythic significance notwithstanding. Further, the dramatised relationship between Amans and Genius in the *Confessio*, or between the dreamer and the Pearl maiden, are also enactments of procedures whereby the Church cascades its knowledge of the same metaphysical truths to its component parts. The vital distinction in all these texts is not that between the literal and the allegorical, nor yet between play and poem. The latter distinction can amount to little more than scribal choice; the scribe of the Bodley *Burial of Christ* changes his mind midway about whether he is copying a treatise or a play. All the texts we have reviewed in this chapter are 'dramatic', as all perform provisional examples of the observable human world and, rather than relating them to broader social or political agenda, relate them to shared understandings about an ultimate higher reality which is theologically determined and morally understood.

NOTES

1. Christopher M. Bellitto, *The General Councils: a History of the Twenty-One Church Councils from Nicaea to Vatican II* (Mahwah, NJ: Paulist Press, 2002), pp. 49–95.
2. Nicholas Watson, 'Censorship and Cultural Change in Late Medieval England: Vernacular Theology, the Oxford Translation Debate, and Arundel's Constitutions of 1409', *Speculum*, 70 (1985), 822–64, 823.
3. W. Pantin, *The English Church in the Fourteenth Century* (Cambridge: Cambridge University Press, 1955), pp. 220–43.
4. T. F. Simmons and H. E. Nolloth (eds), *The Lay Folks' Catechism*, Early English Text Society, OS 118, New Edition (Cambridge: D. S. Brewer, 2006). For the complex history of this text, see Anne Hudson, 'A New Look at the Lay Folks' Catechism', *Viator*, 16 (1985), 243–58, and 'The Lay Folks' Catechism: A Postscript', *Viator*, 19 (1988), 307–9.
5. Malcolm Andrew and Ronald Waldron (eds), *The Poems of the Pearl Manuscript: Pearl, Patience, Cleanness, Sir Gawain and the Green Knight*, Exeter Medieval Texts and Studies (Exeter: University of Exeter Press, 2007), *Pearl* pp. 53–110; *Cleanness* pp. 111–84; *Patience* pp. 185–206. All quotations are taken from this edition; translations also are taken from this edition supplemented by the author's own.
6. John Mirk, *A Critical Edition of John Mirk's Festial, edited from British Library MS Cotton Claudius A.II*, vol. 1, Susan Powell (ed.), Early English Text Society, OS 334 (Oxford: Oxford University Press, 2009); see also Judy Anne Ford, *John Mirk's 'Festial': Orthodoxy, Lollardy, and the Common People in Fourteenth-Century England* (Cambridge: D. S. Brewer, 2006).
7. G. R. Owst, *Literature and Pulpit in Medieval England: A Neglected Chapter in the History of English Letters and of the English People*, 2nd edn (Oxford: Blackwell, 1966), p. 224.
8. G. R. Owst, *Preaching in Medieval England, An Introduction*

to Sermon Manuscripts of the Period c. 1350–1450 (Cambridge: Cambridge University Press, 1926), p. 316.

9. See further Anne B. Thompson, *Everyday Saints and the Art of Narrative in the South English Legendary* (Aldershot: Ashgate, 2003), pp. 39–45; and Thorlac Turville-Petre, *England and the Nation: Language Literature and National Identity, 1290–1340* (Oxford: Clarendon Press, 1996), p. 38.
10. The only edition of the whole poem remains Richard Morris (ed.), *The English Philological Society's Early English Volume, 1862–4* (London: Asher, 1865).
11. Lena Etherington, 'An Edition of Book Five of *The Pricke of Conscience* with Critical Introduction to the Text', unpublished MPhil thesis, University of Lancaster, 2004, pp. 13–28.
12. John Gower, *Confessio Amantis*, ed. Russell Peck (Toronto: University of Toronto Press, 2006 [2000]). All page references are to the 2006 edition.
13. Robert Yeager, 'The Poetry of John Gower', in Corinne Saunders (ed.), *The Blackwell Companion to Medieval Poetry* (Oxford: Blackwell, 2010), pp. 464–5.
14. Ibid. pp. 467–8.
15. Derek Pearsall, 'Gower and Lydgate', in G. Bullough (ed.), *Gower and Lydgate* (Harlow, Essex: Longman, 1969), p. 183.
16. Yeager, 'John Gower', p. 475.
17. Marie Collins, 'Love, Law, and Nature in the Poetry of Gower and Chaucer', in Glyn S. Burgess (ed.), *Court and Poet: Selected Proceedings of the Third Congress of the International Courtly Literature Society* (Liverpool: Francis Cairns, 1981), pp. 113–28 (p. 116).
18. Pearsall, 'Gower and Lydgate', pp. 13–14.
19. Robert Henryson, *Robert Henryson: Poems*, ed. Charles Elliott (Oxford: Clarendon Press, 1974 [1963]), pp. 1–89. All page references are to the 1974 edition.
20. E. P. Dargan, 'Cock and Fox: A Critical Study of the History and Sources of the Medieval Fable', *Modern Philology*, 4 (1906), 38–65.
21. The so-called *arma Christi*, the meditative image of a coat of arms on which are organised the instruments of torture employed in Christ's Passion, quartered by the Cross,

demonstrates the analogy. See further Eamon Duffy, *The Stripping of the Altars* (New Haven, CT and London: Yale University Press, 1992), p. 246.

22. Douglas Gray (ed.), *A Selection of Religious Lyrics* (Oxford: Clarendon Press, 1975), p. 113; Anne Dutton, 'Piety, Politics, and Persona: London British Library MS 4021 and Anne Harling', in Felicity Riddy (ed.), *Prestige, Authority and Power in Late Medieval Manuscripts and Texts* (York: York Medieval Texts, 2000), pp. 133–46.
23. Duffy, *Stripping of the Altars*, pp. 234–5.
24. Gray, *Selection of Religious Lyrics*, p. 30. The other lyrics referenced in the immediately following paragraphs are all taken from this edition, respectively at pp. 41, 18, 22, and 4.
25. A good synopsis of current scholarship is Mishtooni Bose, 'Religious Authority and Dissent', in Peter Brown (ed.), *A Companion to Medieval Literature and Culture, c.1350–c.1500* (Oxford: Blackwell, 2007).
26. Nicholas Love, *The Mirror of the Blessed Life of Jesus Christ*, ed. M. G. Sargent (Exeter: University of Exeter Press, 2005), p. intro 57. All quotations are drawn from this edition, by page and line number. See also Henry Suso, *The Seven Poyntes of Trewe Love and Everlastynge Wisdome*, ed. K. Horstmann, *Anglia*, 10, 1888), 323–89.
27. Stephen Spector, *The N-Town Play Cotton MS Vespasian D.8*, 2 vols, Early English Text Society SS 11 and 12 (Oxford: Oxford University Press, 1991); P. Meredith (ed.), *The Mary Play from the N. Town Manuscript* (Exeter: Exeter University Press, 1997) and *The Passion Play from the N. Town Manuscript* (London and New York: Longman, 1990); James Gibson (ed.), *Kent: Diocese of Canterbury*, Records of Early English Drama, 3 vols in 2 (Toronto: University of Toronto Press, 2002), pp. lix–lxiii; 738, 745–50, 779–94, 1016.
28. See various essays in A. F. Johnston and Wim Hüsken (eds), *English Parish Drama*, Ludus 1 (Atlanta, GA and Amsterdam: Rodopi, 1996).
29. See further Pamela M. King, 'Drama: Sacred and Secular' in Saunders (ed.), *The Blackwell Companion to Medieval Poetry* (Oxford: Blackwell, 2010).

30. Richard Beadle (ed.), *The York Plays: A Critical Edition of the York Corpus Christi Play as Recorded in British Library Additional MS 35290*, Early English Text Society, SS 23 (Oxford: Oxford University Press, 2009), pp. 332–53.
31. F. J. Furnivall (ed.), *The Digby Plays*, Early English Text Society, ES 70 (Oxford: Oxford University Press, 1896), pp. 170–200 and 201–6.
32. Lee Patterson, '"The Living Witnesses of Our Redemption": Martyrdom and Imitation in Chaucer's Prioress's Tale', *Journal of Medieval and Early Modern Studies*, 31 (2001), 507–60 (509–10).
33. There is a rich secondary literature in both areas, for example, T. Head, *Medieval Hagiography: An Anthology* (London: Routledge, 2000); Sarah Salih, Ruth Evans, and A. Bernau, *Medieval Virginities* (Cardiff: University of Wales Press, 2003); P. H. Wasyliw, *Martyrdom, Murder, and Magic: Child Saints and Their Cults in Medieval Europe* (New York: Peter Lang, 2008); and Jocelyn Wogan-Browne, 'Saints' Lives and the Female Reader', *Forum for Modern Language Studies* 27 (1991), 314–32.
34. Norman Davis, *Non-Cycle Plays and Fragments*, Early English Text Society, SS, 1 (Oxford: Oxford University Press, 1970), pp. 58–89.
35. Wogan-Browne, 'Saints' Lives', p. 315.
36. Ad Putter, 'The Metres and Stanza Forms of Popular Romance', in R. Radulescu and C. Rushton (eds), *A Companion to Medieval Popular Romance* (Cambridge: D. S. Brewer, 2009), pp. 111–31 (pp. 123–4).
37. M. Mills, *Six Middle English Romances* (London: Dent, 1973), pp. 46–74.
38. R. Morse (ed.), *St Erkenwald* (Cambridge: D. S. Brewer, 1975). All references are to this edition. See also T. McAlindon, 'Hagiography into Art: a Study of *St Erkenwald*', *Studies in Philology*, 67 (1970), 472–94.
39. See further W. Kamowski, '*St Erkenwald* and Inadvertent Baptism: An Orthodox Response to Heterodox Ecclesiology', *Religion and Literature* 27 (1995), 5–27.
40. See T. Turville-Petre and E. Wilson, 'Hoccleve's Maistir Masy

and the *Pearl* Poet: Two Notes', *Review of English Studies*, 26 (1975), 129–43, for a summary of the debate.

41. For classical critical readings of *Pearl*, see Ian Bishop, *Pearl in its Setting* (Oxford: Blackwell, 1968) and P. M. Kean, *The Pearl: An Interpretation* (London: Routledge & Kegan Paul, 1967).
42. See Julian [of Norwich], *The Writings of Julian of Norwich: A Vision Showed to a Devout Woman and a Revelation of Love*, ed. N. Watson and J. Jenkins (University Park, PA: Pennsylvania University Press, 2006).
43. See further C. W. Bynum, *Holy Feast and Holy Fast: The Significance of Food to Medieval Women* (Berkeley and Los Angeles: University of California Press, 1987), p. 267.
44. Julian, *The Writings*, ed. Watkins and Jenkins, p. 2.
45. See further Elisabeth Dutton, *Julian of Norwich: The Influence of Late Medieval Devotional Compilations* (Cambridge: D. S. Brewer, 2008).
46. See further F. Beer, *Women and Mystical Experience in the Middle Ages* (Woodbridge, Suffolk: Boydell and Brewer, 1992); essays in L. H. McAvoy (ed.), *A Companion to Julian of Norwich* (Woodbridge, Suffolk: Boydell and Brewer, 2008); M. Glasscoe, *English Medieval Mystics: Games of Faith* (London: Longman, 1993).
47. Vincent Gillespie, 'Anonymous Devotional Writings', in A. S. G. Edwards, *A Companion to Middle English Prose* (Cambridge: D. S. Brewer, 2006), pp. 127–49.
48. See Natalie Crohn Schmitt, 'The Idea of a Person in Medieval Morality Plays', *Comparative Drama*, 12 (1978), 23–34.
49. Mark Eccles (ed.), *Macro Plays*, Early English Text Society OS 262 (Oxford: Oxford University Press, 1969); Pamela M. King 'Morality Plays' in Richard Beadle and Alan Fletcher (eds), *The Cambridge Companion to Medieval English Theatre* (Cambridge: Cambridge University Press, 2008 [1994]), pp. 235–62.
50. Dillon, Janette, *Language and Stage in Medieval and Renaissance England* (Cambridge: Cambridge University Press, 1998), pp. 65–6; Paula Neuss, 'Active and Idle Language: Dramatic Images in *Mankind*', in Neville Denny (ed.),

Medieval Drama, Stratford-on-Avon Studies, 16 (London: Edward Arnold, 1973), pp. 41–68.

51. Margaret Jennings, 'Tutivillus: The Literary Career of the Recording Demon', *Studies in Philology*, 74 (1977), 1–95.
52. Wolfgang Riehle, 'English Mysticism and the Morality Play *Wisdom Who Is Christ*', in Marion Glasscoe (ed.), *The Medieval Mystical Tradition in England* (Exeter: University of Exeter Press, 1986), pp. 202–15.

CHAPTER 4

Complaint and Dissent

THE LOLLARDS

Cultural historians warn against narratives of crisis, particularly in cases such as the history of Christianity, which is a story of perpetual tension. What characterises the period from around 1350, however, is that many disputes about religion in England were conducted in English, and that the use of the vernacular for scriptural and doctrinal material was itself one of the foci around which oppositional discourses developed. English had become the language of official record, so why should God not use it too? Similarly, to question ecclesiastical power structures accorded with the scrutiny of secular hierarchies in a period when feudal bonds had been loosened by demographic change. The proliferation of contested religious discourses arose both as part of, and in response to, perceptions of change and decay, in a circular pattern that was to persist through and beyond the Protestant Reformation and the English Revolution. It is prudent to resist imposing simple polarised understandings of heterodoxy and orthodoxy on what was a varied and changing ideological spectrum. Equally the voice of genuine political dissent in a society in which patronage oiled the wheels of power, and punishments were draconian, is hard to identify, something we will return to towards the end of the chapter.[1]

'Lollardy' is understood to be the identifiable institutionalised voice of religious dissent, but the Lollards were so-called by their detractors rather than by themselves, so, as we go on to look at 'Lollardy' in fourteenth- and fifteenth-century writing, we will take the scare-quotes as given. The writings of John Wyclif himself, in Latin, and of his immediate circle, show no evidence that they saw themselves as even incipiently heretical. The ideas debated in Oxford under Wyclif's influence spread, however, from cloister to court where they found a ready audience for an evolving radical and evangelical agenda. After Wyclif died in 1384, the production of texts promoting and developing his ideas proliferated, and the actions of supporters, who also produced translations of the Bible into English, prompted the production of polemical texts attacking them as heretics.[2] Thus the construction of Wycliffite sympathisers as heretical was confected gradually by the ecclesiastical establishment out of a fear of the Pandora's Box effect, climaxing in the passing of the act *De Heretico Comburendi* [For the Burning of Heretics] in 1401. Thereafter the publication of radical ideas was severely curbed, or forced into secret circulation and occluded forms of expression.

Questions of definition become even less clear when we consider the reading audience for Lollard texts. Until legislation made it physically dangerous, a number of readers, including Chaucer, appear to have been familiar with radical religious material and interacted with it in their own writing, without 'converting' to Lollardy. Fiona Somerset has proposed that 'we need to develop an intrinsic, positive account of Lollard belief, practice, and experience that sees binaries only where they are occasionally present'.[3] Accordingly, it is necessary to set out an epitome of the views that came to be characterised as Lollard, before considering a range of literary texts in Middle English which adopt a dissident voice in matters of religion, constructing an established order for the purposes of undermining it.

The best summations of Lollard opinion are embedded in texts written to refute them. The 'Twelve Conclusions of the Lollards' survives embedded in a polemical tract, *Liber contra duodecimo errors et hereses Lollardorum*, presented to Richard II by its author, Roger Dymmock, in 1396. Much of what it ascribes to the followers of Wyclif coincides with the 'Sixteen Points on which the Bishops accuse Lollards', attributed to Richard Ullerston, and written in the early fifteenth century. Lollard theology questioned the nature of transubstantiation, claiming that the bread of the altar, although it was 'verray Goddis body', remained bread 'in kynde'. Confession 'of mouth' was considered unnecessary provided that the penitent was contrite of heart. Prayers were to be directed only to God and not to the Virgin Mary and the saints, and crosses or painted or engraved images were not to be worshipped. Pilgrimages were unnecessary, as was illuminating the Eucharist or images in churches, and exorcisms and other comparable rituals were condemned as necromancy.[4] The implication of this revisionist theology is to simplify the practice of worship, vicariously marginalising the activities of the Church. Lollards also more directly undermined Church hierarchy and authority by claiming that the office of pope was invalid, that neither pope nor bishops had the power to curse nor to pardon a man. They proposed there be only one rank of priesthood, and those priests were to have no temporal possessions but to go on foot preaching the word of God to the populace. In this Church there was no place for the canon law, and tithes, paid voluntarily, were to be distributed to the poor. Finally, hitting at the wider connection between the Church and the secular elite, it was proposed that there was no Christian sanction for killing any man, no matter if he be a pagan or Saracen; that Crusades were against the law of God. Whether or not these views ever did truly represent a coherent sectarian agenda, there is sufficient evidence across a range of literary productions that they were more than straws in the wind. The ambition to democratise religion which crystallised in definitions of Lollardy in fact infused a whole range of writing from the 1370s on.

PIERS THE PLOWMAN

In fifteenth-century literature calling for reform, as in some of the radical peasant texts of 1381, it is not the name of John Wyclif that resonates, but that of a fictional ploughman called Piers. William Langland's creation, *The Vision of William Concerning Piers the Plowman*, is recognised as one of the great visionary works of the Middle Ages. It exposes the limitations, inadequacies, and weaknesses of the Church and the devotional diet of its day, as well as the second estate's loss of spiritual focus. Its reformist agenda is not, however, Lollard; its author calls for better popes, for example, rather than for the abolition of church hierarchy. But the poem, perhaps because it demonstrates so many instances of spiritual crisis, was customarily appropriated to more radical dissenting ideologies in its immediate afterlife.

The fifty-four surviving manuscripts of *Piers Plowman* bear witness to its huge popularity, but also to at least two complete rewritings by the author for whom it was a lifelong project. The three versions are conventionally known as the 'A', 'B', and 'C' texts. The A text is approximately 2,500 lines long and is commonly dated to the late 1360s, recording, for example, vivid memories of the great storm of January 1362. The B text is around 7,200 lines long, probably written between 1377 and 1379, being preoccupied with the schism in the Church, and the minority rule of Richard II. The C text is slightly longer than B and was probably completed in the mid to late 1380s.[5] For many years, scholars favoured the B text as the 'best' version of the poem,[6] but the case for privileging the C text as the poet's last version has grown in recent years.[7] Comparison of B and C affords a rare glimpse into a medieval poet's creative process, but also reveals the elusiveness of the authoritative version of any work in a manuscript culture: the latest editor has concluded that the poet himself appears not to have kept a fair copy of the B text so is 'groping his way back' from a bad copy. There is also evidence that while C tidies up a number of anomalies in B, it is itself an unfinished revision in which some apparent complexities may simply be mistakes.[8]

We know little of William Langland, the poet who wrote his name into his life-work in a cryptogram which appears in the B text only: '"I have lyved in londe," quod I, "my name is Longe Wille"' (B. 15. 152). He has been identified from external evidence as the son of an Oxfordshire gentleman, and was in minor holy orders. The scale of his project and its rewritings explore and moralise the perceivable material and immaterial universe, while also and self-reflexively offering a critique of the adequacies of human discourse to undertake the task. Thus *Piers Plowman* is a complex map of the interplay between an individual intelligence and the political, spiritual, and psycho-social worlds it inhabited, at once exhaustively inclusive and deeply personal. It poses the problem of how to consider it as a critical whole, as it is contrivedly fragmented, full of false starts and new beginnings that are not only narrative but modal. Its progress is constituted as an account of a series of dreams, but the narrator can fall asleep into another dream without having awoken from the previous one. Formally the poem belongs to the 'alliterative revival' but has none of the stylistic virtuosity that characterises *Sir Gawain and the Green Knight* and its companion pieces; Langland goes for plainness. His narrative may be visionary, but it is devoid of marvellous landscapes or people; rather it draws on the real world, exposing its oddity for satirical scrutiny.

The dreamer-narrator begins by having visions focused on the society in which he lives. The reference point is the visionary geography established in the Prologue: a 'fair feld ful of folk' (C. Prologue. 19) is set between the tower of Truth, that is heaven, and a deep dale, evidently representing hell. In the Prologue he observes the activities on the field, attempting to order them according to their merits. The Prologue alone gives due warning to the reader that this will be no orderly explicatory unfolding of devotional guidance; rather the poet assumes familiarity with a range of systematised discourses with which he takes audacious liberties. He is not constrained by the requirements of any unities, including pressure to construct coherently sustained satire. The effect aptly reflects the psychic chaos of the real experience of dreaming.

The poem is conceived as two parts, the *Visio* and the *Vitae*, supported by manuscript rubrics as well as conventional readings. The *Visio* presents a vision of the social world of the 'field full of folk', the corruption of the three estates, and the search for a socially motivated remedy. The *Vitae* begins after the failed attempt at corporate reform, and addresses the proposition that the only way in which society can become more godly is through the reform of the individual. The *Vitae* [lives, or ways of life] is represented as having three grades ascending towards aspired perfection, so is in some respects reminiscent of contemporary mystical writing such as Walter Hilton's *Scale of Perfection*, but with distinctive Langlandian twists.[9] 'Dowell' is the quest for individual improvement conducted through dialogues with allegorical personifications of inner faculties and systems of thought. It ends when the narrator becomes dispirited by his own intellectual confusion and falls into Rechelesness, literally 'ceasing to care less'. 'Dobet' then represents a rejection of the endeavours of Dowell in favour of intellectual quietude focused on the imitation of Christ, and on pursuit of the three theological virtues, faith, hope and charity. 'Dobest' is then a return to the idea of communality in an attempt to reconfigure the ideal Church on earth as a community of reformed believers, but swiftly returns to what the poet proposes to be the crises of his present time, which is an apocalyptic vision of the seven deadly sins walking abroad in a world where the arrival of the Antichrist is imminent and where the persuasive misrule of the friars holds sway. The *Vitae* are one of Langland's etymological jokes. His quest is triggered by his early dialogue in passus I with Lady Holy Church, the personification of the ideal Church on earth. His appeal to her, 'Teche me to no tresor but telle me this ilke, How Y may saue my soule' (C. I. 79–80), enacts the pressing need of the individual Christian for ecclesiastical guidance. Her answer is complicated in exposition but simple in its fundamental message: adhere to the truth, depend on 'kynde knowynge' [innate understanding], and strive to do well, then to do better, and then to do best. The narrator 'misunderstands' these three imperative verbs as nouns, destinations on a journey, and, according to the procedures of allegory, three verbs are realised substantively.

On a smaller scale, the poem is divided into passus, Latin for 'step' (plural *passūs*), and one of the sustaining metaphors of the poem is pilgrimage. As physical journeys, pilgrimages are rejected and replaced by the idea of labour, specifically ploughing, but not real ploughing so much as working towards leading one's life in a spiritually consistent way. This hierarchy of equivalences is unpacked explicitly in the failed social experiment of the ploughing of the half acre in C passus VIII. The division of the poem into passus is also a sign that, for its author, the poem itself is the pilgrimage, his spiritual journey of investigation. The move from *Visio* to *Vitae*, the understanding that spiritual growth can be conducted within the individual only, is presented as the poem's sequentially organised argument, but it is also the premise out of which the poem's re-composition is generated. This is one of the major clarifications offered by the C text in a major insertion in passus V, lines

1–108, a passage of extended direct autobiographical narrative in which the poet offers an apologia for his own life, constructed as a dialogue between his voice, Reason and Conscience.[10]

At the time of writing, he is able-bodied and living with his wife and children in Cornhill in London. Reason interrogates him about why he is not engaged in gainful employment, recalling the distinctions drawn between winning and wasting in the Prologue. He reveals that his parents sent him to 'scole' (C. V. 36), probably university, but he was forced to leave when his 'friends', presumably family financial backers, died. The experience left him unable to settle to a life out of 'longe clothes' (41), that is clerical garb, and the tools of the trade he plies both in London and the country are, therefore, the Lord's Prayer, the Primer, the Office of the Dead, and the Psalter. In other words he performs minor ecclesiastical duties in the care of the souls of the living and the dead, not, he is at pains to distinguish, as a professional mendicant (by 'bagge or botel' (51)), but in order to eat. He justifies his way of life because those who 'ben ycrowned' (59) – tonsured – must follow the law in Leviticus 21 and not engage in material labour, nor bear arms. To do so would be to participate in the very disruption of the God-given social order he sees around him. The personification of his own Conscience chimes in, supporting his eloquent testimony of vocation. The narrator then confesses to his Conscience that of course he has wasted time but,

> . . . as he that ofte hath ychaffared
> And ay loste and loste and at the laste hym happed
> A bouhte suche a bargain he was the bet euere
> And sette al his los at a leef at the laste ende. (C. V. 94–7)

Like the merchant who takes risks and sustains multiple losses in order to find the deal that will change his life, he continues to hope that through God's grace he will come to the moment that will justify all his earlier and apparently fruitless endeavours. So what is the ship that will finally come in? It is defined as 'making' (C. V. 5). 'Making' is the art of poetry, and William Langland's vocation is, at bottom, writing his poem, fashioning it, and honing it. It is his spiritual autobiography in which he inscribes his own experience. He is Will; he is also will, human volition, best governed by reason, and checked by conscience, but also tempted by the inertia of sloth and 'rechelesness' to go through the motions like the clerics he despises.

The logic of the progress from *Visio* to *Vitae* is that the poem cannot be didactically conceived; each individual must undertake the journey according to 'kynde knowynge'. The poem has, therefore, no target audience, but is offered up as a deeply personal record of one man's spiritual journey which is, at the same time, an exemplum of a process which anyone can, or everyone should, pursue. Dreaming becomes an excuse for conducting experiments in reordering and distilling reality so as to examine its deficiencies, while organisational logic is preserved by the passus, each dealing either with a single dominant voice, often that of an allegorical persona, such as Holy Church, Repentance, Patience, and Imaginatif, or with an experiment in a mode of discourse, such as the sermon preached by Holy Church (B and C. I), the confessions of the seven deadly sins (B. V and C. VI), or the direct dramatic narrative of the dreamer-narrator's 'eye-witness' account of the Crucifixion and the Harrowing of Hell (B. XVIII and C. XX).

The figure whose name became a byword for radical ecclesiastical reform appears only sporadically in the poem that bears his name. His first appearance is prepared for throughout the first two visions, which incrementally expose what is corrupt in every branch of the three estates, enacting the conclusion that the seven deadly sins are everywhere to be found, and, moreover, all lead to one another. Given the dysfunctional nature of all authority exposed in the first vision, and in particular in the three passus exploring the power of bribery and corruption personified as Lady Mede, it is clear that a vacuum exists awaiting the arrival of a leader. Suddenly, at this moment of crisis, a ploughman called Peter pops up, claiming to know Truth 'as kyndely as clerk doth his bokes' (C. VII. 182–3). Thus Piers Plowman bursts upon the scene and offers to lead the people on a pilgrimage to the Tower of Truth, or heaven. The 'pilgrimage' involves co-operatively ploughing half an acre of land, an exercise in which they all fail. Piers goes off angrily, and the dreamer vows to make his pilgrimage the search for Piers. Accordingly the inner journey of the *Vitae* is also a search for Piers the Plowman.

That name, Piers, suggests that, as apostolic leader of the universal pilgrimage to God, he signifies St Peter, the 'rock' of Matthew

16: 18 on which Christ built his Church, holder of the key to heaven, and hence to Truth. In this aspect he is also an ideal or alternative pope, but he is also a wandering ploughman. Contrary to the literal and radical readings of the ploughman as idealised alternative ecclesiastical leader taken up by Langland's followers, however, the original Piers is an agricultural labourer in a figural sense only. The figure is derived from the Gospels, specifically from Luke 9: 57–62, which describes Christ's assembling of his disciples, and warns the recalcitrant that 'no man having put his hand to the plough and looking back is fit for the kingdom of heaven'. The enterprise on the half acre becomes a redefinition of feudal society as mutually supporting and godly, but importantly not levelling. Just as the poet sees the proposition that he as a tonsured member of the first estate should take up physical labour as something socially disruptive, he presents the knight on his half acre as someone who cannot plough but whose vocation it is to defend those who properly do. Piers offers to plough for them both in return for the knight's defence (C. VIII. 23–4).

The ploughing of the half acre as an experiment in social reform does not work. People cannot earn their place in heaven; they need pardon for original sin. A pardon does in due course arrive from Truth (C. IX. 3). The status of the pardon in the poem is complex, and changes between the B and the C texts. At one level it is a papal indulgence, and Langland does not question that indulgences issued by the pope are effective in accelerating progress through purgatory, although Dowel is a better guarantor:

> So Dowel passeth pardoun and pilgrimages to Rome
> Yut hath the pope power pardoun to graunte
> To peple withouten penaunce to passe into ioye . . . (C. IX. 324–36)

He counsels penance, however, and direct appeal for mercy to God and to the Virgin Mary. The problem of the pardon sent by Truth is compounded further by its wording: 'those who have done good shall go to eternal life; those who have done evil shall go to everlasting fire' (C. IX. 287–8). These words from the Athanasian Creed appear to offer no prospect of pardon for the penitent sinner. The dreamer wakes while a priest and Piers debate whether the pardon is a true pardon at all. In the B text Piers tears the pardon up 'in pure tene', a passage omitted in C. The tearing of the pardon is central to readings of this section of the B text.[11] Piers as reconstructed priesthood appears not only to be rejecting papal indulgences, but to be acting out of frustration, as the words of pardon simply restate the requirements of good Christian living. At another level the act of tearing up this apparent statement of the Old Law of justice, whereby the sinner goes to the fires of hell, suggests a moment of inspiration and energy:

> And Piers for pure tene pulled it atweyne
> And seide, 'Si ambulavero in medio umbre mortis
> Non timebo mala, quoniam tu mecum es.'
>
> ['Though I walk through the valley of the shadow of death, you are with me']. (B. VII. 115–17)

Possibly Piers's statement of the power of redemption anticipates his later alignment with the figure of Christ himself. However, in the C text, this passage, and therefore this resonance, is dropped, possibly because, as Derek Pearsall suggests, it conflicts with Piers's role as the model unquestioning servant of Truth.[12]

From this point forward, the name of Piers comes to have inspirational force. At the beginning of passus XV the narrator meets with Patience, who begs for food. A feast ensues at which the narrator is placed at a side table with Patience where they are served the bread of penance and the drink of perseverance. Piers intervenes in the ensuing debate, affirming that Patience conquers, then disappears again. Whereas in the ploughing passage earlier, Piers represents the life of active Christianity, he is now a corrective to a figure called *Activa Vita* or Active Life. The argument here is that the greater the engagement with the affairs of the world, the greater is the danger of being absorbed by its ephemera. In the B text this is illustrated through the person of Haukyn the Active Man, whose coat is perpetually being stained with splashes of sin (B. XIII. 272ff). In the C text the name Haukyn is dropped, suggesting that Actyf is to be read as another critical introspective portrait of the narrator himself. His opening question, 'What is parfit pacience?', like the narrator's urgent appeal to Holy Church to tell him how he may save his soul, is one of the extraordinarily dynamic moments in the progress of the poem's overarching argument.

This prepares the way for Piers's part in the climactic account of the Crucifixion (B. XVIII; C. XX), where Christ is described as 'Oen semblable to the Samaritaen and somdeel to Pers the plouhman' (C. XX, 8). In 1 Corinthians 13: 13 St Paul wrote that faith and hope are ineffective without charity – in the Latin sense of *caritas*, selfless love. Langland presents these three theological virtues – faith, hope and charity – as Abraham, Moses, and the Samaritan, in a protracted allegorical sequence through which the ideal of the contemplative life is prepared for by a compressed historical narrative of the transformation from the Old Law of justice to the New Law of mercy. The organisation of all Christian history into the periods of the Old Law of Moses and the New Law of Christ, pivoting on the transformational moment of the Redemption, is then illustrated by the debate of the Four Daughters of God (C. XX. 115ff.). This allegory, whereby Justice and Truth are reconciled with Mercy and Peace in the godhead through the agency of their brother Christ, has its source in an elaboration of Psalm 85 in the Vulgate Bible by St Bernard of Clairvaux, and was commonly rewritten throughout the Middle Ages.[13] Drawing on this range of mainstream exegetical material, the logic of the narrator's vision finally merges his ideal of perfectible humanity with Christ incarnate in the figure of Piers the Plowman.

This approach to uncovering the meaning of *Piers Plowman* and its eponymous hero, however, runs the danger of submerging reception of the poem as poetry, and as spiritual autobiography. Piers the Plowman is, at bottom, the narrator's personal inspirational mentor and magus. In his reading of the B text, James Simpson concludes, moreover, that the poem's central concerns are mirrored by changes in the poetic forms and discourses Langland uses, so that it repeatedly undermines itself through exposing the inadequacies of the authoritarian discourses on which biblical exegesis depends.[14] For many readers the highpoint of the poem lies not in its explications of personal salvation or of the doctrine of atonement, nor even in the vivid satirical attacks on contemporary society as represented by

Meed the Maid or the seven deadly sins, but in the inventive dramatic narrative of Christ's Passion, the debate between Christ and Satan in hell, and the moment of Christ's death on the Cross. The latter is at once universal and affectingly human, and is conveyed, with the insertion of a tellingly hypermetrical line, by means that are wholly poetic:

> '*Consummatum est,*' quod Crist, and comsed for to swoene,
> Pitousliche and pale, as a prisoun that deyeth,
> The lord of lyf and of liht tho leyde his eyes togederes. (C. XX. 58–60)

Piers Plowman is a singular and personal work but is also of its historical moment. Its three versions express preoccupation with the political events in England through which its author lived, and, in his non-aligned theological revisionism, Langland was overtaken by the growth of Wycliffite thought. His earnest engagement with the material realities of his society is perhaps best illustrated through his unresolved struggle with the problem of the poor. The narrator dwells on various difficulties with the fundamental Christian injunction by Christ to perform the acts of alms-giving enshrined in the Seven Works of Corporal Mercy (Matthew 25) as the means to access salvation in a world where wealth has become mobile and beggary institutionalised. Hunger's intervention in the ploughing of the half acre brings to a head the debate that troubles Langland, 400 years before Malthus supplied the formulation, about how the distinction between the deserving and the undeserving poor is to be made. The problem was particularly pressing in a society where, following the social disruption of the Black Death, the peasant family unit subsisting in the manorial system had broken down, and the opportunist and the destitute seem to have taken to the road in equal measure, giving rise to some punitive legislation.[15]

Langland returns to the problem repeatedly, however, and notably in additions to the C text. In passus IX he evokes an image of winter drudgery, as women struggle to fill the bellies of their hungry children, that is far removed from the idealised labours of the months familiar from contemporary calendar art. It is here that he begins to move away from a focus on the undeserving parasitical beggars who disrupt and distort the Christian community, to fashion the concept of patient poverty as a particular virtue. Those who bear poverty patiently will be rewarded in heaven having endured their purgatory on earth, yet the requirement of almsgiving, that is of self-impoverishment, and of discerning the appropriate recipient for those alms, remains a conundrum that dogs him to the end, coming to a head in the arguments put forward by the figure of Need (C. XXII. 1–50).[16] Need persuades the narrator that if he takes, or steals, only what he needs to avoid hunger he is exercising temperance, one of the cardinal virtues. The argument seems not wholly specious, but the proverbial assertion that 'need ne hath no lawe ne neuere shal falle in dette' (10) is dangerously anarchic, in conflict with the principles of charity and divine justice, and swiftly returns the narrator to the problem presented by the friars, their abuse of apostolic poverty, and their traffic in salvation which is contrary to Will's Conscience, who, at the poem's end, sets out in search of Piers once more.

CHAUCER AND THE CHURCH

Some time shortly after Langland completed his C text, Chaucer ended *The Canterbury Tales* with the words 'Oure book seith, "Al that is written is written for oure doctrine," and that is myn entente', concluding the passage in which 'taketh the makere of this book his leve'. We do not have Chaucer's rewritings, but we do have his retractions by name of much of the corpus of his work: everything pleasing he attributes to God; everything displeasing to his own 'unkonnynge' (X (I), 1081–3). He concludes by offering thanks to Christ, the Virgin Mary, and all the saints of heaven, praying that they will assist him in living out his life in penance. To all intents and purposes this is the signature of a conventionally pious, spiritually anxious, medieval layman. It follows The Parson's Tale, not a 'tale' in the strict sense, but a didactic treatise or sermon on vices and their remedies based chiefly on standard Latin pastoralia.

Explorations of the poet's personal religious witness have eddied uneasily in Chaucer criticism, blighted for a time by the long shadow of D. W. Robertson, but necessarily revived as part of the large project of questioning binary divisions between lay and religious, orthodox and heterodox, in readings of late medieval texts. Perhaps in the present context the most helpful summation of Chaucer's position has been offered by Nicholas Watson, who suggests that Chaucer's attitude is close to that which Langland parodies in *Activa Vita*: he does not engage with any of the redefinitions of lay devotional enthusiasm current at his time, but rather makes a pitch for the devotional needs of the good layman, worthy of salvation, the *mediocriter boni* as defined by thirteenth-century scholastic theology.[17] This is not to suggest that Chaucer is unthinking about his Christianity; he is keenly reflective about his laicity and, specifically, about the demands his position makes upon the Church. The layman's first port of call was his parish priest, responsible for elementary education, pastoral care, and for providing his parishioners with the sacramental validation of the significant rites of passage of their lives. Chaucer's Parson is just such a parish priest, and it is appropriate that his Tale should offer a standard, pastoral, relevant examination of the everyday sins which imperil the souls of all the Canterbury pilgrims, and their creator.

Langland had his own singular theological agenda overtaken by Wycliffite sectarianism, probably between the writing of the B and C texts of his poem. Chaucer was around a decade younger, so follows in the wake of Wycliffite thought, and was writing through the period of its condemnation. It is unsurprising, therefore, that, while Chaucer does not dabble in proto-Puritan revisionist theology, he is mobilised as a formidably unforgiving ally of ecclesiastical radicalism in his attacks on failures in the Church's administration of the cure of souls. He targets, with increasing degrees of savagery which coincide with the failings focused on by the Wycliffites, the out-of-touch ineffectuality of the Monk, the Prioress, and to some extent, the Clerk, and the materialism, ignorance, internecine rivalry, self-interest, and cynical exploitation, upon which he unleashes his most scathing satire in the Tales of the Friar, the Summoner, and the Pardoner. Despite his refusal of totalising judgement in the work as a whole, his technique in *The Canterbury Tales* of presenting himself as deficient in literary skill and discrimination but prodigious in memory, throwing judgement back upon the (predominantly lay) reader, is ideally suited for ecclesiastical satire.

What summoners, friars, and pardoners had in common was a particular relationship with economics rather than theology. Summoners, mere policemen of the ecclesiastical court system, could conduct their affairs without the encumbrance of any theological knowledge whatever, and, because it was their job to uncover crimes against morality, their opportunities for extortion were abundant. Chaucer's period saw open season for satirical attacks on the friars. Apostolic poverty as modelled by St Francis of Assisi was hard to pursue in the harsh climate and nascent urban mercantile society of fourteenth-century England. Instead of living on the road, brothers based in lavishly patronised friaries worked the limits of their designated neighbourhood like pedlars. They did not fall within diocesan jurisdiction, and, being relatively better educated than the average parish priest, were perceived as dangerous rivals. As travelling salesmen with salvation as their marketable commodity, pardoners outclassed friars. They traded in material commodities, the written papal indulgences and relics which played to a hunger for comforting talismans, domesticated icons, in the unlettered, impressionable, and superstitious. All could easily fall prey to the temptation to use fear, rather than love, to render their audience tractable. All also had command of exclusive discourses with which to persuade their audiences, and all could, of course, bark in Latin.

Performance becomes thematic in these Tales, as it is presented as a common substitute for the true clerical vocation. These pilgrims enact the typical clerical abuses described by Langland in the Prologue to *Piers Plowman*, and attacked by Holy Church, who asserts that 'faith withouten feet ['fait' = action] is feblore then nautht'(C. I. 181–2). Whereas the Tales of the Miller and the Reeve are set up as the competitive performances of two individuals settling a personal score, the Friar and the Summoner have a professional rivalry external to the tale-telling exercise, and traditional to the larger performative roles they represent. Their archetypicality is encoded in the striking similarities between the friar within The Summoner's Tale and the summoner within The Friar's Tale, and the respective descriptions of pilgrim Friar and Summoner in the framing narrative. This is surely Geoffrey Chaucer's own covert performance in skilful manipulation with malicious intent, as the matter of both Tales is in fact borrowed from traditional sources.

The Friar's Tale of the summoner and the devil is a traditional sermon exemplum. A corrupt summoner meets up with, but initially fails to identify, the Devil, with whom he vies to show off his skill at extortion. The Tale develops as a lesson on the Devil's rights, the belief that after Christ harrowed hell and bound Satan the devil was empowered to seize the souls of only those who refused grace.[18] The summoner proves a fatally slow learner. He demonstrates how he can get things by extortion and the old woman who is his victim curses him to the Devil. The Devil hears her curse, checks that she is in earnest, gives the summoner a chance to retract his intentions, which he refuses, then drags the summoner off to hell. The Friar concludes,

> And God that maked after his ymage
> Mankynde, save and gyde us alle and some,
> And teche this somnour good man to bycome. (III, D, 1642–4)

The passage and its concluding 'prayer' illustrate how the teller is given a special relationship with both the motive and the manner of telling, and becomes an unwitting victim of his own moralisation. He has claimed that he is telling a tale of moral improvement, but his intent is exposed as wholly malicious. In The Friar's Tale both summoner and Devil complain of hard masters. The summoner's is an archdeacon, administrator of the church court system, but the Devil's is God. These Tales are used to illustrate the well-known adage that God sometimes tricks the Devil into doing good despite himself. One of the questions underlying the available readings of all Chaucer's anti-clerical satires is whether corrupt intent in individual scions of the Church compromises the efficacy of their teaching and sacramental duties.

The Summoner's Tale stands in marked stylistic contrast, recreating satirically the unctuous circumlocutions of the professional mendicant friar. The narrative edifice is delightfully constructed as the friar's sermon on anger backfires, so that its target, a sick man, instead of being moved to pay for confession, becomes angry, retaliates and angers the friar by farting into his hand as it gropes in the bed for a promised fee. But the Tale's true climax concerns the division of the fart, which is inflated into a problem of mathematics, 'ars-metric', impelling the reader to make the inevitable equation between the pretentiousness and corruption of the friar's verbal manner and the smelly hot air of the fart. The fart and the groping hand are thus set up as potent images of the nature and value of the pastoral activities of 'limitours'. Both the Summoner and the Friar thus become their own and each other's exempla. Their Tales are explicitly moralised, and both turn the tables on their tellers who ironically embody facets of those very characteristics which their Tales expose. They are presented as wholly unaware of the implications of their actions, a source of sustained comic irony, but they also prepare the way for Chaucer's Pardoner, a portrait of a more successful and more threateningly self-aware representative of the medieval Church.

At the end of The Pardoner's Tale, the response modelled by Harry Bailey suggests that the Pardoner be taken as scapegoat for the whole Church; that castrating him will cure the evils of the whole system. Harry Bailey represents the school of criticism that would impose a fully dramatic reading on *The Canterbury Tales*, something particularly tempting in the case of the Pardoner, who, like the Wife of Bath, presents a social deviant in confessional mode. Such readings generate fantasies of motive. The voice constructed for the Pardoner, like the Wife, may perform an imitation of a plausible mental process, but arguably one of the most menacing features of Chaucer's construct here is precisely his lack of psychology: the Pardoner has no insight, so cannot change; his only existence is as a performance. The medieval Church jealously protected its monopoly over the cure of souls, and exploited the fundamental human fear of death. Chaucer critiques this position by implication in The Pardoner's Prologue and Tale as a performance-sermon, based closely on the structures recommended in preaching manuals, turns into a sales pitch. He also focuses on the vulnerability of the poorest and most ignorant members of the Christian community as victims of ecclesiastical rapaciousness. The Pardoner's text is *radix malorum est cupiditas* – greed is the root of evil. Like didactic burdens of the other two Tales, this has ironic implications for the preacher, but here the process of uncovering that irony is short-circuited as the Pardoner volunteers that he preaches for financial gain. His voice, in its aggressive acquisitiveness, signals someone too clever not to understand his own message, which is why he makes no psychological sense as an individual. He is more than a static allegory of clerical abuse; he embodies the corrupt processes of opportunistic responsiveness in the Church, the institution which validated the clerical profession. Read thus, his implied sexual deviance is not a sign of Chaucer's illiberality but a sign of the sterility that is material gain put in place of spiritual gain.[19]

The distractions of the performative aspects of The Pardoner's Prologue and Tale from its content are modelled by the enraged reaction of the pilgrims. But just as Chaucer systematically undermines the authority of the office of pardoner, he pulls out of the void what is one of the best made Tales in the whole Canterbury compilation, leading the reader to affirm with Langland the moral efficacy of 'making', of poetry. The question of whether corrupt intent compromises the product, however, remains pressingly open. The story of the rioters, death, and the old man, is set within a formal containing structure straight from the preaching manuals. Greed is divided and subdivided to demonstrate that it can manifest itself as gluttony, lechery, gaming, blasphemy, and homicide. Each subdivision is underpinned with learned authority and supported by rhetorical colouring. The exemplum itself, as retold by Chaucer, emerges from its box of formal apparatus as a perfect short story – eery, dark, and economically told. The rioters' quest for gold embodies the truth not only of their way of life, but of the narrator's. As the story equates gold with death, the rioters' project, and by extension the Pardoner's, inverts the Christian mission that is the search for eternal life. Within the story, the Old Man, comprehending the correct relationship between the death of the body and the life of the spirit, stands as a corrective cipher, and one through whose agency the rioters' quest is fulfilled. Correct and misdirected quests are signalled rhetorically by the blasphemy of the rioters and the blessings in the voice of the Old Man, foregrounding the textuality of the entire construct and suggesting the larger equation between spiritual sterility and death, and blasphemous priesthood. The Pardoner is linked with the rioters, who are in turn metonymically linked with the rats for whom the poison that kills them was intended: their distorted fragments of doctrine, their swearing, reflects back on the abused fragments of the faith pedalled by the Pardoner and objectified in his bag of relics. The Church encoded in the Pardoner deals in spiritual death, a parody of the true Church and founded on gold. Chaucer may sentimentalise his unreconstructed parish Parson, but his attack on those who abuse the trust placed in them by his less intellectually acute fellow laymen for the cure of souls is venomous.[20]

PIERCE THE PLOUGHMAN'S CREDE

Both Langland and Chaucer have in common the strategic adoption and rejection of different discourses, and ventriloquised voices, as signs of their own negotiated critical positions. From these the modern reader can take bearings not only on the culture they inhabited but on practices of reading in that culture. Their reception by their immediate successors assimilated Chaucer the courtier-poet as the benchmark of establishment literary culture, as we shall see in Chapter 5, whereas Langland was adopted as a major reference point for texts of resistance. The more overtly sectarian texts whose authors read and appropriated Langland's poem and its eponymous hero demonstrably exploited its textual instabilities to their own ends in constituting a discourse of dissent.

The narrator of *Pierce the Ploughman's Crede* opens by claiming that his immortal soul is in jeopardy because his catechetical education has been deficient, and he consequently does not know the words of the Creed.[21] Ignorance of the words of the Creed is used as a sign that belief falters when it is compromised by institutionalised materialism, and by the obfuscation of biblical truths by sophistic practices of glossing. This poem of evident Lollard sympathies was written at the end of the fourteenth century, when the Church was closing down on the allowable use of ecclesiastical discourses. Using the common method available to writers wishing to defend themselves from charges of sedition, the poet presents himself as an ignorant but devout Christian on a spiritual quest. He thus displaces the theological debate from himself to the fictionalised voices of those he encounters along the way, in this case four friars on one hand, and the figure of Peres, a preaching ploughman, on the other. The narrator's first-person contributions take the form of descriptive observation, laced with disingenuously spontaneous responses.

The poem's direct inspiration derives from Will's meeting with the four orders of friars, which begins the search for Dowell in Langland's poem, but with broader structural affinities to other anti-fraternal writing, including The Friar's Tale and The Summoner's Tale, as the representatives of each order treat the narrator to malicious 'quiting' diatribes on one another, in another animation of the Church's internal market. Where ploughing in Langland's poem is always and only metaphorical, Peres, who becomes the narrator's true pedagogue, is a real ploughman. Hence the poet supports the radical position that sought to supplant Church hierarchy with a real proletarian priesthood. It is through the voice of Peres that the poet will finally explicitly reveal his hand, although the earlier part of the poem is also permeated with encoded references to radical doctrinal positions in the faux-innocent descriptions of the narrator's encounters. There are, as Helen Barr observes, certain key words around which the critiques are mustered. The divine sanction of their orders' foundation was disputed by Wycliffite opinion, so the poet not only has each begin his diatribe with reference to that foundation, but plays with the word 'found' more widely. Equally he returns insistently to the words 'order' and 'rule'.[22] Etymological wordplay is just one of his techniques for managing a potential tension between his demonstration of how elaborate linguistic devices are used to blind the friars' victims, fundamental to his ideological position, and his own chosen medium of alliterative verse as an expression of the preaching voice of the true apostolic vocation.[23] The quiting voice by which each order of friars is condemned out of the mouth of another keeps the narratorial voice clean of accusations of back-biting, condemned by the narrator as unchristian (138–42). The passages of sustained direct speech given to the representative friars are more broadly used to demonstrate unreliable discourses, object lessons in the notoriously manipulative practice of 'glosyng' that is interpreting scripture for the preacher's own ends.

The passages in the narrator's voice rely on the arrangement and selection of detail, and the connotation of comparisons, to carry the burden of criticism, and this is where the poet's command of his verse form comes into its own. The description of the elaborate building-style of the Dominicans' church makes otherwise neutral architectural detail seem somehow fundamentally devious, morally unsound: the pillars are 'queyntili' carved with 'curious' knots (161); there are 'posterns in pryuytie' (165) – secret gates that let the friars come and go as they please – and 'tabernacles y-tight' (168), that is set-in niches. Particular lexical choices set up the opportunity for the narrator to offer comment immediately, for example, that it must have cost the price of a plough-land to decorate one small pillar (170). The tour of the premises uncovers one fabulous building after another with the closing observation:

> And yet thise bilderes wilne beggen a bagg-full of wheate
> Of a pure pore man that maie onethe [scarcely] paie
> Half his rente in a yer and half ben behynde. (216–18)

The description of the friary reaches its climax in the description of the friar who will be the narrator's second interlocutor:

> A greet cherl and a grym, growen as a tonne,
> With a face as fat as a full bledder
> Blowen bretfull of breth and as a bagge honged
> On bothen his chekes, and his chyn with a chol [dewlap] lollede,
> As gret as a gos eye growen all of grece;
> That all wagged his fleche as a quyk myre. (221–6)

The frank disgust embedded in the connotations here is a further indicator of the relative extremity of the ideological position of the *Crede* poet.

The narrator's observations are chiefly directed at the easy target of the materialism of the friars. There are, however, indicators of other dimensions of sectarian ideology embedded in the narrator's descriptions too, which make way for the dogmatic position laid out by Peres in the second part of the poem. For example, there is a side-swipe at religious theatre in the mocking by the Franciscan friar of the Carmelites' enjoyment of 'miracles of mydwyves' (78) and 'gladness in glees' (93), and there is a pervasive suspicion of teaching through images, and of all books except scripture, which has led John Scattergood to observe that 'one can hear not too far off the breaking of stained glass, the closing of the doors of theatres, and the crackle of burning books'.[24]

As the narrator reels away from his final encounter, still ignorant of his Creed and ill-equipped to help himself to salvation, he meets Peres. The poet's choice of the verse form again finds its justification here in the fashioning of an alternative icon in the shape of the ragged ploughman, his team of starving heifers, his wife, wrapped in a shroud to keep her warm, 'barfote on the bare ijs that the blod folwede' (436), their baby and two toddlers crying with cold at the end of the furrow. The ploughman first offers to share what food he has with the narrator, then, when he hears his real plight, becomes the first voice in the poem directly to quote biblical Latin, accusing the friars of being false prophets, and wolves in sheep's clothing (458). Under the guise of fulfilling the narrator's request for information, Peres embarks on a diatribe against the Church which extends to some 350 lines of revisionist dogma, before he finally reveals the words of the Creed to the waiting narrator. Peres not only ventriloquises the poet's dissenting voice in affirming his swingeing attack on the friars, he directly cites Wyclif as his authority, raising him to the status of near-martyr (528–32). He later also makes a contrast between the defensiveness of the friars, who sting harder than wasps when their toes are trodden on (648–50) in contrast to the apostolic ideal of patient sufferance set out by Christ in the Beatitudes and exemplified in his own time by the West Country radical, Walter Brut (657–62), tried as a Lollard by the bishop of Hereford in 1393.[25] The voice of Peres in the latter half of the poem makes clear that, more than just an anti-fraternal diatribe, the poem is intended to be an enactment of a militant Lollard position. Yet Peres confirms belief in transubstantiation, 'in the sacrament also that sothfast God on is, / fullich his fleche and his blod, that for vs dethe tholede' (817–18) accusing the friars, 'as dotards' (820), of having disputed it in the first place. Neither the denial of transubstantiation nor of the value of oral confession, both cornerstones in Lollard heterodoxy according to its detractors, form part of the dogma set out by Peres. Although he takes Langland's invention to places that formed no part in the original *Vision of William concerning Piers the Plowman*, it is in the end important not to position the *Crede* poet too simplistically as exemplifying what is probably in any case a speciously coherent revisionist position.

MUM AND THE SOOTHSEGGER

We ended Chapter 2 on an upbeat note, exploring the empowerment of the third estate through the growth of vernacular literacy that accompanied social change in the latter half of the fourteenth century. The downside of that is, however, evident from the large number of judicial killings that swiftly followed the events of 1381 and the Church's legislative clamp-down on Lollard heresies: writing that expressed dissident views, or told 'the truth' was a dangerous pursuit.[26] Censorship legislation, particularly aimed at containing religious heterodoxy, precedes the Lollard crisis, yet the Middle English period as a whole was witness to a wide tradition of writing that used the truth-telling trope as a cover for expressing dissident opinion through strategies for exposing the very constraints that impeded plain speaking.[27]

Claims to truth-telling have particular force when attached to radical theological propaganda, for central to the range of Lollard arguments is the assertion that the teachings of the individual conscience are true without needing to be validated through the procedures of the sacrament of Penance or any of the other procedures of the Church. John Clanvowe's prose treatise, *The Two Ways*, is a remarkable meditation by a middle-aged warrior-courtier, on Christ's teaching that the way to hell is easy, while the way to heaven is hard and narrow, and found by few (Matthew 7: 13–14).[28] There is no overt Lollard polemic in this work, except by omission; everything is supported by direct reference to scripture without one mention of the Church, nor any reference to the sacraments, priesthood, pilgrimage, confession, or the saints. Clanvowe was a chamber knight at the courts of Edward III and Richard II, one of a circle of educated men from South Wales and the Marches who disappear from political prominence in the late 1380s, the so-called 'Lollard knights', including Richard Stury, Thomas Latimer, William Neville, Lewis Clifford, and John Montague, all of them executors of the will of Joan of Kent who had protected Wyclif when he came under attack. Their history goes back to their war service with the Black Prince, and they stand as a reminder of the long pre-history of Lollardy, of Wyclif's royal support, and that his ideas penetrated English society in a number of ways, not all of them demonstrably sectarian. Lewis Clifford was an associate of Chaucer, and his daughter married Sir Philip de la Vache, the dedicatee of Chaucer's short lyric of 'bon conseill', in which he too ruminates on what constitutes the true and the false.

Central to all those writings which denounce their spiritual leaders for fraudulently serving materialist goals is that they characterise the Church's primary spiritual purpose as being the guardian of and guide to truth. In Langland's system of equivalences, Truth is equated with God, but the passus featuring Meed the Maid in Langland's poem early demonstrate the interpenetrability of all human institutions and their discourses of power, all to be measured against the same yardstick of truth. *Mum and the Soothsegger* is another poem which presents its quest for truth as a test of the full range of authoritarian institutions and their discourses. The poem is set in the poet's present, early in the reign of Henry IV, and is linked with a particular milieu, familiar with the city of Bristol, and probably connected with the circle of Sir Thomas Berkeley, who was closely involved in the removal of Richard II.[29] The narrator of *Mum* reflects the idealism and optimism which attended the early years of Henry's reign, describing a court where truth-telling and openness were encouraged (143–4). Henry is the ideal chivalric king, deserving of robust counsel, but no longer kept in touch with the condition of those he governs, as those who would tell him have been intimidated into silence. What the court lacks is a permanent truth-teller. The poem's opening sequence is, thus, both an audacious critique of Henry's Council as suppressers of the truth and an illustration of the problems of censorship.[30]

The oppositional voice called 'Mum', in the sense 'keep quiet', is introduced in debate with the narrator. The debate, like *Wynnere and Wastoure*, is one-sided: the text develops as an object-lesson in truth-telling by oblique means. Moreover it becomes an enactment of an ethical dilemma, more complicated than the simple choice between speaking out and holding silence, a test for the veracity of a variety of discourses. Truth-telling is a kind of measurable speech to be distinguished from talking too much, or 'bable' (292), while keeping mum can also be misrepresented as circumspection, and includes the value-free discourses of flattery. Like the most effective dissident texts of any oppressive culture, the poem not only comments on its socio-political context, but claims agency for itself within that context.

The narrator's quest for a truth-teller defers to a range of authoritative institutions, then finds them wanting. A fruitless search of the ancient authorities in the literature of wisdom gives way to an approach to the universities. The seven sciences that made up the medieval university curriculum are then dismissed by swift allegorical caricatures before a learned doctor advises that the narrator's concerns are too fashionable to have any bearing on what the universities deal in – 'sum noyous nycete of the newe iette' (375) – and advises him to seek his answer in the world. There was no systematic discipline of political science in the Middle Ages.

The narrator's excursion into the world brings him into debate with the friars, close friends with Mum. It is here, in his second 'privy' or secret point of attack that he aligns truth-telling directly with Lollardy. Originally, he claims, friars conducted themselves like Lollards, referring to the manner in which both addressed the need for poor honest priests free from Church hierarchy, but their recent lies have led them to 'loll' by the neck on the Tyburn gallows (415–20), a reference to certain friars who were hanged for provoking insurgency by claiming that Richard II was still alive. Thus the poem combines satirical criticism of the friars with its own political partisanship. The enclosed orders of religious, whom he visits next, simply refuse to admit him, and the cathedral clergy are too busy eating and drinking. The poet does not engage with the theological dogma represented by the various elements of the Church hierarchy he encounters, but rather denies them all meaningful voice, relegating all to Mum. His final ecclesiastical encounter is with the parish clergy, where a priest's sermon is reduced to a picaresque list of foodstuffs, a little *jeu d'esprit* of the alliterative line as poultry, pears and plums, grapes, garlic, and geese are pushed together, to discredit the practice of tithing. In the following passage, during which seven years of the quest elapse, he contrasts the self-regarding actions of the whole Church with the martyrs of the early church who were prepared to die for 'pure trouthe' (641). Another intervention in the voice of Mum reinforces the point by advising the abandonment of the quest because of the alliance between 'maintenance' and 'mede', probably best understood here as political patronage and financial back-handers.

Mum's exposure of political intrigue, and the techniques of informants, illustrates how the poet distributes truth-telling amongst the various voices of the poem, including Mum's voice.[31] Although the argument is increasingly grounded in early fifteenth-century politics, the reference points remain biblical, and Mum is equated to Pontius Pilate who washed his hands and allowed Christ to die on the Cross. The narrator moves on to seek truth amongst the laity of all classes, only to find Mum everywhere, and controlling the mayor and council – 'for alle was huyst in the halle sauf "hold vp the oyles"' (831) – with the 'oil' of flattery. The civic truth-teller dines with Dread in a chamber apart, out of favour with the mayor who is a friend of Mum (838–40). The construction of the whistle-blower as pariah, exuding fear in a way that leads others to avoid his company, was later to be elaborated more dramatically in John Skelton's poem, *The Bowge of Court*, discussed in Chapter 5; here the message is that candour is unwelcome, indecorous in institutional contexts, and dangerous.

A move into dream mode marks the transition from satirical complaint to the visionary manifesto of an alternate society. The dream landscape is a variation on the conventional idyll of the love vision, a Georgic in which the abundance of nature is farmed by contented bucolics. There he encounters an ancient beekeeper, 'sad of his semblant', and 'softe of his speche' (963). The voice of the beekeeper authorises the subsequent allegory of good government as the weeding of the garden and the expulsion of drones from the hive. Bee society is orderly, governed by a benign king to whom all are answerable through local principals; it is industrious, expelling those whose endeavours do not serve the common good; it is not covetous of what others have; and it is charitable towards those who are unable to play their full part (999–1017). The beekeeper affirms that Mum dominates the church, the law, and parliament. He also, in a move similar to Holy Church's appeal to the dreamer's 'kynde knowynge' in *Piers Plowman*, short-circuits the quest for Soothsayer by advising the narrator that he lives in every man's heart, established there by God. Here the instruction on how the narrator should activate the truth-teller in his heart embeds at a remove a miniature morality play in which the beekeeper animates the workings of Satan, and warns of how Antichrist will obstruct entry to the truth-teller's house, by giving Covetise the key and causing Dread to bar the door (1261). Finally the beekeeper urges the narrator to cast away doubt and pursue the truth by writing his poem (1280–3). The narrator awakes, vows to put an end to his 'long labour and loitryng aboute' (1297), and resolves to counsel the king himself, thereby making the poem its own subject.

The counsel he offers extends the thematic centrality of writing. Mum's exposure is represented emblematically by the opening of a bag of unread writings. The bag becomes a sign of the narrator's despair at the complexity of institutional authority and how it has provided rich opportunities for manipulation and corruption. There is a sustained focus on textuality, and on the withholding of documents of public record. This is exemplified by a volume of ecclesiastical visitations made up of fifteen leaves, an emblematic indictment of bishops who collude in concealing the abuses they uncover, and a roll itemising ecclesiastical rental income which ought to have been distributed to the poor. The king's ministers' lies, flying in the air like swallows' cries, conceal recorded truth. The poem's end also signals how a dissenting position can be deeply conservative. The poet does not advocate complete freedom of speech, but endorses the procedures of correct and incorrupt feudal order, under a strong monarch, and operating constitutionally through Parliament. Popular uprisings are dismissed as both futile and unethical.[32] The reader is enjoined sentimentally to love his king who will reciprocate, and virtuous behaviour will put all to rights. The poet's relatively naïve solution to institutional corruption dissolves in the end to further attacks on the status quo; the poem's strength as an expression of dissent lies in its enactments of corruption in the first and second estates, and in the iconic creation of the old beekeeper as a vision of the possibility of an alternative order.

POLITICAL COMPLAINTS

True dissent in late medieval English society was necessarily expressed in literary modes which are essentially oblique, like the letters attributed to John Ball mentioned in Chapter 2. Furthermore, such were the risks that the spiritual commitments of Lollardy gave rise to the only truly developed and consistently oppositional voice of the period. Other voices of protest tend to address particular grievances, and call for nothing more radical than the proper performance of their duties by all orders in society. That said, it is worth looking briefly at some of those that protested, or just grumbled, to present a wider spectrum of literature's engagement with the period's sense of its own crises.

Drama presents an interesting example of how critical opinion can find expression in a mode of writing that is by its nature public, and offers the modern reader a broader sense of the kind of abuses that were so commonly acknowledged that they had become soft targets to be attacked without apparent risk to the writer. If heresy and treason found no place on the stage, targeting lax and corrupt administrative systems, and the manipulation and abuse of the law, seems to have been topical, safe, and even fashionable. Hence, while both *Mankind* and *Wisdom* are staunchly affirmative of Church hierarchy and doctrine, both also embed pungent criticism of other targets. *Mankind*, like *Mum and the Soothsegger*, politicises idleness of tongue. Its apparently safe and neutral presentation of 'correct' speech as Latinate and liturgical, and incorrect speech as belonging to the tavern, conceals more topical and localised references to continuing Lancastrian partisanship in East Anglia during the reign of the Yorkist Edward IV, demonstrating the dramatist's confidence in finding a consenting audience.[33] *Wisdom* too is full of satirical references to the evils of so-called bastard feudalism, including the maintaining of liveried bully-boys, and the manipulation of the legal system, which appear to assume approving reception from its target audience in contexts now obscure.[34]

W. H. Auden observed in his elegy 'In Memory of W. B. Yeats' (1940) that 'poetry makes nothing happen', but the enthusiastic patronage of flatterers and punishment of detractors suggests that in the late medieval period in Britain the power of the pen was felt, and feared, across a political spectrum which covered every aspect of human activity. The well-placed written opinion in the right kind of circulation can generate its own kind of historical truth; the modern reader's problem lies in recognising and decoding this kind of intervention. Major disruptions to the political continuum reveal how the 'popular voice' which made itself heard was a demonstration of growing affluence and diversification of activity within the third estate. The deposition of Richard II in 1399, for example, left evidence of 'a blizzard of bogus genealogy, false prophesy, anti-Ricardian fabrication and novel ceremonial' generated both within and outside the organised 'Lancastrian propaganda machine'.[35] The combination of growing literacy, the move into the vernacular of documents of official record, constant war with France, and dynastic disruption add to the richness in character of commentary on the times in poetic form.

Political complaint shares rhetorical strategies with the liturgical *planctus Mariae* and the lover's complaint in romance, and comprises everything from complaints against the times, against maintenance, perjury and other juridical abuses, to the author of the *Libelle of Englyshe Polycye*'s disapproval of the import and export habits of foreign merchants, and on currency exchange. Verses complaining simply about modern fashions in dress contribute to the tide of writing which may have done nothing more than provide a therapeutic outlet for its over-aerated authors.[36] Some extraordinarily inventive performances resulted from a period in which the impulse to complain is balanced by the danger of doing so. Frequently the apparent paranoia of the poet is foregrounded as forcefully as the actual circumstances which have prompted the text's creation. At the extreme end is a challenging verse expressing a partisan view, possibly about the overthrow of the whole court in 1381, which depends on understanding a popular game of dice, as the names of those the poet wishes to see deposed and those who will replace them are all represented by little drawings of dice. In another example from the end of Richard's reign, more conventionally literary substitutions are used to remark on the bareness of the 'busch', 'the long gras that semeth grene', and the 'grete bage' that 'is so ytoren', an attack on the unpopular triumvirate of Richard II's corrupt ministers immortalised in Shakespeare's *Richard II*, Bushy, Green, and Bagot.[37]

In the last year of his life, and the first year of the reign of the new Lancastrian monarch, Henry IV, Chaucer, whose income was directly affected by regime change, wrote a complaint to his purse, an intervention in the political process which wittily demonstrates the chief characteristics of the genre, and which is a poem that was certainly designed to make something happen. The poet addresses his empty purse in three rime royal stanzas, as his 'lady dere', crying her mercy, and concluding each stanza with the refrain, 'Beth hevy ageyn, or elles mot I dye'. The characteristics of the full purse are anatomised in the second stanza, its jingling sound and yellow coloration, as the speaker is moved to exclaim in mockery of the hyperbole of the unrequited lover,

> Ye be my lyf, ye be myn hertes stere,
> Quene of comfort and of good companye . . . (12–13)

In the third stanza, he describes his own plight, 'shave as nye [close] as any frere' (28). There then follows a five-line envoy in which the poet turns to address the new monarch, his would-be patron:

> O conquerour of Brutes Albyon,
> Which that by lyne and free eleccion,
> Been verray kyng, this song to yow I sende:
> And ye, that mowen alle oure harmes amende,
> Have mynde upon my supplicacion! (22–6)

This closing address demonstrates Chaucer's fine diplomatic skills. Henry is addressed at the moment when his legitimacy as monarch hung in the balance of opinion amongst the power groups in the nation, as a noble conqueror, but one who is entitled to the throne by hereditary lineage ('line') and also by popular support ('free eleccion'). Above all, in seeking renewal of the poet's royal patronage, the poem, in its manipulation of the stylised convention of complaint as a witty hyperbolic account of an all too urgent personal plight, is a performance of precisely the poetic skill which the poet relies upon to refill his purse.

Failures in spiritual leadership, crises of governance, and simple administrative bungling are, then, variously reflected in a range of texts from the Middle English period, matched by the range of authorial points of view, from the sycophantic to the suicidally committed dissenter. Our reception of this range is coloured by the random survival of texts, our limited understanding of local conditions, and of the precise circumstances of each author. The texts of the private letters and papers that survive from the period, therefore, provide a different order of evidence as snapshots of the times. In particular, the letters of a number of successive generations of the East Anglian Paston family offer access to how the abuses attacked in texts of protest affected individuals, and also an opportunity to eavesdrop on those individuals' responses to disruptions of their personal circumstances.[38] The record from multiple points of view of events leading up to Margery Paston's elopement, against her family's wishes, with the household steward is the popularly cited example of the latter.[39] There are, however, other events charted in the letters which illustrate in a wider arena what it was like to live in a land where more documentation did not confer greater security. With her husband frequently away from home, Margaret Paston experienced great difficulties in holding on to a number of properties the family had amassed. She not only confronted rival documentary claims to the ownership of these properties, but was subject to disturbing sieges in which attempts were made by maintained bullies to eject her and her household physically from their home. Her attitude to her circumstances demonstrates not only the precarious nature of legal title but, in the phlegmatism of her response, the all too common nature of the onslaughts she endured.[40] Margaret Paston's documented experiences some half-century later assist the modern reader to understand why the poet of *Mum and the Soothsegger* advises of causes 'not cleere in the winde' (1548) that it is best to 'gife hit vp with good wille whenne thy grovnde failleth, / and falle of with fayrenes leste fors the assaille' (1555–6).

NOTES

1. George Kane, 'Some Fourteenth-Century "Political" Poems', in Gregory Kratzmann and James Simpson (eds), *Medieval English Religious and Ethical Literature: Essays in Honour of G. H. Russell* (Cambridge: D. S. Brewer, 1986), pp. 82–91.
2. M. Bose, 'Religious Authority and Dissent', in Peter Brown (ed.), *A Companion to Medieval English Literature and Culture, c.1350–c.1500* (Oxford: Blackwell, 2000), pp. 40–55 (p. 42).
3. F. Somerset intervention in *Geographies of Orthodoxy: Mapping*

English Pseudo-Bonaventuran Lives of Christ, 1350–1550, http://www.qub.ac.uk/geographies-of-orthodoxy/discuss/ (2009) (accessed 18 January 2010).

4. Anne Hudson (ed.), *Selections from English Wycliffite Writings* (Toronto: University of Toronto Press, 1997 [Cambridge: Cambridge University Press, 1978]), pp. 19–28.
5. R. Hanna, *William Langland*, Authors of the Middle Ages, No. 3 (Aldershot: Variorum, 1993), pp. 11–24.
6. See the standard edition, William Langland, *The Vision of Piers Plowman: A Complete Edition of the B-Text*, ed. A. V. C. Schmidt (London and New York: Dent/Dutton, 1978). References to the B text of the poem are to this edition.
7. William Langland, *Piers Plowman: A New Annotated Edition of the C-text*, ed. Derek A. Pearsall, 3rd edn (Exeter: Exeter University Press, 2008), p. 3. References to the C text of the poem are to this edition.
8. Derek A. Pearsall, 'The Character of Langland's C-Text', paper given at the meeting of the Medieval Academy of America, 3 April 2008, Vancouver, BC.
9. See Walter Hilton, *The Scale of Perfection*, ed. John P. H. Clark and Rosemary Dorward (Mahwah, NJ: Paulist Press, 1991), discussed in relation to the morality play, *Wisdom*, in Chapter 3.
10. Anne Middleton, 'William Langland's "kynde Name": Authorial Signature and Social Identity in Late Fourteenth-Century England', in Derek Pearsall (ed.), *Chaucer to Spenser: A Critical Reader* (Oxford: Blackwell, 1999), pp. 206–45.
11. Rosemary Woolf, 'The Tearing of the Pardon', in S. S. Hussey (ed.), *Piers Plowman: Critical Approaches* (London: Methuen, 1969), pp. 50–76.
12. Pearsall, *Piers Plowman*, p. 32.
13. C. William Marx, *The Devil's Rights and the Redemption in the Literature of Medieval England* (Cambridge: D. S. Brewer, 1995), p. 58.
14. James Simpson, *Piers Plowman: An Introduction to the B-Text* (London: Longman, 1990), pp. 249–50.
15. See further David Aers, *Chaucer, Langland, and the Creative Imagination* (London and Boston, MA: Routledge and Kegan Paul, 1980), pp. 36–7; N. David Aers, *Community, Gender and*

Individual Identity (London and New York: Routledge, 1988), pp. 20–66.
16. Simpson, *Piers Plowman*, pp. 232–4; Pearsall, *Piers Plowman*, pp. 34–6.
17. Nicholas Watson, 'Chaucer's Public Christianity', *Religion and Literature*, 37 (2005), 99–114.
18. See further Marx, *Devil's Rights.*
19. Stephen Knight, *Geoffrey Chaucer* (Oxford: Blackwell, 1986), p. 131.
20. P. Brown and A. Butcher. *The Age of Saturn: Literature and History in the Canterbury Tales* (Oxford: Blackwell, 1991), pp. 114–56 (p. 115).
21. All references are to the edition in H. Barr, *The Piers Plowman Tradition* (London: Dent, 1993).
22. H. Barr, *Signes and Sothe: Language in the 'Piers Plowman' Tradition* (Cambridge: D. S. Brewer, 1994), pp. 120–2.
23. Ibid. p. 89.
24. V. J. Scattergood, *The Lost Tradition: Essays on Medieval English Alliterative Poetry* (Dublin: Four Courts Press, 2000), pp. 92–3.
25. V. J. Scattergood, 'Lollardy and Texts: *Pierce the Plowman's Crede*', in Margaret Aston and Colin Richmond (eds), *Lollardy and the Gentry in the Later Middle Ages* (Bodmin, Cornwall: Alan Sutton, 1997), pp. 77–94; H. Barr (ed.), *The Piers Plowman Tradition* (London: Dent, 1993), p. 9.
26. Andrew Wawn, 'Truth-telling and the Tradition of *Mum and the Soothsegger*', *Yearbook of English Studies*, 13 (1983), 270–87 (278).
27. James Simpson, 'The Constraints of Satire in *Piers Plowman* and *Mum and the Soothsegger*', in H. Phillips (ed.), *Langland, the Mystics, and the Medieval Religious Tradition: Essays in Honour of S. S. Hussey* (Cambridge: D. S. Brewer, 1990), pp. 11–30 (pp. 11–13).
28. John Clanvowe, *The Works of Sir John Clanvowe*, ed. V. J. Scattergood (Cambridge: D. S. Brewer, 1975), pp. 57–80.
29. All references to both poems are to the editions in Barr (ed.), *Piers Plowman Tradition.* See also H. Barr, *Socioliterary Practice in Late Medieval England* (Oxford: Oxford University

Press, 2001), pp. 161–2. Sir Thomas Berkeley was father to Elizabeth, first wife of Richard Beauchamp, earl of Warwick, discussed in Chapter 1.

30. Simpson, 'Constraints of Satire', pp. 20–3.
31. Ibid. p. 24.
32. James Simpson, *The Oxford English Literary History. Volume 2. 1350–1547: Reform and Cultural Revolution* (Oxford: Oxford University Press, 2002), pp. 216–17.
33. Jessica Brantley and Thomas Fulton, '*Mankind* in a Year without Kings', *Journal of Medieval and Early Modern Studies*, 36 (2006), 321–53.
34. Gail McMurray Gibson, 'The Play of *Wisdom* and the Abbey of St Edmund', *Comparative Drama*, 19 (1985), 117–35; John Marshall, 'The Satirising of the Suffolks in *Wisdom*', *Medieval English Theatre*, 14 (1992), 37–66. See also Pamela M. King, 'Morality Plays', in Richard Beadle and Alan J. Fletcher (eds), *The Cambridge Companion to Medieval English Theatre* (Cambridge: Cambridge University Press, 2008 [1994]), pp. 235–62.
35. Paul Strohm, *Hochon's Arrow* (Princeton, NJ: Princeton University Press, 1992), p. 75.
36. V. J. Scattergood, *Politics and Poetry in the Fifteenth Century* (London: Blandford Press, 1971), pp. 298–349.
37. Ibid. pp. 359; 110–1.
38. Norman Davis (ed.), *Paston Letters and Papers of the Fifteenth Century, Part I*, Early English Text Society, SS 20 (Oxford: Oxford University Press, 1971), and *Paston Letters and Papers of the Fifteenth Century, Part II*, Early English Text Society, SS 21 (Oxford: Oxford University Press, 1976, reissued 2004); Richard Beadle and Colin Richmond, *Paston Letters and Papers of the Fifteenth Century, Part III*, Early English Text Society, SS 22 (Oxford: Oxford University Press, 2006).
39. See Davis (ed.), *Paston Letters, Part I*, pp. 201, 203, 332.
40. See, for example, Davis (ed.), *Paston Letters, Part I*, pp. 36, 131. These events and their background in national politics are valuably interpreted and narrated in Helen Castor, *Blood and Roses: One Family's Struggle and Triumph during the Tumultuous Wars of the Roses* (London: Harper Collins, 2006), pp. 38–59.

CHAPTER 5

The Literary World

THE BOOK OF THE DUCHESS

For neither William Langland nor Geoffrey Chaucer was being a writer a primary occupation, yet for both it was a vocation. Both are cited widely in the voices of those who come after them and use their names to validate their own compulsion to 'make'. In the last chapter we saw something of Langland's legacy, and how his poem and its hero were appropriated by radical opinion. Now we turn to Chaucer's work and how his name resonated in different circles within fifteenth-century literary society, as individuals sought to associate themselves with an English literary heritage made up of a coterie of writers who looked to him as founder. The idea of a distinct 'literary society' in the pre-print period is endorsed in a number of places, but most straightforwardly by the Scots poet William Dunbar. Lying in his sick-bed at the turn of the sixteenth century, he wrote a *Lament for the Makaris*, a dirge for all the poets who had predeceased him, with a Latin refrain taken from the Office of the Dead, *timor mortis conturbat me* ['the fear of death disturbs me'].[1] It is based on the model of the Dance of Death, in which the animated figure of Death invites an array of individuals to dance with him one by one. The Dance was taken up from the French, translated and adapted by John Lydgate in the mid-fifteenth century.[2] Dunbar's poem begins similarly by reminding its audience that all will be levelled by death, before presenting a procession not of the standard representatives of the three estates, but of poets, starting with Chaucer, 'of makeris flour', the 'Monk of Bery' (Lydgate), and Gower (50–5). In this final chapter, we will explore the traces of literary self-consciousness, of the construction of literary coteries whose members address one another, and of literary discipleship, in an age which left no treatises on creative writing in English, and little we would identify as literary criticism.[3]

The whole corpus of Chaucer's work is a more reliable witness to literature than it is to life, despite the popular reputation of *The Canterbury Tales*, and is not only littered with references to the nature of poetry and poetic authority, but reveals the material culture of a network of London and court-based patrons, intellectual friends, and followers. Chaucer's dependence, as a non-noble courtier, on the patronage of great men, and his use of poetry as a tool for capturing and keeping patronage, is something we saw in the short poem addressed to his empty purse. For all his *bon conseil*, his voice never hectors, but is artfully self-deprecating, making gestures away from himself, deferring to ancient authority on the one hand, and to the finer feelings of the socially superior recipient of his verse on the other. Chaucer's most powerful patron was John of Gaunt, earl of Richmond and duke of Lancaster, eldest surviving son of Edward III, uncle of Richard II, and heir by marriage to the vastly wealthy Duchy of Lancaster. His son Henry became the first Lancastrian monarch, Henry IV. Chaucer's earliest complete major poem, known as *The Book of the Duchess*, but referred to as 'the Deeth of Blaunche the Duchesse' in the Prologue to *The Legend of Good Women* (406), was written for John of Gaunt on the death of his first wife.[4] In the poem, a dream-vision based on a number of French models, the 'man in black' is identified with the patron in a rather transparent cryptogram, as he rides home to 'A long castel with walles white, / By Seynt Johan, on a ryche hil' (1318–19), the lady he mourns is 'faire White' (948). It was once fashionable in criticism to insist on the scrupulous separation of the first-person narrator from the person of the poet, and to refer to the 'dreamer' or the 'persona'. In this poem, however, it seems safe to assume that here the first person is the poet's representation, albeit in gentle self-parody, of his own voice. The construction of a fictional dream setting affords the licence of intimacy that may not have been actual, and could not have been directly inscribed.[5]

The poem is a public statement about the private grief of a social superior, so Chaucer's approach is oblique and delicately balanced emotionally. He draws extensively on highly conventionalised French models of dream-visions, deriving from the *Roman de la Rose*, with which the court audience would have been familiar. The dream is approached from the point of view of one troubled, not by unrequited love, nor yet by bereavement, but by eight years' insomnia. The narrator takes up a book, the story of Ceyx and Alcyone from Ovid's *Metamorphoses*, in which Queen Alcyone prayed to Juno to learn the fate of her husband, King Ceyx, who drowned when away from home. Juno ordered Morpheus the god of sleep to occupy the corpse of Ceyx and appear to Alcyone in a dream to explain his fate. But Chaucer's retelling mirrors the preoccupations he affects, dwelling upon the details of the cave of the god of sleep (170–91); the message of Ceyx's death is, by contrast, delivered to his wife with near-brutal directness: 'For certes, swete, I am but dede: / Ye shul me never on lyve yse [see]' (201–5). Alcyone wakes inconsolable, and dies. The narrator puts down the book, prays to Morpheus, and falls asleep. Thus John of Gaunt's insoluble problem, the death of his spouse, is tactfully introduced under the guise of the narrator's successful search for a solution to his own problem.

Chaucer's adaptations from his French models are pressed into service here. From the *Roman* he takes the opening of the dream, the detailed description of a beautiful and highly stylised landscape, but the poem's form, the framed lover's complaint, is derived from the *dits amoureux* of Chaucer's contemporaries, particularly Guillaume de Machaut's *Jugement dou Roi de Behaigne*, *Remede de Fortune* and *Dit de la Fonteinne Amoreuse*, and Jean Froissart's *Paradys d'Amours*. The *dits* 'modernised' the model of the *Roman*, stripping it of its allegorical superstructure, in favour of highly stylised and elaborately framed, dramatic encounters between sympathetic narrators and their grieving love-lorn subjects.[6]

War did not divide the English from the French but, through diplomatic activity and the exchange of aristocratic prisoners, rather created a context for cultural exchange, particularly in the area of modern poetry. Chaucer was in Reims on a campaign in

1359–60, where Machaut was on the other side, and both Chaucer and Jean Froissart were at the Treaty of Calais negotiations in 1360. Moreover, from 1357, Jean III, 'the Good', King of France was a prisoner at the English court, exchanged in 1360 for a number of aristocratic hostages including Jean, duc du Berry, the great patron of the arts, who remained in England until 1367. There were other French poets at the English court too: Gace de la Buigne and Jean de la Mote were older contemporaries, the latter having framed his elegy for Guillaume de Hainault, father of Edward III's queen, as a dream-vision.[7] The Savoyard Oton de Granson, who lived permanently in England from 1368 until 1387, was a close friend of Chaucer.[8]

The move to the central complaint in *The Book of the Duchess* is made as the dreamer wakes into his dream in a chamber, then moves outside, where he encounters the Emperor Octavian's hunt and attempts to follow it. The quarry escapes and the dreamer gets lost following a puppy into the wood. Hunts of the hart, exploiting the obvious homophone hart/heart, are commonplace in love poetry, but here the more elaborated focus is on the association of dreamer and puppy. Both are failures through the inexperience born of youth and lack of opportunity, in the supremely aristocratic hunt, both providing the necessary solitude and establishing the subservient relationship between Chaucer and the 'Man in Black' with whom he now meets.

The complaint of the Man in Black succeeds here precisely because it arrives with credentials set up to mislead an audience familiar with *dits* of unrequited love. This contrived misunderstanding is modelled in the response of the dreamer. He asks, 'Where is she now?' (1298). The man becomes 'dede as stoon' (1300) and reminds the dreamer that he said he had lost more than he thought. The dreamer presses him,

> 'Allas, sir, how? What may that be?'
> 'She is ded.' 'Nay!' 'Yis, be my trouthe.'
> 'Is that youre losse? Be God, hyt ys routhe.' (1308–10)

There is no remedy for death; there can be only 'routhe', pity. The substance of the complaint has, however, allowed Chaucer to pay a long and extravagant compliment memorialising Blanche, and to put it into the mouth of her bereaved husband, thus licensing something far more personal than formal elegiac poetry would sanction. The Knight's complaint is not an emotional outpouring, but an elaborate rhetorical exhibition of the high style, opening with an extended image based on the game of chess. With its king, queen, knights, and bishops, chess offered a popular field of feudal imagery in the period, but in *The Book of the Duchess* it is the stark contrast of black and white that predominates, supporting the poem's structural oppositions between dark and light, sleep and waking, death and life.

In constructing the complaint, Chaucer performs a rhetorical sleight of hand. In *Troilus and Criseyde* he quotes Geoffrey de Vinsauf's *Poetria Nova* (c.1200), a manual of rhetoric, and it is from Vinsauf that he takes the model for the Black Knight's encomium of praise for the fair White, anatomising her physical, temperamental, and spiritual qualities according to text-book order (855–960). This is not, however, what Vinsauf recommends as the matter of elegy: his model is based on an elegy on the death of Richard I, and parodied by Chaucer in The Nun's Priest's Tale.[9] In *The Book of the Duchess*, where Chaucer is writing a real poem of lament on the occasion of a real death, he chooses a set-piece example of how to praise the object of romantic love, transposed from his own voice into that of the chief mourner himself.

The poem concludes abruptly. Once the Man in Black has stated the fact of White's death, the hunt ends, everyone goes home, and the dreamer is wakened by a bell. The poem's linearity can be read as a sign of its meaning: Blanche is dead, so there can be no renewal. As the Gawain-poet observes,

> A ȝere ȝernes ful ȝerne, and ȝeldez neuer lyke,
> Þe forme to þe fynisment foldez ful selden. (II, 7–8)
>
> [A year passes very quickly and does not repeat; the beginning to the ending returns very seldom.]

Unlike the natural world, and green knights, for the human being there is no regeneration in this world, and to suggest otherwise would insult the bereaved. The Church offers hope of eternal life and reunion in the next world; the court poet's strategy, and the consolations that it offers, are of this world, driven by the quotidian possibilities of finding comfort in retrospection. The poem's most vivid and immediate moments come from the indirect experiences to be found in books, in dreams, and in memory, not as escape or denial, but as opportunities to exorcise grief. It has been said that physical medicine in the Middle Ages involved remedies so unpleasant that they offered distraction until the original complaint killed the sufferer or went away through the passage of time. The type of poetry being produced to order in the royal and aristocratic courts in the same period perhaps offered a sweeter emotional and psychological salve.

THE PARLIAMENT OF FOWLS

Chaucer's courtly audience was one which not only consumed the *dits amoureux*, but for whom games addressing the question of love had become fashionable social entertainment. These were generally conducted as debates around *demands d'amours*, unanswerable conundra about romantic love. Such debating points provided the inspiration for the underlying dilemmas about conduct dwelt on in The Knight's Tale and The Franklin's Tale. The English court, emulating the French fashion, had formed two societies, *cours amoureuses*, the Flower and the Leaf, which engaged in debates and poetry-writing competitions about love. Chaucer refers to them in the Prologue to *The Legend of Good Women* (71–3). The early fifteenth-century poem entitled *The Floure and the Leafe*, formerly attributed to Chaucer, presents a stylised and moralised imitation of the type of debate these courtly societies engaged in.[10] St Valentine's Day was the annual festival for these courtly societies and a number of poems were written for the occasion, including Chaucer's dream-vision, *The Parliament of Fowls*.[11] In it, Chaucer, the literary court servant, makes his conventional self-effacing gestures, while the way in which he extends the philosophical range of the love-vision also suggests he had another intellectual audience in mind. The effect is not ironic, as the poem's celebration of refined romantic love is uncompromised, but is framed within a complex textual structure that offers his audience a harmonious range of social and philosophical meaning.

The narrator presents himself as the reader of the section of Tullius Cicero's *De Re Publica*, known as 'The Dream of Scipio' in the version popular throughout the Middle Ages, which includes commentary by fifth-century African-Roman philosopher Macrobius. The book, which contains diagnostic information on the interpretation of dreams, sends the narrator to sleep, and he awakes in a conventional beautiful landscape. At the heart of the garden he finds the Temple of Venus, but overcome by the hot-house atmosphere there, and the tales of turbulent love affairs painted on the walls, he reels outside to witness a parliament of birds debating about the conduct of their spring mating. The debate is supervised by Nature, and when it is resolved the birds sing a harmonious roundel in praise of summer and love, before flying off with such noise that the narrator awakes, and takes up another book, remarking that one day he hopes to read something that will help him do better (698–9).

The *demande d'amour* at the heart of the poem asks which of three suitors is the most worthy to mate with the aristocratic female formel eagle. The mating of the other birds is held up while the three suitors put their cases in show-piece speeches: the tercel eagle, 'foul royale' (394) declares that he will serve her or die (416–27); the second eagle claims to have loved her longest; the third that he loves her best and will be faithful for ever. The debate turns on such nice distinctions; moreover the formel is so refined that she asks for, and is granted with forbearance by Nature (626–8), a further year's grace to make her choice. The debate is, however, not contained within a courtly bubble, but is conducted in front of all the other birds, who wish they would 'Haue don & lat vs wende [depart]!' (492). The courtly game is a time-consuming distraction from life's business of procreation. Other birds represent the views of the other ranks: the cuckoo for the worm-eaters, the turtle-dove for the seed-eaters, the goose for the water-fowl. Stylistic shifts and contrasts are used to illustrate the ways in which the codes of conduct for each order are irrelevant to others, while the debaters are described in terms that entertainingly balance anthropomorphism with bird-ness. The debate enacts understandings of, and failures to understand, elite behaviour, and rhetorical register signifies social meaning, paying a compliment to its courtier audience.

In all this, Nature is arbiter; Chaucer presents himself as having no personal experience in love in the poem: for him, love's contradictions can be resolved only by recourse to learning. The Dream of Scipio is of limited application as Scipio Africanus, who becomes the narrator's dream guide, dismisses human desire because it can compromise 'common profit', that is the benefit of humanity as a whole. The garden landscape beyond the gate nonetheless shows how 'common profit' is applied in nature, every tree defined according to its particular function: the oak for building, the fir for making the masts of ships, and the yew for making bows. In its place at the traditional heart of the garden, the Temple of Venus also fails to answer the narrator's hope of finding a workable model of the 'craft of love'. Its description is drawn from Boccaccio's *Teseida*, a book which is fundamentally irreconcilable with The Dream of Scipio in presenting erotic human desire as the epitome of a sensual ideal. Yet all the lovers depicted around the walls of the Temple died unhappily, many victims of passion, like Dido and Candace, moved to act against nature and take their own lives. The answer to the question about love is signalled by the geography of the vision: it will come not from Scipio in the heavens, and not from the enclosed Temple of Venus, but from a workable synthesis of the two extremes found in the garden itself and in the figure of Nature.

Nature is borrowed from the poem's third book, 'Aleyn' (316), the twelfth-century French theologian, Alan de Lille's, *De Planctu Naturae* [Complaint of Nature]. Nature, as governor of the relationship between human and divine love in De Lille's philosophy, accommodates sexual love within the universal order of things. Essential for procreation, it cannot be innately wrong. The birds in the parliament over which she presides are described according to their attributes in a manner that echoes the narrator's earlier description of the trees in the garden. Setting the debate within a framework derived from the *De Planctu*, full of metaphors taken from the law, also signals to the informed reader that Chaucer is here placing a discussion of different types of love within a philosophical, rather than a purely social, context. The dalliance of the aristocratic birds conforms to models of ideal behaviour, but does not lead to a productive conclusion, submitting instead to the judgement of the rest of bird society. Courtly behaviour is natural, 'of kynde', for the refined in society, and the hierarchical customs and traditions of society are ordered and sanctioned by Nature provided they are not contrary to the good of all, the 'common profit'. Moreover, the turtle dove's view that those who can neither read nor sing of refined behaviour should not interfere in it (518) vindicates the situation of the poet of love. The roundel with which the poem ends offers further reinforcement, using the harmonious circularity of its literary form as a sign of sexual and romantic love's role as a beneficial regenerative force.

THE HOUSE OF FAME AND THE NUN'S PRIEST'S TALE

Chaucer's socio-literary interactions give access to a world in which meaning could be constructed, and social gestures performed, through a shared repertoire of conventional forms of expression. Moreover Chaucer, like the other writers of his time, was conscious of writing himself into a tradition made up of authoritative works of the past, in Latin, in French, and now in English. Thus, although there were no treatises of writing poetry before those of Sir Philip Sidney and George Puttenham in the sixteenth century, Chaucer shows evidence of being conscious of the decorum of the artistic process, and anxious about the adequacy of his form of 'making' for conveying meaning and truth.[12] In *Troilus and Criseyde*, this self-conscious writerliness, as we saw in Chapter 1, becomes thematic. There the narrative voice constantly questions whether a story drawn from another book can provide sufficient information on which judgement can be based, secure meaning constructed. He sets up the dramatic fiction of himself solicitously searching through accounts of the legendary infidelity in search of the truth about Criseyde, thereby throwing the determination of meaning back upon the reader. The transactional relationship between author and reader is further foregrounded in *The House of Fame*, and in The Nun's Priest's Tale from *The Canterbury Tales*, where the familiar themes of experience and authority, of invention and reproduction, become the central subject matter. These texts reveal much about the history of reading in Chaucer's immediate circle, and of the assumed sophistication of a readership prepared to be entertained by poems whose subject matter is their own process.

By the time that Chaucer was writing *The House of Fame*, the love-vision's conventional topoi were sufficiently well established that they could be manipulated to raise questions about the form as a vehicle for enlightenment. The poem opens with a long and self-contradictory sentence, openly parodying the beginning of the *Roman de la Rose*. The device of questioning the reliability of dreams is so inflated here that, when matched with a setting in December instead of May, it genuinely does undermine the value of what follows. The book, which usually helps dreamers get to sleep, is then shifted into the dream itself. The poem's logic moves from questioning the reliability of dreams to, within a dream, questioning the reliability of books. The poem's apparent fumbling for its own form, destabilising the structural utility of dreams and old books, is tantamount to questioning the validity of literary tradition.[13]

Part I of *The House of Fame* reverts to the debate about authority. In The Wife of Bath's Prologue, the dramatised voice of the narrator claims supremacy for experience, but she is simultaneously an object-lesson in the truth of the authorities from which she is constructed. In Book I of *The House of Fame* authority is more directly problematised, as the dreamer-narrator presents two equally authoritative sources for the story of Dido and Aeneas which defy integration. Virgil's version of the story constructs Aeneas as the hero, who rightly breaks free from the embraces of Dido in order to pursue his epic destiny. Ovid, on the other hand, presents Dido as heroine, abandoned by an unfeeling seducer, and tragically moved to suicide. Chaucer thus wittily suggests that the ethical 'truth' concerning Aeneas's action depends on the literary mode in which the story is cast.

What follows performs the proposition that, robbed of confidence in its conventional validating procedures, literary endeavour has nowhere to go. Landscape is the conventional objective correlative of aesthetic success, and this dreamer-narrator, now finds himself in a wasteland, 'a large feld, / as fer as that I myghte see, / withouten toun, or hous, or tree . . .' (482–4). The poem has to embark on another strategy, to become something else. It does this by a literal feat of elevation, a Dantean flight into the heavens which leaves behind the earthbound tradition of the *Roman de la Rose* in which it had become enmired. It renegotiates its visionary frame of reference, and, as another marker of a shift into higher seriousness, introduces scientific matter which validates poetry as the emission of sound, subject to the laws of physics. The trouble is that, unlike Dante's visionary guide in *The Divine Comedy*, Virgil, the poet is guided unpromisingly by one of those talking birds. It may be an eagle that picks up the faltering narrator in his claws, but this one is a bore. His flight is one of rhetoric, as he delivers a disquisition on sound-theory based on a tautological premise, in an almost impenetrable imitation of the high style. His passenger 'Geffrey' suffers a consequent attack of vertigo. Their destination, the eponymous House of Fame, for all that it too is derived from Ovid's *Fama* from the twelfth book of the *Metamorphosis*,[14] underscores the conclusions the dreamer arrived at in his attempt to synthesise two versions of the story of Dido and Aeneas into a meaningful discourse: fame, that is the preservation of accounts of exemplary human conduct, operates entirely arbitrarily. The alternative, however, is the House of Rumour, represented as a whirling sixty-mile wide wickerwork cage made of twigs, whizzing, squeaking and creaking, with noise like the release of stones from a siege-engine leaking out of 1,000 holes (1928–34). This noise with which the House is crammed is described as 'tydynges' on a vast list, enumerated in a sixteen-line *repetitio* of antithetical yet ironically assorted subjects, such as wars, peace, and marriages (1961–76). The eagle leaves his perch on a stone nearby to pick the dreamer up again and drop him into the huge basket which immediately appears to stop whirling. As he wanders amongst the people there, he witnesses unsorted 'tydynges' being passed from one to the other, lies and truths all jumbled up together (2088–9).

What the Houses of Fame and Rumour vividly figure is that all utterance is subject to the discretion of the transmission and reception processes. Chaucer's (medieval) response to what is taken to be one of the markers of modernity, the instability of the sign, is to court divine assistance: '"O Crist," thoughte I, "that art in blysse, / Fro fantome and illusion / Me save!"' (492–4). The poem ends at a point that signals another new departure as the dreamer sees approaching one who seems to be 'A man of gret auctorite . . .'

(2158). At this point the poem breaks off. *The House of Fame*, dominated by an overbearing eagle, turns the poetic process into a matter of anxiety; the world of The Nun's Priest's Tale, dominated by chickens, offers a less reverential approach to the problem of authority. Its proposition about the ethics of writing is playfully masked by the disingenuous choice of its source. The *moralitas* of Aesop's fable of the cock and the fox, the commonplace matter of medieval children's education exposing the dangers of worldly vanity, is adapted to expose the self-congratulatory posturing of texts that claim authority by reference to a process of canonical reproduction.[15] The problem of where to turn for 'matter' is here resolved by opening up the range of 'tydynges', of discourses, on which a poet may draw. In Chanticleer, the romantic hero, the social pretentions of Sir Thopas meet the rhetorical hot air of the Summoner's Friar. He has a dream. His interpretation of it is doubly undercut, first by his chicken-wife Pertelot's homely wisdom (2923–5). For all that it is dressed up in medical terminology, the burden of her message is clear: bad dreams are produced by 'repleccioun', eating too much. Chanticleer the dreamer, undeterred, proceeds to heap authority upon authority, but then, erotically enflamed by the scarlet rings around his wife's eyes, decides to ignore his dream altogether. All the vanities of intellectual endeavour, all epistemology, all authorising discourse is rejected in what Stephen Knight has described as 'a genial front for a cultural holocaust'.[16]

Of course it is not Pertelot's homely voice of experience that is set up as a viable alternative source of truth, but here in *The Canterbury Tales* Chaucer is working with a narrative structure which gave him freedom to devise competing alternative performances, fulfilling what the diffident voices of the dream-visions and *Troilus and Criseyde* gestured towards. The Tale's opening introduces the widow who owns the chickens, and who, in the end, will lead her dogs in pursuit of the fox. The introduction of the widow herself is marked out by the same conservatism that characterises the values of patience and simplicity expressed in The Parson's Tale (2824–7). Here Chaucer directs the reader not so much to the social and spiritual values she embodies, but rather uses her life as a connotative sign of the values of plain style in discourse. She has no need of 'poynaunt sauce' for her meat, just as the Nun's Priest needs no rhetorical colours, for, as he points out to the Monk, it is a text's success as a transaction that alone confers meaning: 'whereas a man may have noon audience, / noght helpeth it to tellen his sentence' (2801–2).

THE CHAUCER CIRCLE

Who was Chaucer's audience for these excursions into literary theory? His life as a courtier brought him into contact with numerous intersecting circles from royalty to commoners in the city of London, as well as associates from continental Europe. It is likely he had audiences in mind other than those specifically catered for in *The Book of the Duchess* or *The Parliament of Fowls*. Paul Strohm cautiously suggests that 'available evidence does permit us to form some opinions about the kinds of poetic features that addressees like Scogan, Bukton, and Vache, and fellow writers like Usk, Scogan, and Clanvowe, did in fact like'.[17] Clanvowe and Vache we have already met in Chapter 4. Thomas Usk, who praises Chaucer in his *Testament of Love*, was mayor of London in 1381–2 and less likely to have been a close associate, being fatally tied up in political factions that Chaucer avoided. Scogan and Bukton, to whom Chaucer addressed short 'envoys', entered the court circle as esquires in the 1390s. Others whom Chaucer mentions by name include Ralph 'philosophical' Strode, to whom, along with John Gower, *Troilus and Criseyde* is dedicated. Strode was an Oxford academic, and author of treatises on logic as well as, possibly, a dream-vision poem that does not survive. He appears then to have taken up a second career as London lawyer in the Court of Common Pleas, and to have lived in the gatehouse of Aldersgate when Chaucer lived in the gatehouse at Aldgate.[18] Merton College, Oxford was also the focus for the study of astronomy, and Chaucer's young son Lewis, for whom he wrote his prose *Treatise on the Astrolabe*, probably went to school in the city. Nicholas in The Miller's Tale may have been named after Merton astronomer Nicholas of Lynn, reminding us that Chaucer's intellectual world extended beyond the bounds of the capital.[19]

Strode, Gower, and Usk died before 1390, and Clanvowe in 1391, but Vache outlived Chaucer, and the addition of Scogan and Bukton as latecomers to the Chaucer circle demonstrates the continuance of his literary influence. The envoys addressed to Scogan and Bukton are particularly illuminating as coterie pieces that nonetheless appear to make gestures to a potentially wider audience.[20] *Lenvoy de Chaucer a Scogan* chides the addressee for giving up his mistress, inviting the revenge of Cupid on all of those 'hoor and rounde of shap', fat, grey-haired men like Chaucer and Scogan. Chaucer defends himself from accusations of self-interest by claiming that his own muse has 'slept in its sheath' for some time. Through swiftly changing points of view, tone, and authorial posturing, the poem deftly suggests connotative associations between erotic love, the writing of love poetry, and the love between a poet at the dull, dead end of his productive career and a younger associate in whom the succession must be entrusted, for '. . . al shal passe that men prose or ryme; / take every man hys turn as for his tyme' (41–2). This little poem, adept in form, reads as a sincere statement of literary fellowship; equally it is free from mawkish sentimentality because of the customary self-parody of the author whose pleas of poverty and fall from favour ring about as true as his apology for waning poetic control. *Lenvoy de Chaucer a Bukton* cites and recycles the anti-feminist warnings of The Wife of Bath's Prologue as relevant to 'this matere we have on honde' (30). The poem concerns the pros and cons of (re)marriage, for the widowed poet and his addressee. Its apparent simplicity, non-committal stance, and the reference to the Wife of Bath all surely signify a text contrived to suggest a meaning that has to be supplied by the addressee by reference to other texts and situations that lie outside the poem but that poet and addressee hold in common.

The 'circle of gentle civil servants and litterateurs' within the royal affinity of which Chaucer was himself a member appears not to have outlasted his death and the reorganisation of the Lancastrian royal household. In the fifteenth century, however, a wide array of poets continued to write within the 'Chaucer cult', witnessed by Dunbar's list of 'makars'. If a literary culture involves identifiable currents of transmission and rhetorical fashions, amongst those who wrote and read, the fifteenth century presents a complicated picture we can only glance at here. Fifteenth-century poets inherited attitudes that became problematic in the upheaval of Richard II's deposition and remained so throughout the political turmoil of the fifteenth century. It has become a commonplace to believe that, just as vernacular religious writing was checked by Arundel's Constitutions, the court politics of the unstable Lancastrian dynasty also impeded development from the vernacular literature of the Ricardian period. The period after the death of Chaucer was characterised, the story goes, by sycophancy – to the reigning monarch and to the memory of Chaucer – conservatism, often exemplified in the prolific output of John Lydgate, and 'dullness'.[21]

THOMAS HOCCLEVE

Thomas Hoccleve, not mentioned by either Chaucer or Dunbar, was a relatively obscure clerk in the office of the Privy Seal, where he met Chaucer in the 1390s. His poetic career, though deeply stylistically indebted to Chaucer, whom he called 'this landes verray tresor and richesse' in a poem lamenting the elder poet's death,[22] was markedly different from Chaucer's own. Difference of poetic temperament, as well as social rank and political circumstances, produced in Hoccleve not a slavish follower of Chaucer, but an early transformer of the 'tradition'.

Hoccleve's most ambitious work was *The Regement of Princes*, written in 1411–12 for Henry, Prince of Wales, later Henry V.[23] It follows the *speculum principis* [mirror for princes] tradition, a convention originating in Aristotle's *Ethics* IV, which addresses the ruler on the subject of the judicious use of power and wealth. The Middle Ages knew the Aristotelian tradition via the *Secreta Secretorum* [Secret of Secrets], and it remained perennially fashionable, a type of writing that became commonplace but 'successfully topical'.[24] Hoccleve strikes a modest pose, claiming that his book, which runs to around 5,500 lines, is a compilation of various redactions; in fact, it performs a more complex cultural exercise.

The *Regement*'s structure intersperses selected narrative exempla with personal reminiscences, reading as if the author were striving to relate all the standard advice to contemporary social problems. After the extended Prologue which occupies almost half the text, and in which the narrator conducts a dialogue with an old beggar, the unmediated advice begins by considering the duties of kingship, how the monarch must weigh his words properly, and honour promises, especially in the repayment of debts. It goes on to deal with justice, with good and bad law, and the virtues of mercy, patience, and chastity. When he then moves on to discuss 'magnaminite', he directly addresses Henry on the humbling of his enemies (3963–6), an instance of what John Burrow calls Hoccleve the good citizen, present as an individuated voice of counsel, opining on contemporary social issues.[25] He constantly urges ending the war with France through a strategic marriage, and encourages Henry to go on a crusade instead. He attacks Lollardy, advising the prince not to get involved in the mysteries of religion, and expresses dissatisfaction with the secular lives led by those in the Church, urging the king to nominate the best men to the pope for appointment as bishops, because of the spiritual charge they bear: 'no small charche is the soules cure / Of al a diocese' (2932–3). This last point is one of those picked up in the main body of the text from the extended Prologue, which is the poem's most radical addition to the *speculum* tradition. In the Prologue the old beggar offers advice that the narrator will later process and pass on to the prince. The voice of the old beggar allows more pungent criticism than the poet might directly dare, attacking the pastoral failures of the Church and of society in general, focusing on ecclesiastical pluralism, the harsh effects of the nobility's self-interest and lack of largesse, the abuse of old soldiers, the extortion by men of rank of money from common people, and the abuse of the law (2822).

Andrew Lynch has observed how all Hoccleve's poetry performs his own personality in a way that strengthens his hand as counsellor 'by helping to set up a clerkly counter-discourse to the norms of chivalric masculinity'. He sets out to redefine princely behaviour, as 'the often comic "confessional" strain in his poetry outlines a sustained personal antipathy to violence which is transformed within the *Regement* in particular into a strategic persuasion against war'.[26] Hoccleve never did join the chorus of those poets who later were to celebrate the Agincourt victory, and although he is opposed to Lollardy, in the Prologue he praises Henry for his personal leniency with individual heretics. His voice is disarmingly self-aware, particularly of the ironies attendant on someone in his social, financial, and temperamental circumstances, offering advice to a prince.

The voice of the old beggar is created as intermediary, the authority and detachment of age affording it the weightiness necessary to offer moral advice. The poet in his own voice can then strike the pose of complainant and frank fan of the royal personage:

> Symple ys my goost and scars my letterure
> Vnto your excellence for to write
> Myn inward loue. And yet aventure
> Wil I me putte, thogh I can but lyte.
> My dere mayster – God ys soul quyte –
> And fadir, Chaucer, fayn wold han me taght,
> But I was dul and lerned lyte or noght. (2073–9)

So, despite all the self-deprecation, Hoccleve is being neither simple nor dull, but is doing something quite innovative within the *speculum principis* tradition: placing himself within the real social context on which he moralises. His is not a voice of moral certainty; that is transferred to the old beggar. He is the complainant, in a literary and conventional sense, but also actual, as royal subject and petitioner, exploiting the anomalous position of what a poem is for.

The poem is cast as serious advice for the young prince, but it is also designed to draw attention to the donor-poet so that he will be paid. This reading is not cynically external to the text's matter, but operates at a level fundamental to the form. For example, the problem of bastard feudalism – if the clerk's fee is not paid by the lord's retainer, there is nothing the clerk can do (1499–1502) – is pointed out by Thomas Hoccleve, clerk. Equally, in the sections dealing with the king's duty of liberality, which should not deviate into prodigality or avarice, Hoccleve disarmingly instances himself as one guilty of prodigality (4362–5). It was an expectation that routine gratuities would be part of a clerk of the Privy Seal's income, and Hoccleve here transparently sets up an opportunity to reveal that his poverty is exacerbated because his annuity from the Crown office is in arrears:

> O liberal prince! ensaumple of honour!
> Vnto your grace lyke it to promoote

Mi poore estat, and to me woo beth boote [and to my woes be the remedy]. (4387–9)

In writing the *Regement*, Hoccleve put himself in a delicate position. Part of a monarch's own strategy of impression management was to surround himself with learned clerks, and to hide behind 'good counsel' in making difficult or unpopular decisions, but there is nothing to suggest that he could not, nor would not, ignore unwelcomely intrusive advice. Chaucer appears to have enjoyed a reputation at court for sagacity, which may also explain why Hoccleve constantly invokes their personal relationship as part of the poem's external context. Within the poem his parallel strategy is to invent the old beggar, and to cast himself as a hapless victim of circumstances.

Once the poem was complete, and it is long, Hoccleve also had to speculate serious money on having it turned into a presentation volume fit for a king. In common with all presentation works, including Chaucer's address to his purse, the *Regement of Princes* as a material object represents the attempt of one chronically underpaid royal servant to stand out from the ranks. Asking for money is another delicate business. Hoccleve complains of poverty while citing his long and faithful service, and attempts to pull whatever strings he holds, chiefly his association with Chaucer. As part of the construction of his presentation volume, probably British Library MS Harley 4866, he determines, and tells his readers, that he will include a true likeness of Chaucer for the benefit of those who did not know him.[27] In the Prologue, the meeting between the poet and the old beggar is set up to embed Hoccleve's own name. This is no place for a cryptogram; it begins two successive lines, as if the old beggar were ever so slightly deaf, and is set in close proximity to Chaucer's:

'What schal I calle the? What ys þy name?'
'Hoccleve, fadir myn, men clepen me.'
'Hoccleve, sone?' 'Iwys, fader, þat same.'
'Sone, I haue herd or thys men speke of the.
Thou were acqueynted with Chaucer, pardee.
God haue hys soule best of any wyght . . . (1863–8)

The beggar's solutions to the problems of the times are Boethian; Hoccleve literally cannot afford to accept this, because, as he went on to illustrate in his *Complaint*, charting his collapse into mental illness, to become a social pariah at court was to risk starvation.

With Hoccleve, court poetry turns from being in and of the court, to being about it. The paranoid discomfiture of the persona dependent on political success, yet somehow unsuccessful in the social and political skills necessary to sustain that success, is nowhere to be found in Chaucer's self-presentation, but emerges in Hoccleve's *La Male Regle*, *Dialogue*, and *Complaint*, and may be followed through court poetry from John Skelton to Sir Thomas Wyatt, notably 'They Flee from Me'.[28] *La Male Regle*, written in 1405/6, is the first poem in which Hoccleve establishes a voice that inverts the usual impression management that characterises court poetry.[29] He uses the conventional complaint to inveigh against social abuses, while admitting that he himself has fallen prey to, for example, drunkenness (161–8) and flattery (206–8). What will be turned to demonstrate the need for reform in the *Regement* begins life here as another instance of medieval life-writing. The organisational scheme is based on the seven deadly sins, so there is a constant tension in the reading of this poem, part personal confession, part conventionally stylised penitential complaint. But although the poem draws sage lessons from the excesses which the narrator's voice recalls of his former conduct, it does not seek to elicit penance in others or to save the speaker's soul; rather it is overtly designed to attract attention in order to extract money because, 'My body and purs been at ones seeke . . .' (409).

La Male Regle acts as a test-bed for the two roles Hoccleve will adopt for higher stakes in the *Regement*: that of the good citizen and would-be moralist, and, authenticating the first, that of the frank confessor of a personal history of misrule. The persona who could never do more than kiss the tavern girls, who could not be bothered to go back to work in summer because it was too hot, and in winter because the Strand was muddy, has fallen on hard times, bad health, and penury. He sets himself up as an exemplum, but the strategy is also to give the poem agency on behalf of the other role he adopts – that of the impoverished petitioner – and to win him a fee. The poem's goal is not penance, but the construction of a begging letter that will stand out in the crowd of other begging letters. The poem not only replicates the poetic conventions of the immediate post-Chaucerian age, but enacts the operation of poetry in culture in a way that particularly characterises the literary world of the fifteenth century. Moreover, the complete integration of the performance of the narrative voice within the poem, and performance of the poet in his society, points to a near-contemporary reading of Chaucer's own work where those two roles are closer than modern readings, which scrupulously divide poet from 'persona', will admit.

The later *Series* poems, particularly the *Complaint* and the *Dialogue with a Friend*, give a further twist to the role Hoccleve constructs for himself through the transmission of his poetry. Here he shows how social contact, and particularly being asked for advice, was, for a sick man, therapeutic. Both poems refer to an illness when, '. . . the substance of my memorie / wente to pleye as for a certain space . . .' (*Complaint*, 50–1), an episode of mental illness looked back on from a later period after the restoration of the poet's wits by a benign God. The poems are written not with the purpose of describing past affliction, but to petition for restored social recognition for the now-sane poet. The *Complaint* and the *Dialogue* discuss the processes of reading, of social interaction, and of writing. In the *Complaint* the author describes how, after his recovery, he had trouble affirming his sanity with others, and overheard, or imagined, talk behind his back about the oddness of his behaviour. This led him to stay at home checking the normality of his appearance in his mirror. In the end he was helped by reading a book, and in particular by the voice of Reason in that book, but unfortunately the book's owner retrieved it before he had finished reading it (372–4). After reading it, however, he cared less about what people thought of him, but just after he finished writing all this down, a friend knocked at his door. Thus the *Complaint* becomes its own subject, a subject written according to the literary conventions of the complaint, and now to be read out to the visiting friend.

What the ensuing *Dialogue* suggests is that the *Complaint* will not be efficacious in convincing the world that its author is sane, on the basis that it protests too much, but that the re-socialisation of the poet will be achieved through the preparation of a longer presentation volume, prefaced by the *Complaint* but containing a more ambitious scheme of works drawn from literary convention. The scheme will become the *Series* of which, in a thorough-going exercise in self-referentiality, the *Dialogue* will also form a part. As James Simpson points out, for the reader there is a tension between 'the fact that the writing slips so readily and so constantly back into literary convention and textuality' and 'the way in which literature springs out of, and answers to, conditions of lived reality'.[30] The exception to the textuality of the *Series* is, however, the *Dialogue*, where its presentation as a recollected conversation about texts effaces its own status and fulfils the poet's need 'to convince his audience that outside his texts there is a sane poet'. Hoccleve may appeal to the modern reader because he borrows Chaucer's weeds to become 'the first modern English poet, beached on the existential foreshore between death and overdraft';[31] he also, nonetheless, represents a trend for writing poetry in his own time which, through a process of self-referencing, considerably complicates the simple binary opposition of experience versus authority.

JOHN LYDGATE

For Chaucer the limitations and the artifice of writing had attendant ethical and philosophical connotations, as he illustrated particularly in his dream-visions. It is rather ironic, then, that his self-appointed successors cited his work as an imprimatur of authority. Chaucer's preoccupation with aesthetic self-examination became something to be emulated and celebrated, and texts were produced in which art, artifice, the writing self, and their own materiality, became thematic signatures of the Chaucerian tradition.[32]

John Lydgate, whose major works include *The Troy Book*, *The Siege of Thebes*, and *The Fall of Princes*, was a self-styled Chaucerian of dauntingly prolific output. The knowledge that he was a member of a regular religious order can obscure the fact that he too operated within networks of secular power in Lancastrian court circles.[33] As we saw in Chapter 1, Lydgate's *Troy Book* illustrates his desire to glorify the present in the light of the past, and to present the monarch with an encomium of the high style. These motives, and the traditional material chosen for his longest works, have led in the past to understandings of his poetry as representative of a recidivist trend in the fifteenth century towards a more conservative, platitudinous, and superficially embellished poetics, by implication less interesting than Chaucer's. Recent trends in Lydgate studies offer new readings of his massive oeuvre, however, suggestive of the creative tensions which we have found in other texts in this chapter. Lydgate too is topical, contextual, and philosophically resistant to that topicality.[34] He is, in a number of respects, the apotheosis of a trend set by Chaucer, of the writer as reader. His rewritings are not a mechanistic regurgitation of old books for new markets even though his reading market was more geographically extended and socially disparate than that addressed by Chaucer.[35]

Among Lydgate's most contextually anchored, occasional texts are those written as narrative recitations accompanying 'mummings', that is refined emblematic dumb-shows. Mummings are theatrical precursors of the Renaissance court masques, and like masques, because they lack the conflict inherent in literary theatre, can be relegated to a literary siding. Yet just as Ben Jonson later wrote a number of masques posing philosophical challenges beyond the necessary scope of a banquet entertainment, so Lydgate, in the verses accompanying court mummings, wrote texts whose literariness exceeds their function. The *Mumming at London* was written as a Christmas entertainment for a great household.[36] It opens with a demonstration of the havoc caused by the goddess Fortune, whose blindness conventionally signifies the apparent amorality of happenstance. Here, by whim, the conventional *locus amoenus*, the beautiful landscape, signifying harmony in human affairs, is destroyed by a sudden wave (28–34). In the ensuing stately and processional action indicated by the text, Fortune is assailed for her random injustices by the four cardinal virtues. Prudence, who carries the mirror of providence, represents foresight; Righteousness with her scales, represents impartial judgement; Fortitude, with her sword resists vice; and finally Dame Fair and Wise Temperaunce, with her cousin Soberness, protects the others. The performance finishes with all four sisters gathering round the fire to sing, Fortune having been ousted.

The matter of this *Mumming* is deeply conventional and reassuringly transparent, but the devil is in the detail. The text ventriloquises the speeches of a procession of embodied emblematic characters, which ties it to a particular performative context. Its internal referents indicate the particular occasion of its performance. Fair and Wise Temperance is accorded particular status, suggesting that Christmas is a hazardous time for the intemperate. But there is also a sterner social message embedded in a text which has already asserted that the exercise of righteousness, that is the law, mitigates the risk of favouritism, whether procured by influence or rank; for Temperance

> . . . dooþe hir power preove
> A communaltee for to releeve,
> Namely vpon a grounde of trouthe. (235–7)

The *Mumming* is a compressed morality play. Moreover it is one whose available readings address virtue as a code of responsible behaviour in those in a position of influence, something developed by John Skelton in *Magnificence*, and which more radically presages the concern with the effects of that behaviour on the 'communaltee', a preoccupation to be developed in plays like *Respublica* and Sir David Lindsay's *Ane Satyre of the Three Estaits* a century and more later. Maura Nolan has made a case for Lydgate's occasional works being 'distinctly literary . . . semantically dense, self-referential, allusive, and above all Chaucerian'.[37] This can be qualified: while Lydgate is 'Chaucerian', he is originally so, addressing ethical issues indicative of the increasingly variegated audience which had become the consumers of 'Chaucerian' texts in the early Lancastrian period.[38]

WILLIAM DUNBAR

'Chaucerianism' became the validator of an increasingly disparate range of literary production as the fifteenth century progressed, and particularly when the mantle was adopted by those poets who wrote in Scots, or what they called 'Inglis' to distinguish their courtly production from the Gaelic of the 'wild' Scots.

> Quha wait gif all that Chauceir wrait was trew?
> Nor I wait nocht [don't know] gif this narratioun
> Be authoreist, or fenúeit [made up] of the new
> Be sum poeit, throw his inuentioun . . . (64–7)

These lines were written by another monk, Robert Henryson, in his *Testament of Cresseid*. Chaucer was by now not only an authority, but the liberator who had brought the writing of new vernacular fictions into the mainstream. Two further court poets, one Scots, the other English, bring us to the official end of the 'Middle Ages', and offer illustrations of the continuing afterlife of Chaucerian literariness. William Dunbar, not unlike Lydgate, wrote a number of poems to accompany occasions organised by and for the royal court, of which *The Thrissel and the Rose*, mentioned in Chapter 1, and *The Goldyn Targe* are examples. Dunbar's poetry also, however, illustrates a range of intertextuality in the vernacular for which the bird voices in Chaucer and Henryson are only a warm-up act. *The Tretis of the Tua Mariit Wemen and the Wedo* begins like a conventional love poem, only to move rapidly into a robustly burlesque *demande d'amour*, indebted variously to the Wife of Bath and to The Merchant's Tale, as the two married women debate the various merits of the married state. Dunbar brings the non-literary language of the street into his poetry here to give created voices immediate vitality; his self-representation too is marked by confident and strategic code-switching, from the liturgical language of the *Lament to the Makaris* to the invective in the *Flytyng of Dunbar and Kennedie*. He clearly anticipated an audience equally familiar with the English 'Chaucerian' literary tradition and the language of the Edinburgh marketplace.

When he comes to write for and about the court itself, Dunbar's range includes the burlesque of *A Dance in the Quenis Chamber*, where the ungainly movements and involuntary bodily noises of the dancers are given *fabliau* treatment, and the ostentatiously literary language of *The Goldyn Targe*. In the latter instance, 'aureation', literally the gilding of poetic language with Latinate terms, is central to the poem's performance and meaning. The poem opens by describing the effect of the sunrise upon an otherwise conventional dream landscape:

> Doune throu the ryce [brushwood] a ryvir ran wyth stremys
> So lustily agayn thai lykand lemys [pleasant flames]
> That all the lake as lamp did leme of licht,
> Quhilk schadowit all about wyth twynkling glemis
> That bewis [boughs] bathit war in secund bemys
> Throu the reflex of phebus [the sun's] visage brycht:
> On every syde the hegies raise on hicht,
> The bank was grene, the bruke was full of bremys,
> The stanneris [pebbles] clere as stern[stars] in frosty nycht.
> (28–36)

The passage showcases literary language as signifier, a conceit which is itself signalled by the animation of the narrator by the rising sun:

> Rycht as the stern of day begouth to schyne
> Quhen gone to bed war Vesper and Lucyne
> I raise and by a rosere [rose arbour] did me rest;
> Up sprang the goldyn candill matutyne [of the morning]. (1–4)

As the dream begins, the relationship between the compositional process and the matter on which the poet is working is reinforced by close verbal echoes of that first stanza.[39] As the narrator-dreamer wakes at the end of the poem, metaphors of embellishment are directly applied to the poetic process, affirming that narrator, dreamer, and author are one Chaucerian disciple who addresses Chaucer as 'rose of rethoris all' (253), 'all the lycht' (259) of English who 'This mater coud illumynit have full bryght' (258). By adding Lydgate and Gower, who 'Oure rude langage has clere illumynate' (266), Dunbar, like the others before him, foregrounds the writer as reader, but his envoy is addressed to the poem itself, ending with a flourish of Chaucerian feigned modesty:

> . . . draw the out of sicht.
> Rude is thy wede, disteynit, bare and rent;
> Wele aucht thou be aferit of the licht. (277–9)

The Goldyn Targe is another poem which suggests the existence of a sophisticated coterie readership, familiar not only with Chaucer,

Gower, and Lydgate, but with the French tradition of love poetry going back to the *Roman de la Rose.* From Guillaume de Lorris, Dunbar borrows a dreamer who is an eavesdropper and voyeur, watching beautiful ladies disembark from a ship, but in Dunbar's poem the dreamer is the author, aware of his own inadequacies not only in dealing with aggressive women, but in faithfully recounting his dream (64–72). The allegorical women in his dream are taken from the *Roman* too, but they just will not leave him alone, and so he is drawn into his own aesthetic edifice which fast takes on nightmarish proportions. The account of the dream has pageant-like qualities, with the auspices of a court mumming, drawing its audience into its structure at the end. As a proto-pageant it could offer the monarch (James IV of Scotland) as audience a covert warning about the predatory nature of women, but the moral implication that is dressed up as the dreamer's unsavoury personal experience has wider application. The light image which links the creative process with the creative matter in the narrative frame, and which celebrates the compositional process, takes on a different connotation within the dream, as the dreamer's Reason is blinded by the onslaught of women. The restoration of Reason lies outside the text, anticipated as the dreamer-poet awakes to resume his literary role.[40]

JOHN SKELTON

As Dunbar was writing *The Thrissel and the Rose* to celebrate the marriage of his king to Margaret, the daughter of Henry VII, John Skelton was retiring from his role as tutor to Margaret's brothers, the ill-fated Arthur, and Henry, later Henry VIII. Skelton, who went on to chart his uneasy later relationship with Henry, and with Cardinal Wolsey in a range of satirical poems, like Dunbar, gives the lie to simple periodisation, and offers another instance of writers as readers, who looked to Chaucer as their reference point. Skelton's early poem, *The Bowge of Court*, is another Chaucerian dream-vision which uses the traditional forms and conventions of poetry written for court readership to construct a poem in which the external context of the poem's envisaged reception becomes its internal setting, and in which the author becomes his own subject. This dream takes place in autumn, the season of unreliable dreams,[41] and there is no book to put the narrator to sleep beyond the one he is failing to write himself in homage to earlier authors:

> Wherby I rede theyr renome and theyr fame
> Maye never dye, bute evermore endure.
> I was sore moved to aforce the same,
> But Ignorance full soone dyde me dyscure
> And shewed that in this ame I was not sure;
> For to illumyne, she sayde, I was to dulle,
> Avysynge me my penne awaye to pulle . . . (15–21)

The conventional progress from reading to dreaming to writing is here undermined as the dream is presented as an alternative to the generation of the text. The poem ends when the poet has failed to learn anything about how to survive at court from his dream, but at the point at which he finds he has material on which to write a poem. As with *The Goldyn Targe*, lack of success in life is compensated by success in writing, a development of the Chaucerian theme which saw the narrator pushed through the gates to the garden of love in *The Parlement of Fowls* as their message did not apply to him. Skelton's dream is not, however, about love, but about life at court, so, dream-setting notwithstanding, it has more in common with Hoccleve's auto-referential writing than Chaucer's own. For Skelton, like Hoccleve, 'the press' of court life is good for the writer, because it both furnishes material and social favour, but is bad for the man, thereby undermining the chances of writerly success. Like Hoccleve too, Skelton uses his own world, and its topical issues, to supplement the traditional contexts of his textual medium as a vehicle for philosophical and social truths. Moreover, because this poem recounts a dream, there is a basic inversion whereby the dream-world is 'real', and the waking state in which the poet can retreat into art is his escape (530–2). The confused and anxious narrator is here reincarnated as the personification of Dread, trapped on board a ship representing the court, and the dream becomes a nightmare. Court life is satirically explored through Dread's failure to transmit constructive information about it, as he is either excluded from conversations or lied to:

But there was poyntynge and noddynge with the hede,
And many wordes sayde in secrete wyse;
They wandred ay and stode styll in no stede.
Me thoughte alwaye Dyscymular [Dissimulation] dyde devyse [point to];
Me, passynge sore, myne herte than gan aryse;
I dempte and drede theyr talkynge was not good. (421–6)

The unreliability of text is here signified by fragmentation, in a poem which deconstructs its own potentiality as authoritative. Skelton was later to move beyond models inherited from Chaucer,[42] but he went on to develop the device of the inadequate narrator, so that the eponymous bird of *Speke Parott*, all-seeing but completely uncomprehending, resonates with a number of earlier voices including that of the incompetent narrator who retells all the stories he heard on his pilgrimage to Canterbury.

THE KINGIS QUAIR

We are going to finish by returning to the early fifteenth century to look at a poem that is steeped in literary allusion like no other. *The Kingis Quair* is a literary mirror not for but of a prince, and with an irony born of actual circumstance, the mirror is no mirror at all but a window on the events of a real life. We have encountered a number of texts which masquerade as performances by plausible medieval voices, which have been exposed as purely textual constructs, medieval literary concatenations of lived experience and the authority of old books. Here the voice is another construct of identifiable texts, but the protagonist of this royal autobiography is also real, a portrait of the author's younger self. It is the story of a young king who lived vicariously through reading and writing because of the deferral of real lived experience enforced on him by a long period of imprisonment. Thus the matter of books, chiefly the English Chaucerian tradition, supplies the substance of the narrated life, a perfect image of active readership. The poem is, therefore, the last word on the 'trouthe' of literature, as experience and authority merge.

At the age of twelve, Prince James of Scotland set off for France on the orders of his father, Robert III, to improve his education, but also because, as heir to the Scottish throne, his life was at risk because the brother of his sickly royal father, the Lord Lieutenant Albany, aspired to claim the throne for himself. The young prince's winter journey in 1406 took him to the Bass Rock, to await the ship that would take him onward. Sir David Fleming, who had escorted him there, was murdered on his way home, and James's small entourage was left stranded for a month. They re-embarked on the Maryenknecht, a ship from Danzig (modern Gdansk), but on 14 March were boarded off the Yorkshire coast by merchant-pirates. The cargo was restored by the English crown, but Henry IV, presented with a valuable bargaining piece in the Anglo-Scottish power game, had James conveyed to the Tower of London. On hearing the news, Robert III went into his final decline and died, and Albany became governor of Scotland.

The years that followed saw a number of momentous events, while James remained a prisoner. In 1420, the year that Albany died, James, aged twenty-six, was persuaded to go to France in Henry V's service, and in 1421 was dubbed a knight and invested with the Order of the Garter. He returned to England with Henry V's body, and finally in 1423 a treaty for his release was concluded. England charged Scotland £40,000 for his keep, but a sixth of this was remitted as the dowry for Joan Beaufort. His bride, who was to bear him eight children, was Henry V's cousin, granddaughter of John of Gaunt and his third wife, Catherine Swynford (Chaucer's sister-in-law). James made some progress in imposing strong royal government in Scotland, modelled on what he had witnessed in England, but was murdered in February 1437.[43]

The poem opens with a Prologue in which the sleepless narrator takes up Boethius's *Consolation of Philosophy*, a work written in prison. In a knowing reversal of the dream-vision convention, the book keeps him awake. He is preoccupied until morning by moral reflections on the circumstances of his youth, which he vows to write down. From the outset, his recollections focus on the vicissitudes of fortune in the world, and compositional failure in writing. He determines to write 'sum new thing' (88), invoking the Muses to assist with his renewed attempt to order and make sense of his lived experiences through the writing process. Timescales are complex: the experience of reading Boethius is set in the past, so the writing it prompts, although it gives the impression of being written in the author's present, is, logically, being rewritten from memory. Composition is established as a parallel to life's process as the author's recreation of his youth recreates the experience of being an incompetent writer as he rereads himself. His former failures are described according to the conventional metaphor of the rudderless ship on a stormy sea, threatened by the 'rokkis blake' he borrows from The Franklin's Tale:

> The rokkis clepe I the prolixitee
> Of doubilnesse that doith my wittis pall:
> The lak of wynd is the deficultee
> In enditing of this lytill trety small;
> The bote I clepe the mater hole of all;
> My wit, unto the saile that now I wynd
> To seke connyng, though I bot lytill fynd. (120–6)

The book will be a voyage of his youth to find a guide for his will equivalent to Boethius's Lady Philosophy. Compositional failure imitates life's process, but the image of the rudderless ship is here also the sign of the poem's overall project of remarking not that art imitates life, but that life imitates art. James's predicament commenced on board a ship in winter seas, as he will go on to relate at lines 148–68. Disaster at sea both is, and is a sign of, his bad fortune.

Before the narrative moves into flashback, however, the book within the book relates a new beginning that puts the protagonist in his prison cell. Here in solitary confinement he takes consolation not from philosophy but, in conscious parallel with Palamon in The Knight's Tale, from the psychological comfort of looking out at a perfect springtime garden. The garden is itself evoked as a textual construct, the *locus amoenus* of dream-visions since the *Roman de la Rose*, and one in which he is able to quote the 'text' of the birdsong, reminiscent of the concluding roundel of the *Parliament of Fowls* (232–8). The material world is indissolubly textual, made of the stuff of books.

In this garden the prisoner-protagonist sees a beautiful woman with whom he instantly falls in love. His passion is described as occurring both 'sudaynly' (285) and 'for euer' (286), as the overwhelming emotion is shared by both narrator and protagonist. The lady is described in graphic detail as the image of natural perfection, drawing on the Knight's portrait of Emilye but enhanced by reference to the whole poetic resource of conventionally superlative descriptions of ideal womanhood. The effect of this moment is to bring on a positive change of mood as he persuades the silent nightingale that sits beside his beloved to sing. His response to the nightingale's song is then to compose a lyric. As he languishes love-lorn in his prison, as day turns to night, his physical condition then becomes that of the Man in Black in *The Book of the Duchess*, robbed of all vitality, until eventually he falls asleep and has a dream: 'And quhat I met [dreamt] I will you now deuise' (511). The bringing together of past events with future writing, unified through the action of present memory, is at the bottom of the poem's self-conscious structure in which all past reality is processed through literary experience. At this point in the narrative the nature of the transposed convention becomes clear: the book which kept him awake did not inspire a vision but supplied a night's wakeful reading which made possible the interpretation of a past dream.[44]

The dream-vision that follows takes the dreamer on a flight upward into the spheres, reminiscent of Geffrey's journey in *The House of Fame*. He calls at the Temple of Venus, startlingly similar to the description in *The Parliament of Fowls*, and is shown a history of love, painted on the walls, and has pointed out to him the presence of love poets there (591–5): all life is the stuff of art, of poets and their topoi. But Venus is not his final calling point, as the dream, mirroring the autobiographical maturation process, has him move on from a preoccupation with erotic desire, which leaves him still 'weltering' in the 'wawis fell', the high seas that threaten his boat, to wisdom, and thus to the Palace of Minerva whose gates are guarded by Patience.

Minerva is more like Boethius's Lady Philosophy, except that she is able to equip him with something concrete that he can enjoy in this world, so long as his love is based on virtue and not what she calls 'nice lust' [foolish infatuation]. Minerva sums up what

Lady Philosophy says, and what Chaucer's Troilus finds from his vantage point in the spheres after he dies, about fortune and free will, but concludes more optimistically that if one has a modicum of foreknowledge and wisdom, it is actually possible to minimise fortune's effects.[45] He is returned to earth equipped with self-governance, and finds himself by the river from the garden at the opening of the *Roman de la Rose.* He comes to meet Fortune and gazes in horror at her wheel from which people fall into a pit as deep as hell. Fortune mocks his aspirations, suggesting he is too feeble to stretch himself on her wheel without good words or volition in his heart (1179–83). Her words again equate vigour in life and in love with literary success, as his tongue-tied condition parallels his struggle to maturity. Fortune then seizes him by the ear and he wakes up (1203).

Awake once more in his prison chamber, the protagonist is visited by a dove, bearing in its beak yet another text, a statement about divine grace which he pins above his bed's head. The remainder of the poem acts as an extended epilogue to the main narrative, in which the narrator questions why the account is being written. He answers his own question that, once one is in 'heaven', it is good to be mindful of time formerly spent in 'hell', and to urge others that have 'no curage at the rose to pull' (1298) to take example from his experience, for he actually got the girl, and was released from prison into the new and delightful captivity of love. Finally, the envoy is addressed to the now-completed book itself, instructing it to pray the reader have patience, not in love, but as forbearance in reading. The final stanza dedicates the poem to Gower and to Chaucer, and them, 'my maisteris dere' (1373) to heaven's bliss.

In *S/Z* (1970), his literary analysis of Balzac's short story 'Sarrasine', Roland Barthes revised his earlier view that denotation comes first in the transaction between author, text, and reader. He proposes instead that denotation is the last of a text's connotations, which brings about closure. He draws attention to how connotation is the mechanism by which the simple denotation can be contested. Denotation generates simple 'truth'; connotation the 'signifying diversity', that is literature.[46] As Middle English emerged as a confident literary vernacular, a tradition of readerly writing developed which understood this insight very well.

NOTES

1. William Dunbar, *Selected Poems*, ed. Harriet Harvey Wood (London and New York: Routledge, 2003), pp. 98–101.
2. John Lydgate, *The Dance of Death*, ed. Florence Warren, Early English Text Society, OS 181 (Oxford: Oxford University Press, 1929). For more on the tradition, see Sophie Oosterwijk, 'Of Corpses, Constables and Kings: The *Danse Macabre* in Late Medieval and Renaissance Culture', *The Journal of the British Archaeological Association*, 157 (2004), 61–90.
3. See Jocelyn Wogan-Browne, Nicholas Watson, Andrew Taylor, and Ruth Evans (eds), *The Idea of the Vernacular: An Anthology of Middle English Literary Theory, 1280–1520* (University Park, PA: Pennsylvania State University Press, 1999) for extracts and essays that expand this theme.
4. In addition to Geoffrey Chaucer, *The Riverside Chaucer*, ed. Larry D. Benson (Oxford: Oxford University Press, 2008), see Geoffrey Chaucer, *Chaucer: The Book of the Duchess*, ed. Helen Phillips (Durham: Durham and St Andrews Medieval Texts, 1982).
5. Derek Pearsall, *The Life of Geoffrey Chaucer* (Oxford: Blackwell, 1992), pp. 86–7.
6. See Charles Muscatine, *Chaucer and the French Tradition* (Berkeley and Los Angeles: University of California Press, 1957); James Wimsatt, *Chaucer and the French Love Poets: The Literary Background of the Book of the Duchess* (Chapel Hill, NC: University of North Carolina Press, 1968); Barry A. Windeatt, *Chaucer's Dream Poetry* (Woodbridge, Suffolk: Boydell and Brewer, 1982); and Piero Boitani, 'Old Books Brought to Life in Dreams: *The Book of the Duchess*, *The House of Fame*, and *The Parliament of Fowls*', in Piero Boitani and Jill Mann (eds), *The Cambridge Companion to Chaucer* (Cambridge: Cambridge University Press, 2003), pp. 58–77.
7. Chaucer, *Book of Duchess*, ed. Phillips, p. 50.
8. Pearsall, *Life of Chaucer*, pp. 70–3.
9. *Troilus and Criseyde*, Book I, 1065–71 describes Pandarus's planning in the same terms that Vinsauf uses to describe how a story should be planned in advance. See Geoffrey of Vinsauf,

'*The New Poetics*', in James J. Murphy (ed.), *Three Medieval Rhetorical Arts* (Berkeley and Los Angeles, CA: University of California Press, 1971), p. 34. For the model elegy, see pp. 47–9.
10. Derek A. Pearsall (ed.), *The Floure and the Leafe; The Assembly of Ladies; The Isle of Ladies* (Kalamazoo, MI: Medieval Institute Publications, 1992).
11. See Geoffrey Chaucer, *The Parlement of Foulys*, ed. D. S. Brewer (Manchester: Manchester University Press, 1972).
12. Robert O. Payne, *The Key of Remembrance: A Study of Chaucer's Poetics* (New Haven, CT and London: Yale University Press, 1963).
13. See Sheila Delaney, *Chaucer's House of Fame: The Poetics of Sceptical Fideism* (Chicago and London: University of Chicago Press, 1972); Pamela M. King, 'Chaucer, Chaucerians, and the Theme of Poetry', in Julia Boffey and Janet Cowen (eds), *Chaucer and Fifteenth-century Poetry* (London: King's College London Centre for Late Antique and Medieval Studies, 1991), pp. 1–14; and Winthrop Wetherbee, *Chaucer and the Poets: An Essay on* Troilus and Criseyde (Ithaca, NY and London: Cornell University Press, 1984), p. 17.
14. Geoffrey Chaucer, *The House of Fame*, ed. Nicholas R. Havely (Durham: Durham and St Andrews Medieval Texts, 1994), p. 154.
15. David Aers, *Chaucer*, Harvester New Readings (Atlantic Highlands, NJ : Humanities Press International, 1986), p. 9.
16. Stephen Knight, *Geoffrey Chaucer* (Oxford: Blackwell, 1986), p. 144.
17. See Paul Strohm, *Social Chaucer* (Cambridge, MA: Harvard University Press, 1989), p. 71 and passim for a detailed study here.
18. Ibid. pp. 41–6; Pearsall, *Life of Chaucer*, pp. 128–35.
19. Pearsall, *Life of Chaucer*, pp. 217–18.
20. Strohm, *Social Chaucer*, pp. 72–3.
21. David Lawton, 'Dullness and the Fifteenth Century', *English Literary History*, 54 (1987), 761–99.
22. The poem is widely anthologised, and available online at http://www.englishverse.com/poems/lament_for_chaucer (accessed 22 March 2010).

23. Thomas Hoccleve, *The Regiment of Princes*, ed. Charles R. Blyth (Kalamazoo, MI: Medieval Institute Publications, 1999).
24. Lawton, 'Dullness', 774.
25. J. A. Burrow, 'The Poet as Petitioner', *Studies in the Age of Chaucer*, 3 (1981), 61–75. Also Nicholas Perkins, *Hoccleve's* Regiment of Princes: *Counsel and Constraint* (Cambridge: D. S. Brewer, 2001).
26. Andrew Lynch, '"Manly cowardyse": Thomas Hoccleve's Peace Strategy', *Medium Aevum*, 73 (2004), 1–17 (1).
27. Pearsall, *Life of Chaucer*, pp. 286–7.
28. See Wyatt's famous lyric, 'They flee from me . . .'
29. Thomas Hoccleve, *'My Compleinte' and Other Poems*, ed. Roger Ellis (Exeter: University of Exeter Press, 2001), pp. 64–78.
30. James Simpson, *The Oxford English Literary History. Volume 2. 1350–1547: Reform and Cultural Revolutions* (Oxford: Oxford University Press, 1976), p. 22.
31. Lawton, 'Dullness', 763.
32. Lois Ebin, *Illuminator, Makar, Vates: Visions of Poetry in the Fifteenth Century* (Lincoln, NE and London: University of Nebraska Press, 1988), p. 18.
33. Derek A. Pearsall, *John Lydgate (1371–1449): A Bio-biography* (Victoria, BC: University of Victoria Press, 1997), pp. 17–24.
34. See, for example, Larry Scanlon and James Simpson, *John Lydgate: Poetry, Culture, and Lancastrian England* (Notre Dame, IN: University of Notre Dame Press, 2006).
35. See further Simpson, *Oxford English Literary History*, pp. 34–67 (p. 64).
36. John Lydgate, *Minor Poems of John Lydgate*, ed. Henry Noble McCracken, Early English Text Society, ES 107, and OS 192 (Oxford: Oxford University Press, 1910 and 1933), II, pp. 682–91.
37. Maura Nolan, *John Lydgate and the Making of Public Culture* (Cambridge: Cambridge University Press, 2005), pp. 2–3.
38. See Paul Strohm, 'Hoccleve, Lydgate and the Lancastrian Court', in David Wallace (ed.), *The Cambridge History of Medieval Literature* (Cambridge: Cambridge University Press, 2002), pp. 640–61.
39. Ebin, *Illuminator, Makar, Vates*, p. 76.

40. See further Pamela M. King, 'Dunbar's *Golden Targe*: A Chaucerian Masque', *Studies in Scottish Literature*, 19 (1984), 115–31; A. C. Spearing, *The Medieval Poet as Voyeur: Looking and Listening in Medieval Love-Narratives* (Cambridge: Cambridge University Press, 1993), p. 86.
41. A. C. Spearing, *Medieval Dream Poetry* (Cambridge: Cambridge University Press, 1976), p. 197.
42. See further in Jane Griffiths, *John Skelton and Poetic Authority: Defining the Liberty to Speak* (Oxford: Clarendon Press, 2006).
43. John MacQueen, 'Tradition and the Interpretation of the *Kingis Quair*', *Review of English Studies*, 12 (1961), 117–31.
44. Julia Boffey, 'Chaucerian Prisoners: The Context of *The Kingis Quair*', in Boffey and Cowen (eds), *Chaucer and Fifteenth-century Poetry*, pp. 84–99 (p. 91); and William Quinn, 'Memory and the Matrix of Unity in *The Kingis Quair*', *Chaucer Review*, 15 (1981), 332–55.
45. See Lois Ebin, 'Boethius, Chaucer, and *The Kingis Quair*', *Philological Quarterly*, 53 (1974), 321–41.
46. Kaja Silverman, *The Subject of Semiotics* (New York and Oxford: Oxford University Press, 1983), pp. 8–9; 240.

Conclusion

In Chapter 1 we saw how Chaucer in *Troilus and Criseyde* highlights the differentness of the remote past in which his matter is set as part of his strategy to withhold totalising judgement. In reading the literature of his period, we would do well to follow his example. It would be folly to suggest that any general conclusions can be drawn about 200 years' literary production from a culture as remote from our own as that covered in the foregoing pages. This book has, however, sought to move the reader away from the straitjacket of a limited range of canonical texts, as well as to move Chaucer away from being read in isolation and under the illusion of his peculiar accessibility to modern sensibilities. As the Introduction warned, chapter divisions have been permeable and, to some extent, arbitrary, so that no general conclusion may be reached beyond the particularities of the book's various explorations. Nonetheless, certain cross-cutting critical themes have emerged which reflect some of the current trends in the criticism of medieval literature, and which we may draw together here.

Some specific literary relations in a polyglot society have emerged, as we have read texts written in different dialects of English, texts which present themselves as 'translations' in the sense of adaptations of texts from other cultures, and texts by authors who wrote sometimes in English, sometimes in French or Latin. The apparent growing pains of English as a mature literary language are referred to by Chaucer in particular, with the attendant anxieties about its appropriateness for serious matter, but these need to be set alongside the evidence that Middle English was a language more than adequate technically for literary production across the full stylistic register, so that anxious murmurings should be associated more with social decorum than any actual deficiency. 'Authority' remains Latin for the most part when it is drawn attention to for validatory purposes, but there is also rich, and often unacknowledged, cross-fertilisation from the literatures of other European vernaculars, and not just from French.

We have met a number of dramatised voices and in possibly surprising places. Characters in plays turn out to be largely demonstrative embodiments of particular moral positions, with, perhaps, the honourable exception of some of the biblical figures realised in the N. Town collection. The Canterbury pilgrims, deceptively like fully-fledged dramatic characters, often turn out to be constructions pieced together from pre-existing texts and given the illusion of individuated personality by the application of some well placed verbal tics, like the Wife of Bath, or they turn out, like the Miller, to be implausible as tellers competent to deliver the matter attributed to them. Frequently adapted for the stage, *The Canterbury Tales* is not a play, and its dramatic characteristics require caution. Even Margery Kempe's *Book* and King James I's *Quair*, although ostensibly sustained autobiographical narratives, present complications: the first was dictated to a male amanuensis and contaminated by discourses to which Margery was unlikely to have access, the second was another extraordinary cut-and-paste. And yet current trends are to be not over-scrupulous in separating out authors' voices from the narrators in their work. There is no reason to doubt that when Chaucer uses the first-person singular, or calls his protagonist 'Geffrey', as he does in *The House of Fame*, he intends himself – albeit in some self-parodying form – particularly in his short lyrics and envoys. Equally, passus V in the C text of *Piers Plowman* appears as a significant moment in that poem's reincarnation at which the poet rejects all the superstructures of dream-vision and allegory in order to confide in his reader, to talk about himself and his need to write. And Thomas Hoccleve probably did drink too much, worry about the impression he made on others, and have a breakdown. Even when authors call less attention to themselves, their readers may be given access to their worlds through their eyes, and there is nothing inherently wrong with believing in reliable access to William Dunbar's derision of what he saw one day in the Queen's Chamber, nor to his fear of joining his predecessors in the choir eternal on an occasion when he was unwell.

Medieval texts also talk about themselves. The self-begetting novel was a literary fashion associated with the critiques of realism and modernism which characterised the late twentieth century. It traced a respectable history back to Lawrence Stern's *Tristram Shandy*. But in the fourteenth and fifteenth centuries too we find a number of texts which construct themselves as their own subjects. A fundamental intertextuality is natural in a literary tradition that places so much importance upon written authority, and that is the mainspring not only of *The Canterbury Tales*, but of the longer works of Lydgate and of Malory. Most authors speak to their readers about what they are doing and where their material comes from. It is but a small step from that to having books which tell their own prehistories, and finally, like *The Bowge of Court*, end with the moment at which the recounted events concluded and the author took up his pen. Writing can be a denotative or, more commonly, a connotative reflection of empirical reality, but is also a real event within the continuum of that reality.

We began by considering how medieval elites used literary production as part of their project in impression management, 'spin'. All the texts we have visited are cultural performances in their different ways. This might be said of all literature, but, in a society where the book was a unique and significant material object, and where transmission was a much more palpably physical act of donorship and reception than is the case with mass publishing, the performative role of texts has particular resonance. Indeed a number of texts include frontispieces in which an artist has been employed to paint an image of the author handing over his book to an aristocratic patron. Frequently the relationship between authorial voice, material, and envisaged audience has been described in the foregoing using the word 'gesture': according to understandings of performativity, it is fruitful to see all medieval texts as significant physical gestures in a highly stratified world of constructed and determined social identity.

Student Resources

GLOSSARY

allegory	a metaphorical mode in which characters and/or events represent other things, generally with religious, moral, or political meaning
apocalypse	version of the end of the world, particularly with reference to the events recounted in the book of Revelations at the end of the New Testament
chanson de geste	French epic song of heroic deeds from the twelfth century
conceit	an unusual, witty, or far-fetched idea, theme, or proposition
connotation	implied additional meaning apart from the direct
denotation	specific, direct meaning, as opposed to connotations
dialectic	investigation through debate, particularly the Socratic method of arriving at truth via disputation
discourse	language relating to a particular context or subject
effictio	set-piece, rhetorical, descriptive inventory of a person's characteristics from head to toe
ekphrasis	the description in words of a work of art designed to make the thing described be visually present for the reader

encomium	a formal, detailed, and descriptive expression of praise
exegesis	systematic critical interpretation of a religious text
fin amor	refined romantic love as modelled in romance fictions
fitt	thematic division of a poem
hagiography	biography of a saint
homophone	word that sounds the same but is different in meaning and spelling
lists	enclosed area for a tournament
macaronic	verse in which words and phrases from more than one language are combined
metonymy	rhetorical device by which a thing is defined by relating it to things to which it is proximate
motif	a unifying, sometimes repeating, theme inhering in an object, design, action, pattern, or particular idea
palimpsest	a text in which old words are written over, but can be read beneath the new ones
patristic	relating to, or deriving from, the ideas expressed in the writings of the early Church fathers, such as St Augustine
phatic	utterance designed to share mood rather than convey information
prolepsis	an expression anachronistically anticipating later events or circumstances
redactor	one who edits and revises previously published material
signifier	(semiotic terminology) a sign is a transaction between the signifier and that which is signified
syllogism	a process of systematic deductive reasoning
teleology	the study of the relationship between causes and their ends
topos (*pl.* topoi)	traditional theme, particularly one developed rhetorically
typology	a kind of allegory, whereby one character or episode (often Old Testament) is identified as prophetic of another (New Testament)

REFERENCE MATERIALS

Primary Texts

Accessible editions of Middle English texts are increasing through the publications of the TEAMS Middle English Texts series, produced by the Medieval Institute, Western Michigan University, Kalamazoo, MI. The online catalogue is found at http://www.lib.rochester.edu/camelot/teams/catalog.htm (accessed 22 March 2010). There is a link from the same site to METS, the Middle English Texts Series, for texts available on line only. The following list refers to standard print editions of authors and individual works cited in this volume, alphabetically by author where known, by editor where not. Alternate editions which contain useful supplementary apparatus and explanatory material are cited in the notes.

Editions of Works by Known Authors

Chaucer, Geoffrey, *The Riverside Chaucer*, ed. Larry D. Benson, 3rd edn (Oxford: Oxford University Press, 2008) – the standard complete edition of all Chaucer's work.

Chaucer, Geoffrey, *Troilus and Criseyde: A New Edition of 'The Book of Troilus'*, ed. B. A. Windeatt (London and New York: Longman, 1984) – includes parallel texts of Chaucer's sources.

Dunbar, William, *Selected Poems*, ed. Harriet Harvey Wood (London and New York: Routledge, 2003).

Gower, John, *The Complete Works of John Gower*, ed. G. C. Macaulay, Early English Text Society OS 81 and 82 (Oxford: Oxford University Press, 1900–1).

Guillaume (de Lorris) and Jean (de Meun), *The Romance of the Rose*, trans. and ed. Frances Horgan (Oxford: Oxford University Press, 1999).

Henryson, Robert, *Robert Henryson: Poems*, ed. Charles Elliott (Oxford: Clarendon Press, 1974 [1963]).

Hoccleve, Thomas, *The Regiment of Princes*, ed. Charles R. Blyth (Kalamazoo, MI: Medieval Institute Publications, 1999).

Hoccleve, Thomas, *'My Compleinte' and Other Poems*, ed. Roger Ellis (Exeter: University of Exeter Press, 2001).

Julian [of Norwich], *The Writings of Julian of Norwich: A Vision Showed to a Devout Woman and a Revelation of Love*, ed. N. Watson and J. Jenkins (University Park, PA: Pennsylvania University Press, 2006).

Kempe, Margery, *The Book of Margery Kempe*, ed. Barry Windeatt (Cambridge: D. S. Brewer, 2004).

Langland, William, *Piers Plowman: A New Annotated Edition of the C-text*, ed. Derek A. Pearsall, 3rd edn (Exeter: Exeter University Press, 2008).

Langland, William, *The Vision of Piers Plowman: A Complete Edition of the B-Text*, A. V. C. Schmidt (London and New York: Dent/Dutton, 1978).

Love, Nicholas, *The Mirror of the Blessed Life of Jesus Christ*, ed. M. G. Sargent (Exeter: University of Exeter Press, 2005).

Lydgate, John, *Troy Book – Selections*, ed. Robert R. Edwards (Kalamazoo, MI: TEAMS Middle English Texts, 1998).

Lydgate, *Minor Poems of John Lydgate*, ed. Henry Noble McCracken, Early English Text Society ES 107, and OS 192 (Oxford: Oxford University Press, 1910 and 1933).

Malory, Thomas, *The Works of Sir Thomas Malory*, ed. Eugene Vinaver (Oxford: Oxford University Press, 1966).

Anonymous Works and Anthologies

Andrew, Malcolm and Ronald Waldron (eds), *The Poems of the Pearl Manuscript: Pearl, Patience, Cleanness, Sir Gawain and the Green Knight*, Exeter Medieval Texts and Studies (Exeter: University of Exeter Press, 2007).

Barr, H. (ed.), *The Piers Plowman Tradition* (London: Dent, 1993).

Beadle, Richard and Colin Richmond (eds), *Paston Letters and Papers of the Fifteenth Century, Part III.* Early English Text Society SS 22 (Oxford: Oxford University Press, 2006) – see Davis for Parts I and II.

Benson, Larry D. (ed.), *King Arthur's Death: The Middle English Stanzaic Morte Arthur and the Alliterative Morte Arthure* (Kalamazoo, MI: Medieval Institute Publications, 1994).

Davies, R.T. (ed.), *Medieval English Lyrics* (London: Faber and Faber, 1973).

Davis, Norman (ed.), *Paston Letters and Papers of the Fifteenth Century, Parts I and II*, Early English Text Society SS 20 and 21 (Oxford: Oxford University Press, 1971 and 1976).
Eccles, Mark (ed.), *The Macro Plays*, Early English Text Society OS 262 (Oxford: Oxford University Press, 1969).
Gray, Douglas (ed.), *A Selection of Religious Lyrics* (Oxford: Clarendon Press, 1975).
Hudson, Anne (ed.), *Selections from English Wycliffite Writings* (Cambridge: Cambridge University Press, 1978; 2nd edn Toronto: University of Toronto Press, 1997).
Mills, M. (ed.), *Six Middle English Romances* (London: Dent, 1973).
Morse, R. (ed.), *St Erkenwald* (Cambridge: D. S. Brewer, 1975).
Trigg, Stephanie (ed.), *Wynnere and Wastoure* Early English Text Society OS 297 (Oxford: Oxford University Press, 1990).
Walker, Greg (ed.), *Medieval Drama: An Anthology* (Oxford: Blackwell, 2000) – most of the plays referred to may be found in this anthology; for those that are not, see the single editions referred to in the notes.
Wogan-Browne, Jocelyn, Nicholas Watson, Andrew Taylor, and Ruth Evans (eds), *The Idea of the Vernacular: An Anthology of Middle English Literary Theory, 1280–1520* (University Park, PA: Pennsylvania State University Press, 1999).
Zupitza, Julius (ed.), *The Romance of Guy of Warwick*, Early English Text Society ES 42, 49 and 59 (Oxford: Oxford University Press, 1883, 1887, 1891).

Secondary Sources

An exhaustive bibliography is impossible to reproduce here, so the following should be treated as a selection of useful starting points and/or studies that have contributed particularly to the approaches taken in this volume. It is organised into Collections of Essays and Individual Studies. Many of the collections are volumes in *Companion* series, and offer excellent introductions to current critical approaches. Many studies that relate to specific sections of this book only are cited in the notes but not repeated here.

Collections of Essays

Archibald, Elizabeth, and Ad Putter (eds), *The Cambridge Companion to Arthurian Legend* (Cambridge: Cambridge University Press, 2009).

Arnold, John H. and Katherine J. Lewis (eds), *A Companion to 'The Book of Margery Kempe'* (Cambridge: D. S. Brewer, 2004).

Bawcutt, Priscilla, and Janet Hadley Williams (eds), *A Companion to Medieval Scottish Poetry* (Cambridge: D. S. Brewer, 2006).

Beadle, Richard, and Alan J. Fletcher (eds), *The Cambridge Companion to Medieval English Theatre* (Cambridge: Cambridge University Press, 2008 [1994]).

Benson, C. David (ed.), *Critical Essays on Chaucer's Troilus and Criseyde and His Major Early Poems* (Toronto: University of Toronto Press, 1991).

Boitani, Piero (ed.), *The European Tragedy of Troilus* (Oxford: Oxford University Press, 1989).

Boitani, Piero and Jill Mann (eds), *The Cambridge Companion to Chaucer* (Cambridge: Cambridge University Press, 2003).

Brown, Peter (ed.), *A Companion to Medieval English Literature and Culture, c.1350–c.1500* (Oxford: Blackwell, 2007).

Cooper, Helen (ed.), *The Canterbury Tales*, Oxford Guides to Chaucer (Oxford: Clarendon Press, 1989).

Duncan, Thomas G. (ed.), *A Companion to the Middle English Lyric* (Cambridge: D. S. Brewer, 2005).

Edwards, A. S. G. (ed.), *A Companion to Middle English Prose* (Cambridge: D. S. Brewer, 2006).

Edwards, Robert, and Stephen Spector (eds), *The Olde Daunce: Love, Friendship, Sex and Marriage in the Medieval World* (Oxford: Blackwell, 1991).

Erler, Mary C., and Maryanne Kowaleski (eds), *Gendering the Master Narrative: Women and Power in the Middle Ages* (Ithaca and London: Cornell University Press, 2003).

Field, Rosalind, and Alison Wiggins (eds), *Guy of Warwick: Icon and Ancestor* (Cambridge: D. S. Brewer, 2007).

Fulton, Helen (ed.), *A Companion to Arthurian Literature* (Oxford: Blackwell, 2009).

Griffiths, Jeremy, and Derek A. Pearsall (eds), *Book Production and Publishing in Britain, 1375–1475* (Cambridge: Cambridge University Press, 1989).

Hilton, R. H. and T. H. Aston (eds), *The English Rising of 1381* (Cambridge: Cambridge University Press, 1984).

Huot, Sylvia, Alastair Minnis, and Patrick Boyde (eds), *The Romance of the Rose and Its Medieval Readers: Interpretation, Reception, Manuscript Transmission* (Cambridge: Cambridge University Press, 1993).

Hussey, S. S. (ed.), *Piers Plowman: Critical Approaches* (London: Methuen, 1969).

Kratzmann, Gregory, and James Simpson (eds), *Medieval English Religious and Ethical Literature: Essays in Honour of G. H. Russell* (Cambridge: D. S. Brewer, 1986).

McAvoy, L. H. (ed.), *A Companion to Julian of Norwich* (Woodbridge, Suffolk: Boydell and Brewer, 2008).

Ormrod. M. and P. Lindley (eds), *The Black Death in England* (Stanford: University of California Press, 1996).

Phillips, H. (ed.), *Langland, the Mystics, and the Medieval Religious Tradition: Essays in Honour of S. S. Hussey* (Cambridge: D. S. Brewer, 1990).

Saunders, Corinne (ed.), *A Companion to Romance: From Classical to Contemporary* (Oxford: Blackwell, 2007).

Saunders, Corinne (ed.), *The Blackwell Companion to Medieval Poetry* (Oxford: Blackwell, 2010).

Scattergood, V. J., and J. W. Sherborne (eds), *English Court Culture in the Later Middle Ages* (London: Duckworth, 1983).

Wallace, David (ed.), *The Cambridge History of Medieval Literature* (Cambridge: Cambridge University Press, 2002).

Individual Studies

Aers, David, *Chaucer, Langland, and the Creative Imagination* (London and Boston, MA: Routledge and Kegan Paul, 1980).

Aers, David, *Community, Gender and Individual Identity* (London and New York: Routledge, 1988).

Barr, H., *Socioliterary Practice in Late Medieval England* (Oxford: Oxford University Press, 2001).

Beer, F., *Women and Mystical Experience in the Middle Ages* (Woodbridge, Suffolk: Boydell and Brewer, 1992).
Bishop, Ian, *Pearl in its Setting* (Oxford: Blackwell, 1968).
Brown, P., and A. Butcher, *The Age of Saturn: Literature and History in the Canterbury Tales* (Oxford: Blackwell, 1991).
Burrow, J. A., *Thomas Hoccleve* (Aldershot, Hants, and Brookfield, VT: Variorum, 1994).
Clanchy, M. T., *From Memory to Written Record: England 1066–1307* (Oxford: Blackwell, 1993).
Cooper, Helen, *The Structure of* The Canterbury Tales (London: Duckworth, 1983).
Crane, Susan, *Insular Romance: Politics, Faith, and Culture in Anglo-Norman and Middle English Literature* (Berkeley, CA: University of California Press, 1986).
Crane, Susan, *The Performance of Self: Ritual, Clothing, and Identity during the Hundred Years War* (Philadelphia, PA: University of Pennsylvania Press, 2002).
Davenport, W. A., *The Art of the Gawain Poet* (London: Athlone Press, 1978).
Dillon, Janette, *Language and Stage in Medieval and Renaissance England* (Cambridge: Cambridge University Press, 1998).
Dobson, R. B., *The Peasants' Revolt of 1381* (London: Macmillan, 1970).
Duffy, Eamon, *The Stripping of the Altars: Traditional Religion in England, 1400–1580* (New Haven, CT and London: Yale University Press, 1992).
Ebin, Lois, *Illuminator, Makar, Vates: Visions of Poetry in the Fifteenth Century* (Lincoln, NE and London: University of Nebraska Press, 1988).
Glasscoe, M., *English Medieval Mystics: Games of Faith* (London: Longman, 1993).
Hanna, R., *William Langland*, Authors of the Middle Ages, No. 3 (Aldershot: Variorum, 1993).
Hanna, Ralph, *London Literature 1300–1380* (Cambridge: Cambridge University Press, 2005).
Hansen, Elaine Tuttle, *Chaucer and the Fictions of Gender* (Berkeley, Los Angeles, London: University of California Press, 1992).

Justice, Steven, *Writing and Rebellion* (Berkeley and Los Angeles: University of California Press, 1994).

Kean, P. M., *The Pearl: An Interpretation* (London: Routledge & Kegan Paul, 1967).

Keen, Maurice, *Chivalry* (London and New York: Yale University Press, 2005).

Keen, Maurice, *English Society in the Later Middle Ages, 1348–1500* (Harmondsworth: Penguin, 1990).

Kerby-Fulton, Kathryn, *Reformist Apocalypticism and Piers Plowman* (Cambridge: Cambridge University Press, 1990).

King, Pamela M., *The York Mystery Cycle and the Worship of the City* (Cambridge: D. S. Brewer, 2006).

Kipling, Gordon, *Enter the King: Theatre, Liturgy, and Ritual in the Medieval Civic Triumph* (Oxford: Clarendon Press, 1998).

Knight, Stephen, *Geoffrey Chaucer* (Oxford: Blackwell, 1986).

Mann, Jill, *Chaucer and Medieval Estates Satire* (Cambridge: Cambridge University Press, 1973).

Mills, D. A., *Recycling the Cycle: The City of Chester and its Whitsun Plays* (Toronto: University of Toronto Press, 1998).

Minnis, Alastair J., *Chaucer and Pagan Antiquity* (Cambridge: Cambridge University Press, 1982).

Minnis, Alastair J., *Chaucer's Boece and the Medieval Tradition of Boethius* (Woodbridge, Suffolk: D. S. Brewer, 1993).

Nolan, Maura, *John Lydgate and the Making of Public Culture* (Cambridge: Cambridge University Press, 2005).

Pantin, W., *The English Church in the Fourteenth Century* (Cambridge: Cambridge University Press, 1955).

Patterson, Lee, *Chaucer and the Subject of History* (Madison, WI: University of Wisconsin Press, 1991).

Payne, Robert, O., *The Key of Remembrance: A Study of Chaucer's Poetics* (New Haven, CT and London: Yale University Press, 1963).

Pearsall, Derek A., *The Life of Geoffrey Chaucer* (Oxford: Blackwell, 1992).

Pearsall, Derek A., *Arthurian Romance: A Short Introduction* (Oxford: Blackwell, 2003).

Putter, Ad, *An Introduction to the* Gawain *Poet* (London and New York: Longman, 1996).

Putter, Ad, and Jane Gilbert, *The Spirit of Medieval English Popular Romance: A Historical Introduction* (London, New York: Longman, 2000).

Scanlon, Larry, and James Simpson, *John Lydgate: Poetry, Culture, and Lancastrian England* (Notre Dame, IN: University of Notre Dame Press, 2006).

Scattergood, V. J., *Politics and Poetry in the Fifteenth Century* (London: Blandford Press, 1971).

Scattergood, V. J., *The Lost Tradition: Essays on Medieval English Alliterative Poetry* (Dublin: Four Courts Press, 2000).

Simpson, James, *Piers Plowman: An Introduction to the B-Text* (London: Longman, 1990).

Simpson, James, *The Oxford English Literary History. Volume 2. 1350–1547: Reform and Cultural Revolution* (Oxford: Oxford University Press, 2002).

Spearing, A. C., *Medieval Dream Poetry* (Cambridge: Cambridge University Press, 1976).

Staley, Lynn, *Margery Kempe's Dissenting Fictions* (University Park, PA: Pennsylvania State University Press, 1994).

Strohm, Paul, *Hochon's Arrow* (Princeton, NJ: Princeton University Press, 1992).

Strohm, Paul, *Social Chaucer* (Cambridge, MA: Harvard University Press, 1989).

Turville-Petre, Thorlac, *England and the Nation: Language Literature and National Identity, 1290–1340* (Oxford: Clarendon Press, 1996).

Windeatt, Barry A., *Troilus and Criseyde*, Oxford Guides to Chaucer (Oxford: Clarendon Press, 1992).

Windeatt, Barry A., *Chaucer's Dream Poetry* (Woodbridge, Suffolk: Boydell and Brewer, 1982).

Woolf, Rosemary, *The English Mystery Plays* (Berkeley and Los Angeles, CA: University of California Press, 1972).

Index